WIMBLEDON

WIMBLEDON

CENTRE COURT OF THE GAME

MAX ROBERTSON

BRITISH BROADCASTING CORPORATION

Published by the
British Broadcasting Corporation
35 Marylebone High Street
London W1M 4AA

ISBN 0 563 17923 6

First published 1977 by
Arthur Barker Ltd
under the title *Wimbledon 1877–1977*
This edition first published 1981
© Max Robertson 1977, 1981

Printed in Great Britain by
Butler & Tanner Ltd, Frome and London

CONTENTS

	Foreword by Fred Perry	viii
	Preface	ix
1	Wimbledon is Magic	1
2	The Beginnings and the Brothers 1877–96	16
3	The Dos and other Doers 1897–1914	28
4	Lenglen and Tilden	49
5	The 'Four Musketeers' 1922–31	65
6	Perry Predominant 1932–9	91
7	American Take-over 1946–50	112
8	Mighty Little Mo 1951–5	133
9	Waltzing Matilda and Queen Maria 1956–60	153
10	Mortimer, Smith and Truman too 1961–5	171
11	King High 1966–8	187
12	Twilight of the Gods 1969–72	197
13	Connors asks the Questions 1973–6	212
14	The Centenary is the Greatest	228
15	Borg, Borg and more Borg 1978–80	255
	Appendices	287

PICTURE CREDITS

The author would like to thank the following for permission to reproduce photographs:
Allsport Photographic (Steve Powell), 15(t).
Associated Press, pages 108(b), 109(b), 308.
BBC Hulton Picture Library, 19(b), 21(b), 24(tr, br), 26, 31 (tl), 35(tr, bl), 37(t), 39, 42, 44(tr, b), 45(tl), 46, 47(tr, b), 53(b), 55, 58, 59, 62, 63(b), 66(b), 67(tl, b), 70, 71, 73(tl, b), 77(bl), 80, 81, 82, 85, 86(t, bl), 87, 89, 92, 93, 95(b), 98, 99, 101, 103(tl, b), 105(b), 107, 108(tl), 109(t), 116(tr), 123, 125(t), 127(b), 131(t, bl), 135(t), 139(t, bl), 141(t), 149(b), 150(tr), 154(b), 157, 159(br), 161(b), 165(t).
Beaverbrook Newspapers Ltd, 5(b), 19(t), 31(tr), 35(br), 44(tl), 47(tl), 66(t), 76, 77(t), 96(tl) 116(tl), 199(t).
Fox Photos, 105(tr), 108(tr).
Keystone, 9(tl, b), 173(tl, b).
Lawn Tennis and Badminton, 245 (bl).
Arthur and Michael Cole and Le-Roye Productions Ltd, vii, xii, 5(t), 8, 9(tr), 12, 14, 15(b), 24(tl, bl), 31(b), 35(tl), 63(t), 67(tr), 73(tr), 77(br), 86(br), 95(tr), 103(tr), 105(tl), 111(b), 113, 116(b), 118, 119, 122, 124, 125(b), 127(t), 128, 129, 131(br), 134, 135(b), 138, 139(br), 140, 141(b), 144, 145, 148, 149(t), 150(tl, b), 152, 154(t), 155, 156, 159(t, bl), 161(t), 165(b), 167, 168, 169, 172, 173(tr), 175, 177, 180, 181, 183, 185, 191, 194, 195, 198, 199(b), 202, 205, 207, 209, 213, 216, 217, 219, 222, 223, 226, 227, 229(b), 237, 241, 245(t, br), 249, 253, 258, 259, 263, 266, 267, 273, 277, 283, 285, 286.
P.A. Reuter, 45(tr).
Press Association, 229(t).
Max Robertson, 21(tr).
Michael Searle, 21 (tl).
Sport & General, 111(t).

Abbreviations: b=bottom; l=left; r=right; t=top.

TO THE CHAMPIONSHIPS
AND ALL WHO PLAY THEIR PART IN THEM

Rain on Ladies Final day
Centre Court, Friday 6 July 1973

The British are a patient lot,
God wot.
On the Centre Court they stand and stare
At the ghosts of players who are not there
And grim and bear
Their lot.

They've queued all night, they've stood all day,
So they have to stay –
To display their ardour, quite undismayed,
'Til the decision, so long delayed,
Gives rain again the Final say –
Call it a day.

FOREWORD

An event of such importance as the hundredth anniversary of Wimbledon will undoubtedly bring forth many books and pictorials.

When the writer of such a book is Max Robertson, it bears the stamp of authority and an insider's perspective. Since the war, Max Robertson has been the voice of the BBC. His play-by-play commentaries and word pictures of actual events have carried the aura of this magnificent spectacle into millions of homes all over the world. It has been my good fortune to work closely with him during many Wimbledons. His knowledge of players and spectacular descriptions of matches never cease to amaze me. Who better than Max Robertson to write the story that appears in these pages?

For the player, Wimbledon has become the pinnacle of achievement. For the spectators who endlessly wait in queues overnight to gain admission for the following day's matches, and for those who breathlessly send for their tickets in the cold of January, it is a 'must'.

For me, it is Wimbledon . . . and that says it all. No other name carries the mystique or prestige generated from this commuter bedroom suburb of London SW19. It is simply Wimbledon, the home of *the Championships*.

I know Max Robertson and I know Wimbledon. The two are an unbeatable combination. I heartily recommend this book and wish it the greatest success.

FRED PERRY
PO Box 668
Pompano Beach
Florida 33060
USA

PREFACE

Writing this book has been a new experience and it leaves me with only one real regret – that, when one is telling the story of a hundred years, one year gets very little space. So much that was worth recording has had to go, so many of the very fine players who did not reach the final stages (or whose talents lay in doubles) do not even get a mention in this despatch. I hope they or their shades will understand.

Apart from the introductory chapter the book is a narrative in chronological form. At the end, as well as the results of all Finals, I have put together some appendices, which I hope will be of use to readers who enjoy either instant or esoteric information.

Many people have helped in the writing of this book. Time was short and worthwhile allies at a premium, so that I was doubly lucky in the ones I found and who gave so freely. Mavis David gave me several hours to tell me stories of her beloved Herman – many of which will be found in the opening chapter. Rex Sterry talked to me at length about the old days and that determined Champion, Charlotte Sterry, his mother. Duncan Macaulay, Wimbledon's far-seeing and efficient post-war Secretary and pre-war assistant in the Referee's office, confirmed much that I had been told and added knowledge and story new to me.

Brian Burnett, the Chairman and David Mills, the present Secretary, told me the sort of stories that are manna to a chronicler. David, his assistant, Chris Gorringe, and Enid Stopka, who runs the office, were helpful far beyond any bounds of professional duty in verifying facts and answering questions. Tony Cooper, Curator of the new Museum, which has been so brilliantly conceived and carried out by Robin Wade, saved me hours by providing copies of many of the earlier results sheets.

Alan Little, the Museum's honorary librarian, was a constant and most generous source of reference and checking, both personally and by allowing me to borrow his own early records of the Championships. Arthur Cole let me ransack his Le-Roye Productions Limited library to look for illustrations that were different. That we did find some was due to his, Susie's and Mike's wholehearted and sporting co-operation. Buzzer Hadingham and John Barrett of Slazengers' and Ken Weatherley of John Beddington & Partners have all given me amusing and illustrative stories.

To all these I owe a considerable debt. To Fred Perry, who has written such a heartwarming foreword, I can only say, 'Fred, you have made me feel very proud – though I doubt I deserve a tenth of it.' Fred and I have indeed worked closely during many Wimbledons (not difficult in a commentary box) and his deep knowledge of the game, its performers and their tactics, together with our other experts' comments, has been the warp and weft of the fabric of our broadcasts.

Another former star of the court, who now twinkles in the commentary box, is Christine Truman Janes. Chris not only gave me valuable assessments of her leading contemporaries but took time off from her very busy life to read the post-war chapters and pass them for content.

My debt to earlier writers is profound. Personal experience only takes me a third of the way back in the Championships' history. But here I have been so lucky that I could refer to facts established by such contemporaries of the older Wimbledon scene as that eminent *Daily Telegraph* correspondent, A. Wallis Myers (*Leaders of Lawn Tennis*, Amateur Sports Publishing Co. Ltd and *Fifty Years of Wimbledon, The Field*, 1926); that most respected of referees, F.R. Burrow (*The Centre Court and Others*, Eyre & Spottiswoode, 1937); and another *Daily Telegraph* man, John Olliff, fine player and evocative writer (*The Romance of Wimbledon*, Hutchinson & Co.).

Other invaluable reference sources have been Duncan Macaulay's and Jackie Smyth's *Behind the Scenes at Wimbledon* (Collins, 1965) and the latter's *Lawn Tennis* (Batsford, 1953); for the description of the Lambert Chambers/ Lenglen Challenge Round *The LTA Book of the Game* (Max Parrish, 1957); *The Encyclopedia of Tennis* (Allen & Unwin, 1974); E.C. Potter's *Kings of the Court* (Charles Scribner's Sons, 1936): Norman Cutler's *Inside Tennis* (Evans Brothers Ltd); Fred Perry's *My Story* (Hutchinson's); *The Field*, whose editor kindly made me free of its fascinating archives; and unfailingly The B.P. and Commercial Union *World of Tennis* edited by John Barrett. To all these goes my unstinted thanks.

Debt, too, to Judith Morden, my secretary, who typed the fair copy; to Liza, my wife, who subordinated the wants of her own publishers to those of mine; whose editor, Simon Dally, did his best to accommodate my never-ending demands for more pictures; and to Peter Knight of London Express, whose guile and Beaujolais Nouveau persuaded me to have a go.

My deepest thanks go to Dennis Hart, without whose help and guidance as a professional writer, without whose patience and unflagging good humour, this book would never have been finished within its limits of space and time. To you, Dennis, I shall always be very grateful.

And last but greatest of these acknowledgements is without doubt to Wimbledon itself, to the past Champions (some of whom were unable to resist the bright lure of another crack – at *Centenary* titles), and to the BBC and my colleagues there who have allowed me to enjoy so far over four hundred of the best days of my life – at the Championships.

PREFACE TO THE 1981 EDITION

This book was originally published in 1977 by Arthur Barker Ltd under the title *Wimbledon 1877–1977*. It was written against an acute deadline and inevitably mistakes of fact were included – most of them minor, but still irritating – and one or two real howlers. Though most were discovered well before publication, it was too late – perhaps too expensive – to correct them. Consequently it has always been my ambition to bring out a revised edition, which may be trusted to 99.9 per cent as a reference book.

This I think we have succeeded in doing, and at the same time I have taken the opportunity to update it with descriptions of the recent years. These narrations are much fuller than the originals (some of which have been slightly expanded), and I hope that this – together with the greater number and variety of illustrations – will serve to make this chronicle more comprehensive and interesting. Every singles champion, as well as many others, is now illustrated.

The appendices have been corrected, tidied up and considerably added to, so that they should now provide most statistics that either a reporter under pressure or a wanderer amongst bypaths might seek.

All this has again been done with the help and co-operation of many people, notably Tony Cooper, Valerie Warren and Mrs Olive Jukes of the Wimbledon Museum and Alan Little, their Honorary Librarian; Chris Gorringe, now firmly in his All England Club Secretary's saddle, and his new assistant Paula McMillan; Arthur Cole of Le-Roye Productions; the very helpful staff of the BBC Hulton Picture Library; and Sara Fisher who typed the new chapters.

Having worked for them since 1939 and having commentated at Wimbledon for them every day since the war, I am grateful to the BBC, whose adoption of this book will give it, I hope, prestige and longevity; and particularly so to their Books Editor, Tony Kingsford, whose profound professionalism, loyal friendship and unbounded enthusiasm for the subject have ensured a finished and better article. I do hope you, the reader and Wimbledon officionado, will enjoy it and profit from it – not just once but over and over again.

Anyone for tennis?
The main concourse,
scoreboard and venerable
water tower.

Vantage points. The
stands between Nos. 2 (*left*)
and 3 Courts, the players'
restaurant and rooftop.

I

WIMBLEDON IS MAGIC

Once, in the Royal Box, Mavis, wife of Herman David, the then All England Club Chairman, said to her neighbour when watching two players hitting up before a match, 'Oh, I know who I want to win, that one, he looks so nice.' Field-Marshal Lord Montgomery leant forward and rebuked her for a flippant viewpoint. 'This is a battle,' he said, 'and you must watch how each player uses the forces at his command.'

Monty liked to come to Wimbledon. He always arrived at 12.30 and expected to be met by the Referee, Colonel W.J. Legg, and escorted round Wimbledon on a tour of inspection. It was no part of the duties of the Referee, who is a very busy man, but to Monty he was the GSOI running the show and it was only right and proper that his senior officer should take an interest.

For anyone in the tennis world – players, spectators, administrators alike – Wimbledon is more than a show, Wimbledon is magic. It is without question the most important title any player can aspire to. In 1913 it was granted the official title of the 'World's Championships on Grass Courts', a title voluntarily relinquished after 1923. It did not matter. Wimbledon still remains the premier championship in the world.

It is this partly by right, as being the earliest, but also because it always has been and still is the best run, and with the best facilities for players and public. Admittedly, things can go wrong. An order for the usual 300,000 lavatory rolls lost a couple of noughts one year. In another, after a long day and an enthralling match, a record crowd gave real meaning to the old cliché 'flushed with victory'. They ran the tanks dry.

The courts are the best grass courts in the world and the Centre Court on opening day is like the proverbial billiards table, smooth with a green, velvety sheen as if the marker has just put the brush over it. Even when turning, twisting and skidding feet have bruised it and Wimbledon sun has tanned it, the Centre Court surface produces a true bounce. There are exceptions but usually these are caused by the ball hitting the actual lines, which from year to year have to be in the same place. So with the constant marking, the lime sediment builds up to produce a hardness that has almost the effect of a metal tape and varies the bound of the ball.

The Centre Court is almost completely resown every year and is used only for the Championships or a Final Round of the Davis Cup (that last happened in 1937, when Britain as holder, but without Perry who had turned professional, were challenged and beaten 4/1 by the United States). The Wightman Cup was also played on it in the even years from 1924 to 1938. There has been one exception when during the 'Open' Tennis controversy an experimental pro tournament, sponsored by the BBC to mark the introduction of colour television, was held on the Centre Court in 1967. The outside courts have to be used for ordinary members during the season, so they are not resown but returfed from the sides of the court and the sides in turn are replaced by turf grown in a nursery.

During the Championships the Head Groundsman and his staff are hard at it from the end of play till late into the evening, watering, patching and, next morning, cutting (just a light trim), rolling and remarking. Some players cut up the court much more than others. Adriano Panatta, the Italian ace, is one whom Jack Yardley, the Head Groundsman, hates to see scuffing up the baseline turf with his service action. Sometimes when things got too much for Edwin Fuller, a great groundsman after the last war, he used to retire to the pond in his cottage garden and soothe his feelings by contemplating the goldfish.

The Centre and No. 1 Courts have tent-like covers which can quickly be raised by a well-drilled team of groundsmen, and the sixteen outside courts have covers that can be laid flat on the ground. So it is only prolonged or repeated rain that will dislocate the playing schedules. There is one small tradition that has grown up in the preparation of the Centre Court. On the Saturday before the Championships four lady members play it in with a double. On the Monday after, the Chairman's four plays a double which officially closes the use of the Court.

Nowhere is the player better looked after than at Wimbledon. His entry is given hyper-critical consideration as it is weighed against the claims of the 500 or so others who want to get in. Direct acceptance will go only to 200 players of most proven past performance and current computered form. Those next in precedence will be asked to take part in the dreaded Qualifying Competition for sixteen places for men and eight for women left vacant in the draw, and the rest, except those given grace-and-favour entry by 'wild card', are politely told that their record does not justify their acceptance.

The Qualifying Competition has caused more agony, ecstasy, drama and heartbreak than even the most thrilling Centre Court match. To the qualifier getting into Wimbledon means almost as much as for the accepted player to win the title. There was one occasion on a very wet day when normally play would not have been allowed (the Qualifying tournament has an absolute deadline as the Championships cannot wait) and two players had been struggling for hours. One reached match-point. His opponent, who was spreadeagled on the baseline after diving despairingly to retrieve, put up a short lob. The first, playing safe, waited for the ball to bounce. It hit the ground with a squelch – and stayed there. He never recovered and lost the match.

Once in the draw the overseas player is cosseted. Cars bring him from his hotel or from the Queen's Club if he is practising there. The dressing-rooms have every facility, including trained masseurs and physiotherapists. Duncan Macaulay, the post-war Secretary, tells of a request just after the last war by Margaret Osborne du Pont and Louise Brough for a male masseur, as women were not strong enough to work properly on some muscles. The problem was solved by engaging a blind masseur – another instance of the versatility of Wimbledon's administration.

The players have their own restaurant. On the roof is a marvellous position for viewing play on the outside courts and there are competitors' enclosures in the two show courts. They are given very good warning of when they will be needed for their matches. The press and other media are not allowed in the restaurant or dressing-rooms, so the players are able to relax and feel free from unwanted interference.

On court they have experienced umpires and linesmen, ball-boys trained specially for the job, the extras a player needs like iced squash drinks or resin for sweating palms at the umpire's chair, balls of tested size and pressure that since 1955 are changed every nine games, and courts prepared to as near perfection as weather will allow. On top of this they are living for the two or three weeks in London, so their wives, husbands and sweethearts can go shopping in Bond Street or visit the many sights and places that they have heard and read about all their lives.

The public is superbly catered for. When the gates are opened at twelve noon and the queues surge in, everything in the luncheon and tea-bars, on the lawns, in the concourse and aisles and in the stands is fresh and clean – as if there had been no crowd of 30,000 there the day before, dropping news-papers and sweet-wrappings, cigarette ends and matchboxes and all the other dross that even a well-behaved crowd leaves behind. This rebirth is the handi-work of a posse of students, who clean up as soon as the courts are empty. They also help in the groundsmen's court-covering drill when it is raining. They are hired through the students' union and they have their own tented camp in the grounds.

The ushers are drawn from the various services and they see to it that queuing is orderly. The WRVS operate the information desks. The St John Ambulance is at the ready and how essential it is – especially in a heatwave year like 1976. There are sweet kiosks and soft-seat hirers. There is a mobile Post Office and there are the tea-bars and tea-lawns.

Wimbledon is at once a spectacle and an industry. The 300,000 or so enthusiasts who flock there each year are really getting their money's worth, but it is a two-way bargain. They in turn are giving the appreciation of the world's most knowledgeable tennis audience and are providing the income that enables the Championships still to be organised so beautifully, that keeps the Centre Court and others so pristine in appearance (except for the welcome ivy), that allows the All England Club to remain *the* lawn tennis club in the world, and that still provides a sizeable income to the LTA, with which it can further the game at club level in this country.

Wimbledon is always refining and perfecting its operation. During the Championships the Committee is split into sub-committees which each have responsibility for a variety of functions. They are constantly looking for and sifting ideas for improvement. These ideas and suggestions from the public are scrutinised and very often acted upon by the Secretary, who will put any radical change before the Committee. A very important addition to the Wimbledon amenities in 1977 was the Centenary Museum, which is open all the year round. Finely designed, it reflects faithfully the history of the Championships and the development of the game.

At each Wimbledon there are changes and sometimes changes are changed again – even after only one year – when the particular idea that seemed good has been found wanting. Everything possible is done to dot the 'i' and cross the 't' of perfection. Prime examples of this are the arrangements for the press, TV and radio, which undergo changes almost every year. And to ensure smooth relations there is a Press Sub-Committee that meets daily with press representatives, and a member of this Sub-Committee is always available to arrange the many interviews with players requested by the media. These interviews are held in the special press interview room or TV and broadcasting studios built for the purpose.

And the result is more and more players want to enter, more and more spectators want to come, more and more media representatives come each year, and Wimbledon is more and more the hub of the lawn tennis world and the high season of its calendar. All this has happened and continues to happen because the club has always been served by men of practical vision who, while preserving the marvellous tradition that is Wimbledon, have never been frightened of change and development, when the time has been judged ripe for it.

Take fashion, for instance. For many years – right up to World War I – women players were fettered by the garments that convention forced upon them. Long skirts, choker necks, long sleeves, petticoats galore and straw hats. No wonder women found it difficult to serve over-arm. But exceptions there were – like Lottie Dod's calf-length skirts and sensible cap in the late eighties and early nineties, May Sutton's short skirt in 1905 (just above the knee), acceptable because she was a girl, Suzanne Lenglen's one-piece knee-length dresses that gave her room for her acrobatic leaps, Lili de Alvarez's trouser dress and Billie Tapscott's omission of stockings in 1929, Helen Jacobs' short-sleeved shirt and Bermuda shorts in 1932, Alice Marble's T shirt and shorts in 1939 – these were the leaders of change before the Second World War.

Afterwards, largely under the influence of Ted Tinling, dresses became more and more decorative and glamorous. The first lace dress was worn by

Champions all.
ABOVE Jimmy Connors receives the Doubles Trophy on behalf of himself and Ilie Nastase, 1973. *Left to right:* Club Chairman the late Herman David, Connors, Club Secretary Major David Mills, Club President HRH the Duke of Kent.

Dressing from the right. *Left to right:* Virginia Wade, Evonne Cawley, Ted Tinling, Rosie Casals, Billie Jean King.

Maria Weiss of the Argentine in 1950, and the same year saw Pat Ward wearing the first nylon dress. In 1947 and 1948 Joy Gannon and Betty Hilton wore coloured trims and in 1949 came Gussie Moran's lace panties. Then the golden girl, Karol Fageros, in 1959. However, efforts in the sixties to introduce all coloured clothes met with rebuff from the Committee and the rule now is for 'predominantly white throughout', which allows fashion some leeway without handicapping opponents by looking camouflaged, or making a harlequinade of what should be a classic tennis scene.

Mavis David, the then Chairman's wife, tells a story of Maria Bueno's panties. Maria was playing on No. 1 Court and the Club's President, Her Royal Highness Princess Marina, Duchess of Kent, wanted to watch her. She and the Chairman went on ahead while Mavis attended to one or two arrangements in the Royal Box. When Mavis got to the No. 1 Court box she found the Princess and Herman convulsed with laughter. When Maria bent over to receive service Princess Marina exclaimed, 'She's wearing purple panties.' 'Oh no, Ma'am,' replied Herman, 'I'm sure they're green.' A half-crown bet was made and suddenly all was revealed. Maria's panties were quartered in purple and green, the All England Club colours, to which Maria had a perfect right, being an automatic member as a Champion.

Once when the Queen was coming to lunch before watching play, her Equerry sent a message saying she had been delayed by a visit from U Thant and would be late. Temporary confusion arose. Play must start at two o'clock but lunch would not be over in time. 'Cut the first course [soup] then,' said Herman. 'But we can't,' said the caterer's representative. 'All the menus show the full lunch.' 'Then withdraw the menus,' ordered Herman with common-sense inspiration. This was done. Nobody seemed to notice the loss of the first course and Her Majesty was in the Royal Box for the start of play at 2 pm.

Another aspect of Herman David's pragmatic and firm approach to a problem was when there was a hint in the air that, because of their opposition to apartheid, the Russians might scratch their players if they happened to be drawn against South Africans. It was at a period when much political capital of this kind was being made. He asked the Russians and their team manager to come and see him and told them quite bluntly, 'If you think you might scratch if drawn against South Africans, I want you to say so and scratch now. If you should do so later I promise you I shall personally see to it that no Russian player is accepted here in future.' The Russians played. It was the sort of language that Mr Molotov would have found an interesting Cocktail.

Herman David, who took over from Dr Colin Gregory, was a great Chairman of the Club. Having discovered that he almost invariably voiced their collective thoughts, the Committee backed him all the way. They were right behind him on the issue of Open Tennis, of which Herman was the leading advocate – even as far back as 1935 when, in an article in *Tennis Illustrated and Rackets Review*, he wrote, 'Just one subject more, that may have a great effect on future Wimbledons. I believe that open tournaments between professionals and amateurs will definitely come. It may be a good thing. It would certainly clear up a lot of cloudy problems.'

Herman was the ideal man to take up the baton of this issue from Colin Gregory, who had been wholeheartedly carrying it when he suddenly died in 1959. In 1964 the All England Club put forward a motion to the AGM of the LTA, asking permission to stage an Open Wimbledon in 1965. The motion, if passed, would have meant that the LTA was seceding from the ILTF, whose policy was at the time rigidly against such adventures. The motion was lost by 88 votes to 40. Although it failed then the motion was a wedge hammered by the progressives into the sickly trunk of the ILTF. Soon it was splitting and Open Tennis did come about in 1968. It still has its problems but at least there is no Shamateurism and for that the All England Club and Herman David can largely be thanked.

The 'cloudy problems' of amateur tennis recall the problems of wet weather when the patient crowds wait, huddled under their umbrellas, the court-covering crew swing into action and the Referee's office becomes awash with enquiries and the ever-changing pattern of the order of play, as he seeks to nullify the inroads on the playing time left to him.

There was no one better at juggling with his charts than F.R. Burrow, who ruled for most of the inter-war years. A crossword addict (and one who made them up, too), he had the sort of brain that could compute the permutations and quickly compile the order of play that would ease his way out of the latest predicament. Since the war the longest-serving referees have been Colonel Legg and his son-in-law, Captain Mike Gibson.

The weather, of course, affects attendances but not as much as one would imagine – Wimbledon crowds are a hardy lot and once they have set their minds on a particular day and everything is arranged (including perhaps meeting up with friends they see annually at the Championships) they are not easily put off. Year by year the crowds have increased. 1967 was the first year that the fortnight's total topped 300,000 and the record was set in 1979 with 343,091. The record for a single day, 38,291, was set on the first Wednesday of 1979, 27 June.

The Club and Wimbledon have been served well by many. Dan Maskell has been a mainstay of strength and support in various capacities. Before the war he was coach to the All England Club and to the great Davis Cup teams that won and held the cup and his advice, analysis and ever readiness to play practice games were invaluable to Perry, Austin, Hughes and the other team members. After the war he remained the Club's coach until in 1955 he became the LTA's Training Manager. For thirty years he has delighted millions with his TV commentaries, and done much to enhance the prestige of the Club and the Championships.

No Secretary has done more than Duncan Macaulay to make the Wimbledon

Some post-war British Davis Cup and
Wimbledon stalwarts.
Tony Mottram (represented Great Britain
1947–55) and Geoff Paish (1947–55).

Mike Davies (1955–60).

Bobby Wilson (1955, 1957–61, 1963–8).

Mike Sangster (1960–8).

Mark Cox (1967–9, 1973, 1978–80).

Roger Taylor (1964–7, 1973, 1975–6).

Buster Mottram (1975–6, 1978–).

machine what it is. In 1948 Major David Mills was appointed as his assistant and, having understudied him for years, he was able to slip smoothly into the saddle in 1963. He immediately introduced (1964) the idea of having the programme on Finals days opened with music by one of the leading Service bands. During the Championships he and Duncan lived on the job in the cottage by the Somerset Road gates. On one first morning the telephone rang at 7.30. David answered, groaning a little, and eventually a foreigner came on.

'Are you the Wimbledon Courts?' he asked. 'Yes,' replied David. 'What time am I appearing?' enquired the voice and gave his name, which was not immediately recognisable. 'Hang on,' said David and started thumbing through the order of play. But nowhere did the name occur. 'You're not on the list,' said David politely. 'Are you sure the Referee has put you on today?' 'Oh yes,' said the voice confidently. 'He told me I was remanded for one week.'

But if Wimbledon has been lucky in the men behind it, it has certainly been fortunate in its Royal patronage. The name of the late President, Princess Marina, will always be remembered with a special affection. Not only was her interest in tennis and her delight in watching these great Championships patent to the crowds, as well as to those near her in the Royal Box, but her sincere concern for people is instanced time and again by those who talk of her.

Mavis David tells how the Princess often asked her to go to the Ladies' Dressing Room and enquire after players who had been injured or shown distress. And once, when a small ball-boy was hit in the eye by a ball, the Princess summoned him to the Royal Box and told him how sorry she was and how brave she thought he had been. Rex Sterry tells, too, of the very genuine letter and telegram he received from Princess Marina on the death of his mother, five times Champion, Chattie Cooper, who was thirty-seven when she won in 1908 as Mrs Sterry – the oldest woman to do so. On Princess Marina's death in 1968 her son, the Duke of Kent, became President, since when he and the Duchess have shown the same warm interest in the Championships.

Herman David's birthday was on 26 June and so invariably fell during Wimbledon. One year, soon after he became Chairman, the Committee decided to give him a party, so they sent a message to him saying that something awful had happened and he must come at once for a plenary session. Full of foreboding and wondering what this terrible event could be, he came into the Committee Room and was promptly almost knocked out by a champagne cork rebounding from the ceiling. Later Princess Marina joined in what became a double celebration, for her first grandchild, the Earl of St Andrews, was born that day.

Herman, too, was always concerned to know what was going on. One day, after the Committee had given rather grudging permission on a trial basis for iced lollies to be sold in the grounds, Herman asked the caterer how they were doing. He replied, 'I regret to say, sir, they're selling magnificently.'

Rex Sterry, as Herman's deputy, was his standard-bearer when it came to making speeches. Rex's wit is very dry – vintage champagne. He, too, has had his mishaps in the Royal Box. One very ticklish job that he has to undertake is requesting ladies with very large hats to be kind enough to remove them. Usually his powers are persuasive enough, but he was utterly routed by one regal lady who made no bones about refusing him.

On another occasion Rex was making polite conversation to an African monarch, who had been given into his care by Foreign Service request. As the King, who had said nothing all afternoon, was rising to leave Rex asked him what his impressions had been, to which the reply came 'Yes, thank you. I have enjoyed myself here at Henley.'

Everybody has their Wimbledon story – some many. And Wimbledon is made up of the sum of these stories and all that lies behind them. The Wimbledon press is acknowledged to be the best in the world. Their facilities are good and they make use of them. In such a big tournament, involving the best players in the world, with a crowd that is cosmopolitan, too, there is always plenty of scope for the feature writers – as well as the straight reporters.

For years BBC radio and television have provided many hours of transmission that cover not only the big show courts but several others too. The BBC's Overseas Service sends out daily reports and commentaries to every part of the world. Each year Wimbledon is like a miniature Olympic Games and gets almost the same media coverage. The name of this London suburb is known worldwide, and worldwide it is the blazing ambition of tennis youngsters perhaps one day to play at Wimbledon.

One of the most enthralling and young-inspiring matches ever seen at Wimbledon, and one which gave the media and the crowds a very happy time, was not during the Championships, but in the 1976 Davis Cup European Zone B Final against Italy. It was played on No. 1 Court and the Italians eventually won 4/1, but not before drama of the highest quality had been enacted on the second day.

Leading 2/0 after the first day's singles, the Italians seemed to have the tie in their pockets when in the doubles Panatta and Bertolucci led the Lloyd brothers, David and John, by two sets to love. David, the elder, largely kept the brothers in the match and they won the third set. The fourth was a set of Homeric proportions. For one thing there had never been a Wimbledon crowd like this one. Italian partisans were there in their droves and kept up an almost continual chanting of 'Ee-ta-lee-ah, Ee-ta-lee-ah'. For a day and a half there had been plenty for them to chant about and their fervent support had unquestionably raised the morale of their players at vital moments. The British support was to begin with nonplussed and produced no real opposition.

But on the second day, led by a stalwart from Essex who possessed a strident car-horn of indeterminate note, the British crowd fought back. And so did the Lloyd brothers. Battle was really joined, between the players on the one hand

Davis Cup. European Zone B Final, No. 1 Court, 1976. The Lloyd brothers, John (*left*) and David, bring off a sensational doubles win to keep Britain in the fight.

But Adriano Panatta's flying forehand volley seals the tie for Italy.

and the partisans on the other. It was much more like a World Cup football occasion than a scene at Wimbledon.

That fourth set was a humdinger. The British led 2/0 and 3/1, the Italians 4/3. At 5/4 David Lloyd had a set-point but put a backhand cross-court volley out. He had two more set-points, one of which was brilliantly saved by Panatta's return of serve that arrowed down the line. In a seven-deuce game the Italians only broke for 5-all at their fifth game-point. The Italians now led with their service game and at 9/10, 30–40 on his service John Lloyd saved the match and tie with a backhand cross-court chip and a deadly drop-volley.

At 14/15, 15–40, it was David's turn to be beleaguered, with two match-points to save. The first was lost by Bertolucci whose backhand return of serve was mishit. The second David saved with a terrific service to the forehand. Two more were saved by David, one with a backhand dink and the other with a fierce volley. At this point the Lloyds were playing an inspired game and the cacophony of the crowd was overwhelming. The Italians were broken in spirit and only won three more games. The final score to the Lloyds was 6/8, 3/6, 6/3, 18/16, 6/2 in a match which lasted four hours three minutes, including the sixteen-minute interval. It was the greatest Davis Cup doubles most people could remember and an inspiration to those who saw it.

Each year as Wimbledon ends the Secretary, now Chris Gorringe, and his very capable office staff start the ball rolling gently towards the next. Now it is rolling and gathering speed into its second century. Its present Chairman, Air Chief Marshal Sir Brian Burnett, his Vice-Chairman, Bimby Holt, and his Management Committee will face many new problems in the years to come, but they will be foreseen, met and dealt with just as sagaciously as in the past. For Wimbledon must continue and Wimbledon will continue. As an enthusiastic American visitor said to Brian Burnett in 1975, 'There may not always be an England but by God, sir, there'll always be a Wimbledon.'

Arthur Ashe, superb Wimbledon Champion of that year, echoed this verdict just before the American Championships, when he said, 'One thing is clear to me. Notwithstanding the prize money, Wimbledon is bigger than Forest Hills, or anywhere. It is in a class by itself like the world series or your cricketing tests.'

To one man, Pancho Contreras of Mexico, Wimbledon meant so much that he named his son after it. Somewhere there is a Wimbledon Contreras. Perhaps it was enough to turn him to hai-lai (South American pelota).

And now, as the various services and organisations gather and combine to weave the threads of Wimbledon's readiness together, suddenly another year is round, and the magic carpet of Wimbledon is rolled out again. We are transported to delight. It is two o'clock on the first Monday and the Centre Court is already nearly full. The Champion is opening the programme. 'Are you ready?' the umpire asks the players. They should be. Wimbledon certainly is – it has been getting ready for the past fifty weeks.

Eureka! We've done it!
Davis Cup 1981. First round v. Italy. *Left to right:* **Mark Cox** (coach), **Andrew Jarrett, Jonathan Smith, Richard Lewis, Buster Mottram** and **Paul Hutchins**, the national team manager and architect of victory.

Andrew Jarrett celebrates the doubles win.

Wightman Cup 1978 – an
Albert Hall spectacular.
Anne Hobbs, Sue Mappin,
Michele Tyler, Sue Barker,
Virginia Wade.

An overjoyed Sue
Barker, with team coach
Roger Taylor in the
background.

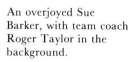

2

THE BEGINNINGS AND THE BROTHERS 1877–96

1877   On 9 June 1877 readers of *The Field*, an English publication which covered sporting and recreational pursuits, were greeted with this announcement:

> 'The All England Croquet and Lawn Tennis Club, Wimbledon, propose to hold a lawn tennis meeting open to all amateurs, on Monday July 9th and following days. Entrance fee £1.1.od. Two prizes will be given – one gold champion prize to the winner, one silver to the second player.'

This simple statement heralded the world's first lawn tennis championship.

Subsequently *The Field* told its readers that it would be putting up a silver challenge cup worth twenty-five guineas. The prizes and the publicity caused interest, but it cannot be said that the sporting world was taken by storm. The announcement was not a mass appeal aimed at attracting a big gate. *The Field*'s sphere of influence and circulation was among Britain's middle and upper classes. These had already established sporting priorities. One of these was cricket and indeed the playing schedule for that first Wimbledon Championship contained a two-day break on the first Friday and Saturday, to avoid a clash with the Eton–Harrow cricket match at Lord's. In the event, rain on the following Monday caused the postponement of the Final until the Thursday.

Some two hundred spectators made their way by carriage, bicycle and by the new railway to the then outer London suburb of Wimbledon to watch Mr Spencer Gore and Mr W. C. Marshall, the survivors of the original entry of twenty-two, face each other across the net to do battle for the first Wimbledon title.

The scene was recognisable as a tennis tournament as we know it today, but the differences were as marked as the similarities. The rackets were heavy and snow-shoe shaped, players served round-arm, and the net itself, five feet high at each wing, dipped to a height of three feet three inches in the middle. These differences were directly inherited from the ancient game of court tennis (Real Tennis), from which the infant game of lawn tennis had recently been derived.

It was this net shape which gave Spencer Gore his opportunity. He saw that with the net rising to five feet on either side, passing shots would not only be difficult but virtually out of the question. So he decided that by getting to the net he could dominate the rallies, in the manner of today's exponent of the big serve–volley game, but of course in those days there was no big serve.

Spencer Gore, an Old Harrovian, was a skilled rackets player – indeed none of the original entry of twenty-two were lawn tennis players – he was quick on his feet and had supple yet strong wrists. So he decided that, instead of playing a gentle baseline game, the main object being merely to keep the ball in play, he would go for the kill. This he did with volleys which were not smashes but which deftly directed the ball wide of his opponent. He did this alternately to the forehand and the backhand, giving the poor fellows such a run-around that one of them subsequently remarked he 'was ready to drop'.

Gore had come to win and he had won – in the Final handsomely, 6/1, 6/2, 6/4. The first All England Lawn Tennis Championship had been staged, the first name inscribed on the roll of honour.

The game, hitherto exclusively a leisurely pastime for leisured classes, had been, unknowingly, launched on the road which was to lead it to becoming a multi-national, multi-million dollar 'industry', followed by millions and creating its own superstars.

The causes of this initial launching lay deep in the character of Victorian Britain. The births of the game and of the first Championships were essentially products of their time.

Britain had a growing middle class. This middle class had energy, energy which developed the industrial revolution, which set up Britain as a colonial power. Some of this dynamism was channelled into the development – and export – of sport. Cricket and football had been well established. These, like indoor rackets and Real Tennis, were more for the skilled and/or enthusiastic exponent. What was still needed was a game which could be played casually, without particularly elaborate facilities.

So, on the spacious lawns behind those solid 'Forsyte' homes, forms of outdoor tennis and rackets were evolved, which provided something just a little more physically stimulating than croquet. Like croquet, tennis offered the chance for a young gentleman to converse and mix socially with young ladies. Tennis had the added prospect of the sight of a long skirt, momentarily uplifted, revealing an ankle. But in many circles lawn tennis or 'lawners' was looked down on as 'cissy' and referred to contemptuously as 'pat-ball'.

The All England Club had been founded in 1868 (at the office of J.H. Walsh, editor of *The Field*) with grounds rented in 1869 at Worple Road, Wimbledon, for playing croquet and holding croquet tournaments. One of its committee members was a certain Henry Jones. Jones was a man of energy and an innovator. He was a keen student of many games and was one of the foremost authorities on whist.

He saw the possibilities in the new game of lawn tennis. In 1875 he persuaded the Committee to set aside part of the ground for a tennis court and also got £25 allocated for equipment. In devoting himself to the cause of developing tennis, Henry Jones did not entirely overlook opportunities for personal reward. When the greater physical exertions of tennis than those of croquet demanded more than the post-game washing of hands, he came to the Committee's rescue (finances being low) by setting up at his own expense a bathroom, all fees for the use of which were to be paid to H. Jones.

With fellow committee members Julian Marshall and C.G. Heathcote he drew up the rules for the first Championship, which he refereed. Those rules have, with minor amendments, governed Wimbledon and world tennis ever since. The scoring terms of real tennis – fifteen, thirty, forty (all minute points on a form of clock scoring) and 'deuce' or 'à deux', i.e. parity (going back to French origins) – were retained and a set was won by the first to get six games.

Before the All England Club produced its rules the emerging game of lawn tennis had in theory adopted a set of rules drawn up by the Marylebone Cricket Club, the controlling body not only of cricket but also of Real Tennis. These embraced at least some of the features introduced by Major Clopton Wingfield, self-styled inventor of Lawn Tennis. Major Wingfield was an incredible character, an entrepreneur in true Victorian style, but who had in his make-up more than a dash of the Elizabethan buccaneer, and even a passing resemblance to the great Sir Francis Drake, a resemblance increased by a favourite garment which was a cross between a waistcoat and an Elizabethan doublet.

Wingfield, a cavalry major, had seen active military and sporting life in the Far East before returning to Britain. He was fascinated by the various racket and ball games beginning to become popular as garden recreation. He saw that this growing popularity had commercial possibilities so he 'invented' the game, calling it Sphairistike or Lawn Tennis, took out a patent and had boxed sets made up comprising equipment and the rules, which he sold. The court was hour-glass shaped, the net being shorter than the baselines.

The rules drawn up by Henry Jones and his colleagues have not only stood the test of time, they had to withstand fierce criticism after that very first Championship. For the net tactics which brought Spencer Gore victory had many declaring that the rules should be changed to counter them.

1878 The All England Club, doubtless realising that continual rule changes would bring confusion and ill repute, yielded, but compromised by lowering the net by only three inches throughout. The club was immediately vindicated in 1878 (34)* through the person of P.F. Hadow, a young planter in Ceylon. He was home on leave in Britain, was introduced to tennis, liked it and played it well (he was a good rackets player) under the tutelage of L.R. Erskine, a friend of the family, who suggested he should enter for Wimbledon.

He won his way through to the All-Comers Final, where he ungratefully beat Erskine, his mentor, in straight sets, so qualifying to meet the much-feared Spencer Gore and his killing net tactics in the Challenge Round (before 1922 the holder did not have to play through). Here Gore, who had shrewdly 'thought' his way to victory the year before, was himself outschemed. Hadow

* Up to 1914 figures in brackets indicate the number of players in the All Comers' draw.

A group of distinguished nineteenth-century British players. *Left to right:* E. de S.H. Browne, E. Renshaw, J.T. Hartley, Lilian Watson, C.W. Grinstead, Maud Watson, H.F. Lawford, W. Renshaw.

'A smashing pair' – Willie and Ernest Renshaw at Wimbledon in 1882.

saw that the counter to the net-rusher was the lob, which he constantly employed to send Gore scurrying back to the baseline.

Hadow's record was truly remarkable. A newcomer to the game, he played through without losing a set – the first of only five men to do so. He beat Gore 7/5, 6/1, 9/7. He then returned to planting in Ceylon and later big game hunting in India. He next appeared at New Wimbledon to receive his commemorative medal in Jubilee year, 1926.

1879 The Champion of 1879 (45), the Rev. J.T. Hartley, was another who did not allow Wimbledon success to interfere with his calling. He survived the first week of the Championship, and modestly he had not arranged for another preacher to take his place in the pulpit. His parish was in Yorkshire, so he made the then long journey back after his match on the Saturday, took his Sunday service and returned in time for service on court on the Monday. In the All-Comers Final Hartley beat V. St Leger Goold, who was later to be convicted of murder in France and sent to Devil's Island where he died. Hartley 'walked over' in the Challenge Round for Hadow was back in Ceylon.

1880 By 1880 (60) the Championship had become a sporting occasion, stands and new dressing-room accommodation had been built, the entry had increased to sixty, the number of courts to twelve and the price of admission was raised from one shilling to half-a-crown. The vision of Henry Jones was being more than justified. The fortunes of the All England club were transformed. In 1879 the profit for the year was a modest 1s. 10d. which in 1880 shot up to £230 and £760 the following year. This was due entirely to the Championships, which not only contributed most of the money but the success of which drew more and more members to the club. Hartley retained his title. Net posts were reduced from 4 ft 9 inches to 4 ft.

The crowds were being swelled by the attraction of the personalities now developing. The most notable and the first great lawn tennis player was Willie *1881* Renshaw, who beat the Rev. J.T. Hartley in the Challenge Round of 1881 (48). Willie Renshaw and his twin brother Ernest were not only great players by the standard of their time, but, even with the succession of great players through the years, the name Renshaw keeps a special place in the lawn tennis hall of fame. They matched their own ability by their dedication and application. From their early days they would watch and make notes on the styles of other players. They came from a wealthy family which allowed them to indulge their tennis to the extent of building a court at a hotel in the south of France, on which they could keep up their régime of constant practice in the winter.

They brought to tennis a new concept in doubles play and above all they introduced 'the Renshaw smash'. Unlike the deft Gore flick, this was a fierce overhead volley and it was this which Willie used to counter the lob and win the first of his seven titles, six of them in succession, three of them in finals against brother Ernest (1882 (28), 1883 (23) and 1889 (37)).

1882–3 In 1882 the height of the net-posts was reduced to today's 3 ft 6 inches.

Champions and pioneers.
Spencer W. Gore, 1877.

P.F. Hadow, 1878.

J.T. Hartley, 1879–80.

H.F. Lawford, 1887.

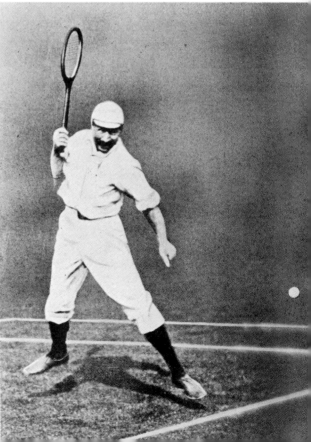

The idea of a service 'let' had been introduced in 1880; previously this had been deemed a good service. In addition players were forbidden to touch the net or volley the ball before it had crossed the net.

In three successive years, 1884–5–6, the beaten Finalist was H.F. Lawford, who had first unsuccessfully challenged in 1880 – against Hartley. Lawford was another of the great characters of Victorian tennis, a broad-shouldered, upstanding man of firm countenance who, in his shirt with wide horizontal stripes, cavalry-style trousers tucked into socks just below the knee and the whole rig topped with a cap resembling a pith helmet, looked as though he was about to set off to discover the source of the Nile, rather than play tennis. His main asset was his strength and power, which he unleashed in full measure in his forehand drive, like a shell from a cannon.

His clashes with Willie Renshaw contained every thrill for the layman, a fascinating contrast in styles for the connoisseur. Their duels were given added spice by reported retorts from both players in the revived controversy about whether volleying should be inhibited by a change in the rules. Declared Lawford: 'It is always possible to pass a volleyer, and I know that when I lose a stroke by being volleyed it is my own fault.' To this Willie responded with, 'Before many years taking the ball off the ground will be quite the exception.'

The principle is still being argued but there was no denying that the nimble, elegant Willie Renshaw had the measure of his powerful, older opponent. In
1884 their first Challenge Round meeting in 1884 (28) Willie took the first six games in eleven minutes and the match in straight sets. This was the signal for Lawford
1885–6 to drive himself harder. The following year (23) he took a set from Willie and in 1886 (23), after losing the first set to love, by dint of volleying much more he got on level terms at one set all, but Willie won the next two to keep the title. As the Renshaw–Lawford rivalry went on, the box office boomed. In 1885, although the Men's Singles Championship attracted only twenty-three entries, the Challenge Round was watched by 3500 spectators.

1887 The Willie Renshaw–Lawford battles were interrupted in 1887 (16) when Willie had to withdraw from the Championships with the first recorded case of tennis elbow, brought on by his severe use of over-arm service, first introduced by A.T. Myers in 1878. So it was left to Ernest Renshaw to carry the family honour. In the All-Comers Final Ernest ran to a two sets to one lead, but then seemed to become over-cautious and Lawford, ever the relentless battler, powered his way through to the victory which his hard efforts had earned. In
1888–9 1888 (24) a more determined Ernest Renshaw redeemed the family and gained his revenge over Lawford with a straight sets win.

The following year (24) the Renshaw monopoly was re-established when Willie, although in failing health, fought his way through the All-Comers Championship for the right to meet Ernest in the Challenge Round. To do so he engaged in an incredible battle for survival in the Final of the All-Comers Singles. His opponent was Harry Barlow who took a 2–0 lead in sets and then went to match-point in the fourth. Even in this dire situation Willie still attacked and got to his favourite net position.

Then, in a hectic rally, he dropped his racket. Barlow, with any shot open to him, played a gentle lob over Renshaw's head. Willie snatched up his racket, raced back to the baseline, retrieved the ball and the point and went on to win the set. Barlow, undaunted, then raced to a five-game lead in the final set, at which point a spectator offered a hundred to one in sovereigns against Willie. He got no takers, and saved himself the hundred sovereigns. For Willie won, surviving altogether six match-points. He went on to beat brother Ernest in the Challenge Round to win his seventh Wimbledon Singles title – a record that has never been equalled in the Men's Championship.

1890 In the 1890 (30) Challenge Round Willie defended against Irishman, Willoughby Hamilton, and gained a 2–1 lead in sets. Hamilton, two years before, had become only the second player to beat Willie at Wimbledon (the first was O. Wodehouse in 1880) and also had wins over both Renshaws to his credit in Dublin. Maybe this gave him a psychological edge, for this thin, pallid Irishman, known as 'the Ghost', fought back against a very weary Willie to win the last two sets 6/1, 6/1. The Renshaw reign was over. Willie was never well enough to compete again. Ernest played in 1891 but lost easily in the All-Comers semi-finals to Wilfred Baddeley and tried only once more – in 1893.

omen By this time male players, for whom an official Doubles Championship
4-97 was started in 1884 at Wimbledon, were having to compete for the limelight with the ladies. Once again it had been Henry Jones, the great innovator, who had persuaded the committee in 1884 to stage a ladies' championship. There were only thirteen entries. Maud Watson came to the Championships with a record of being unbeaten for two years. She maintained her form to win the first All England Ladies' Singles crown in a close final with her sister Lilian, and she successfully defended it against Blanche Bingley in the following year (10).

In 1886 (8), attempting a hat-trick, she was again challenged by the persistent Blanche Bingley, whose strength lay in a forehand which would have been an outstanding shot today, but which in the more genteel women's tennis of the day was truly formidable. She used this weapon to such effect that she won the title. She lost it to the incomparable Lottie Dod in 1887 (5). She consoled herself by marrying (her husband, Commander G.W. Hillyard, was later to be a great Secretary of the Club). As Mrs Hillyard she was to win the title five more times and incredibly remain a force in women's tennis until well after the turn of the century.

But first, Wimbledon was to witness the meteoric career of Charlotte Dod. Even allowing for the limited opposition, Lottie Dod merits a special place in Wimbledon history. She did for women's tennis what the Renshaws had done and were still doing for men's tennis. Having initially forged her game by playing with her sister and two brothers, she then modelled it on that of the

Champions who fashioned the game.
Maud Watson, 1884–5.

Blanche Bingley (Mrs Hillyard), 1886,
1889, 1894, 1897, 1899, 1900.

Lottie Dod, 1887–8, 1891–3.

Lena Rice, 1890.

Renshaws. A tall tomboy, she brought speed to women's tennis, and with it the smash and attacking net play.

And she did it all by the time she was fifteen. She beat her challenger, Mrs Hillyard, again in 1888 (6). She went on to win five titles in seven Championships and in four of the Challenge Rounds she beat the indefatigable Blanche Hillyard. In 1889 she was on a yachting cruise and did not challenge again until returning triumphantly in 1891 (9). Such was Lottie's supremacy in women's tennis that her first four titles were gained for a total loss of twenty-four games. She never lost at Wimbledon and dropped only one set there. It is said that in her entire tennis career she was beaten only four times.

The Dod meteor burned with fierce brightness. It never died out, but disappeared as suddenly as it had come, when at twenty-one the Champion forsook tennis to devote herself to golf – and become English Champion. She was also a first-class archer and an international hockey player. All in all she had good claim to being called a superstar of sport – perhaps the greatest woman all-rounder the world has known.

During Lottie's absence on the high seas Mrs Hillyard won the title for the second time in 1889 (6) but did not defend in 1890 (4) when the title went to the only Irish girl ever to win, Lena Rice, who had to win only two matches. With Lottie Dod off the stage in 1894 (11) Mrs Hillyard won easily but did not play again until 1897 (7), leaving 1895 (9) and 1896 (6) to be won by Charlotte (Chattie) Cooper, later Mrs Sterry and mother of Gwen, a Wimbledon player between the wars, and of Rex, the Club's Vice-Chairman during Herman David's reign. Rex Sterry recalls that at the time of her first win Chattie was staying with her brother, Dr Harry Cooper. She bicycled home to Surbiton and found her brother in the garden pruning roses. 'What have you been doing, Chattie?' he enquired. 'I've just won the Championship,' she replied. Her brother said nothing and went on pruning his roses.

1891 Meanwhile, on to the men's stage, following the departure of the great Renshaws, strode another set of twins, Wilfred and Herbert Baddeley. Their arch rival was Joshua Pim, an Irish doctor. Pim's brilliance became a legend. Here was a true artist of the court, whose game was at once powerful and delicate. His art meant more to him than gaining points and victories. He delighted in playing the drop-volley and it was said that he could even deliberately produce a winning net-cord. Here was no percentage player. For Pim the more difficult the situation, the more daring the stroke. He considered a winner should be possible from any position.

Wilfred Baddeley, on the other hand, was a skilful player who knew how to deploy skills to best advantage. With the Champion, Hamilton, not defending, this he did to beat Pim in the 1891 (22) All-Comers Final and conquered him *2–4* again in the Challenge Round next year (27), but Pim got his revenge in 1893 (27) and held off Baddeley's challenge in 1894 (23) whereupon he retired from top tennis.

Champions and Pioneers.
W.J. Hamilton, 1890.

Wilfred Baddeley, 1891–2, 1895.

Harold Mahony, 1896.

Joshua Pim, 1893–4.

1895–6 Back came Baddeley to regain the crown in 1895 (18) after a tremendous struggle against the Australian doctor, W.V. Eaves. Baddeley was once within a point of a straight sets defeat. Baddeley lost the title the following year (31 entries, including the Americans, A.E. Foote and W.A. Larned – the latter winning two rounds) to a genial Irishman called Harold Mahony who could attack with volley, smash and even backhand but whose forehand did little more than keep the ball in play. He was a character who came regularly to Wimbledon, taking his defeats and victories in the same carefree way and his eventual success in a fluctuating five-setter was a popular one.

But at that time there were not so many Wimbledon spectators with whom to be popular. After the stirring Renshaw–Lawford battles the tennis of their successors, while being of fine technique, did not have the spectator appeal of their predecessors. And unlike cricket and football which through grass roots participation had already established themselves firmly as popular spectator sports, tennis – once its novelty had worn off – lived by the quality of the show it presented. The evidence of this decline in public interest was revealed in the 1895 loss of £33 on the Championships, a serious matter in those days. In desperation croquet was reintroduced and the extra subscriptions proved a life-saver. The tide was further turning. Three other saviours were at hand, the Doherty brothers and Archdale Palmer, a most astute businessman who became Secretary in 1899.

3

THE DOS AND OTHER DOERS 1897–1914

Reggie and Laurie Doherty, 'Big Do' and 'Little Do', could have stepped straight from the pages of Victorian schoolboy fiction. They exemplified the current ideals of heroism, they played superbly, showed grace and sportsmanship on court and modesty off it. Lawn tennis owes them a huge debt. They not only rescued Wimbledon when interest was flagging critically, but helped to stimulate interest in tennis throughout the world.

They were supreme stylists who played just about every shot in the book – by the book which their play was writing. They were fast about the court, but their strokes hardly ever seemed hurried. They were to dominate Wimbledon for a decade and the crowds were to come flocking to see the contrast in styles, as players with varying individual techniques came to try and wrest the title first from Reggie, who won and held the crown for four years, and then from Laurie, Champion for five years. In addition, for eight of those years the brothers combined to hold the Doubles title, engaging in many fascinating battles and holding off many fierce challenges.

There were in fact three Doherty brothers. The eldest, the Rev William Vernon Doherty, was good enough to captain Oxford University, but although a good player, he did not pursue tennis seriously. However, he made an historic contribution to the game by stimulating the interest of his two younger brothers.

R.F. (Reggie), the older by three years, known as 'Big Do' and H.L. (Laurie) as 'Little Do', were both natural sportsmen. At Westminster School both were good at cricket and football. Reggie played in the Wimbledon Singles of 1894 and 1895, the year the brothers first appeared as a pair. They came as undergraduates who had swept all before them at Cambridge, and they took C.F. Simon and W.G. Bailey to a hard five-setter before going out in the first round. Reggie had also played in the 1894 Covered Court Championship. He can be said to have reached the Final for due to the dwindled interest in tennis the Singles Championship attracted only two entries. Reggie lost the one and only match to E.G. Meers, an established player, but had done enough to earn mention in *The Field* as 'a young player of great promise whose lawn tennis future will be watched with interest. He has capital ground strokes, volleys hard and clean, serves a capital length and keeps a cool head.'

Reggie and Laurie both entered for the 1896 Wimbledon Singles Championship. Reggie took Mahony, the eventual winner, to five sets in their first-round match while Laurie extended C.H.L. Cazalet to four sets. He then reached the Final of the All England Plate, instituted that year as an event for early round losers, where he went down only 7/5 in the final set to A.W. Gore, the man who, six years later, was to interrupt the Dohertys' unbroken run of singles successes.

1897 The Doherty reign began in 1897 (31). And what a beginning! Reggie progressed regally, disposing of reigning Champion H.S. Mahony and Wilfred Baddeley, the previous Champion, and W.V. Eaves who for the third successive year had reached the Final of the All-Comers Singles – all without losing a set. Reggie Doherty, over six feet tall and with finely cut features under dark wavy hair would, in a later age, have had teenagers swooning – as it was he brought colour to many a Victorian lady's cheek. But, suffering from dyspepsia, he endured indifferent health. Most affected were his speed and his stamina.

1898 The following year (37) Mahony made a determined bid to regain his title. But, having reached the All-Comers Final, he had there to get past Laurie Doherty in order to get a second crack at Reggie. Laurie, tenacious as ever, seemed even more determined that no-one should get past him. Three times in the fifth set Mahony, leading 5/4 in games, was at match-point. Each time Laurie denied him. This gruelling set was to go to twenty-six games before Laurie earned the right to meet his brother in the Challenge Round, where he pulled back from being two sets down to square 2/2 before Reggie established his superiority in the final set.

In 1898 the reviving interest brought about by the Dohertys' fluent and comprehensive game produced a profit of £70 on the Lawn Tennis Championships. The next year, through the good offices of Palmer, this had leapt to £200 and even the Croquet Championships made £19. A new pavilion was built for £1200 and the Club was restyled The All England Lawn Tennis and Croquet Club.

1899 With Laurie Doherty unable to take part in the 1899 (37) Wimbledon through illness, Reggie was the lone Doherty standard-bearer. But he was not at top fitness nor top form and found himself two sets down in the Challenge Round to A.W. Gore. Gore, playing in his tenth Wimbledon, looked what he was – a successful hard-working Victorian businessman. For him tennis was only a relaxation. But he was a man who played hard as well as worked hard. He was strong, fit and fast. He played from the baseline, happy to engage in long exhausting rallies. His main attacking weapon was his fierce forehand drive. He was so quick on his feet that he was often able to run round the ball and get in a forehand on what should have been a backhand shot. It was such tactics which brought him to the two-set lead against Reggie Doherty. 'Big Do' showed the same coolness which had impressed as a youngster. Refusing to become rattled, he concentrated on accurately placing down the line, so that Gore was forced to play off the backhand which Reggie invariably met on the volley. So Reggie won two sets to square the match and then took the decider.

An experiment was introduced this year with an unofficial Ladies Doubles, which was won by Mrs Hillyard and Miss B. Steedman. This ran till 1907 but the Championship Doubles only began in 1913, as did the Mixed Doubles.

1900   Reggie's Challenger next year (34) was one of the most remarkable players tennis has ever seen, Sidney Smith, who in the same year became the first All England Men's Badminton Champion. A leg disability prevented Smith from being very mobile. To compensate for this he developed a flat, bludgeoning forehand of such power that it gained the name of Smith Punch while, in the manner of prize-fighters of the era, the player himself was linked with his hometown to become known as 'Smith of Stroud'.

Smith won the first set of the Challenge Round against Reggie Doherty, but the Champion again got the measure of his baseliner opponent to take the next three sets. The likely prospect of this match of contrasting styles, and a by no means wholly predictable outcome, kept interest high and the crowds flocking. The match also showed that for the title-holder not to be required to play through the tournament, but to appear only in the Challenge Round, had its disadvantages. Playing through the All-Comers Singles could be tiring, but it could also serve to put the Challenger into high gear against a Champion who might be a bit sluggish, especially at the start.

1901   The year 1901 (36) saw a Wimbledon drama to match any of the stage melodramas of the time. Reggie Doherty was in such poor health that his doctor forbade him to play. Indications were that Reggie would take this advice. These arose from Reggie's belief that Laurie would win the All-Comers Singles and that, if he himself scratched, the title would remain in the family.

But after winning the first two sets of his third round match, Little Do was beaten by George Hillyard, the future Club secretary, then better known as a county cricketer who had taken tennis seriously only after his marriage to Blanche Bingley, who between 1886 and 1900 won the Ladies' title six times. Hillyard then met the redoubtable Gore and reached match-point in the fourth set. Gore saved this with a net-cord, going on to beat H. Roper Barrett and C.P. Dixon to win the All-Comers Singles and so earn the right to challenge Reggie Doherty.

So Big Do had to decide. Should he face Gore in the Challenge Round or should he withdraw? Against the advice of his doctor and the pleading of his mother, Reggie decided to play. If the title were to leave Doherty hands, the passing should not be by default. He took the court against Gore, won the first set and went to a 5/2 lead in the second. But he was having to overcome the handicap of his own ebbing strength and Gore's relentless baseline returns. The Challenger took five games in a row to square the match at one set all and, pressing home the initiative he had gained, went on to win the next two sets and the match.

The Dos – R.F. 'Big Do' and H.L. 'Little Do' – and how to do it. 'Big Do' shows perfect backhand counterpoise.

The Dos get down to it against G.C. Ball-Greene and G.W. Hillyard, 1897.

Big Do had finally been beaten. But the Dohertys were not prepared to bow out of Wimbledon or bow down to a successor. Laurie was now ready to assert his game. Hitherto, he had played well at Wimbledon but with chequered results. Maybe, subconsciously even, he did not want to challenge a brother over whom he had a physical edge. The two brothers never wanted to meet in serious competition, though they enjoyed playing hard-fought friendlies against each other, but Reggie would retire if the pace began to have ill effects on him.

The name of Doherty was not to be kept from the Championship rolls that year. In the Doubles the two brothers held on to their title in a match which marked yet another Wimbledon landmark, for their Challenge Round opponents were the American pair, Dwight Davis and Holcombe Ward. The previous year Dwight Davis had donated the trophy which was to bear his name and he had helped America to win it. Now the Americans were turning ambitious eyes on Wimbledon.

They came to Britain as men of mystery. The crowds were initially intrigued by their black shoes. Players were more concerned with the 'secret weapon' which the Americans brought – the top-spin service which could cause the ball to swerve and break. At the outset the Dos found difficulty in coping with the American spin tactics. One thing that surprised spectators was the way Little Do would try to play back every service, including the faults. The reason was to become apparent. Even as that first set ended Laurie was playing the American service with much greater confidence, and the Dohertys won the next three sets, although the fourth went to sixteen games.

There were those who had had misgivings about the coming of the Americans, feeling that the peaceful family calm of Wimbledon would be broken. But as A. Wallis Myers records: 'By their sportsmanship as by their play the Americans had caught the favour of the crowd.'

1902   The Dohertys came back to defend their title again in 1902. In those Championships Reggie did not enter the Singles (42) but Laurie did. He showed a new authority in taking the title back from the player who had ended his brother's reign. Little Do beat Gore in four sets, the final one to love. But in the Doubles (20) the Dohertys lost their title to Sydney Smith and Frank Riseley (usually unlucky to be in their shadow), whose one up, one back formation flourished on Smith's famed forehand and Riseley's power and speed at the net. For the next four years these same doubles pairs were to fight out the Challenge Round. In the first three, the Dohertys were winners but in 1906 (28) Smith and Riseley came out on top at the end of a gruelling and stirring five-set struggle.

1903–4   Little Do meanwhile was nobly bearing the mantle he had gained by right of conquest. In 1903 (42) and in the following year (62) he beat Riseley in the Challenge Round. Riseley's path to the Challenge Round was marked by a unique incident. As in 1903 Smith and Riseley met in the fifth round. The first time, after a hard five-set battle, Riseley won 7/5, 6/3, 7/9, 1/6, 9/7. In

1904 (62) fifty fiercely fought games saw them at two sets all and at the start of a fifth set. The two contestants, who were again doubles partners, settled for tossing up to decide the winner, rather than subjecting themselves to more punishment.

1905   In 1905 the American Davis Cup team came over to try to wrest the Cup back from the British Isles. In the Championships at Wimbledon their progress and styles of play were keenly watched and analysed. W.J. Clothier was only just beaten in the fourth round by Tony Wilding of New Zealand, who got home 10/8 in the final set; while in the same round Beals Wright, who played in the Davis Cup doubles, took A.W. Gore to four sets. So the leading home players were able to contain this invasion, and at the same time they learned much from the Americans, particularly in the variety of their spin services. This experience was put to very good use at Wimbledon in the Davis Cup tie when the British made a clean sweep.

By now new names were beginning to appear in the lists of entries. Along with the Americans other overseas entries included Tony Wilding and the Belgians P. de Borman and W. Lenaire. Also entered for 1905 Wimbledon was N.E. Brookes (Australia). Norman Brookes was to become the Grand Old Man of Australian tennis and give the game a lifetime of service. The 1905 (71) crowds were anxious to see how this early exponent of the serve–volley game would fare against the home players. Brookes provided the answer by getting through to the Final of the All-Comers Singles and just emerged victorious over baseliner Smith.

Brookes thus became the first winner of the Renshaw Cup, donated by the Renshaw family in honour of the great brothers, to be awarded to the winner of the All-Comers event. Following the abolition of the Challenge Round it has been awarded to the Champion. So it was to be Brookes versus Laurie Doherty. Brookes nearly had to default when, owing to the crush, a zealous gatekeeper barred him from entry. From the start he attacked with serve and with volley. 'Little Do' countered with his all-court game, using the lob to turn his opponent's menacing advance into scampering retreat – and to win the match 8/6, 6/2, 6/4.

906   The next year (69 entries) saw an all-domestic Challenge Round, with Laurie again seeing off the persistent advances of Riseley. But in the Doubles this last year of the Doherty era ended in defeat. Smith and Riseley combined to put on a show of remorseless power, which in the fifth set eventually broke the brave but failing strength of Reggie Doherty, still immaculate in his court manners but physically strained and distressed, a gallant warrior to the last.

It was perhaps fitting that the Doherty Wimbledon reign should end with a mixture of victory and defeat. For as well as the standards of play and sportsmanship they set, they revived the Club's fortunes by establishing new heights of competitive interest. The Dohertys were superlative at the all-court game, but were not so crushingly invincible that they ruled out speculation on whether the various challengers who came up against them would succeed. So, more and more, tennis became talked about and more and more it became watched.

And more and more players came to challenge from overseas. A pair of English brothers had been the centre of the lawn tennis world. Now from the Southern Hemisphere came two men who between them were to share most of the honours until the First World War. Australia had been quick to follow the British lawn tennis lead. The Victorian Championships were held in Melbourne in 1880 and those of New South Wales in Sydney in 1884.

But as in Britain – even more perhaps – it had been purely a social game for the most part and it was not until Norman Brookes, with his devastating volleying game, first hit the headlines in the Old Country that tennis really began to be taken seriously in Australia. Brookes was fortunate to find an ally in Tony Wilding, a brilliant player from New Zealand, and, having wisely formed the Australasian Lawn Tennis Association in 1904, these two were able to team up for Davis Cup matches.

The partnership was of two contrasting characters and styles. Wilding's father, who had emigrated to New Zealand in the 'seventies, had been a good all-round sportsman at home in England. Tony and his brothers and sisters had every chance to grow up in the same way, for there was no shortage of facilities at the Wilding home. He might well have preferred cricket and football to tennis, which so many regarded as cissy. However, a schoolfellow whom Tony disliked heartily, was good at tennis so young Wilding decided to beat him. This he did after six weeks' practice and he realised he could become a champion if he were determined enough.

Going up to Cambridge, he was soon persuaded that tennis offered a greater scope to him than did cricket. He entered Wimbledon in 1904 and in the second round gave the old Champion, Mahony, a very good fight, though he appreciated that his strokes could be improved, especially his backhand, for which he did not change his grip. For another thing, he realised that a baseline driving game must be backed by the ability to volley. His top-spin forehand was fierce, and deceptive, though somewhat uncontrolled. With the help and advice of those backhand experts, Mahony and Reggie Doherty, he improved noticeably and in 1905 was chosen for the Davis Cup team. He had a good eye and strong wrist, as is illustrated in this story told by Wallis Myers. 'He once challenged a friend to a match, agreeing to use only a cricket bat – and very nearly won.' This is strongly suggestive of Don Bradman practising batting with a cricket stump.

Well-built and possessing perfect health, he still took no chances, training hard for any important match and being careful afterwards to change quickly, before sweat could grow cold and a chill be caught. This dedication to condition went with the desire for fresh air and he loved sleeping in the open. Careful as Wilding was about his own condition, he was careless about dress and other

The first invaders. The 'Wizard', Norman Brookes, father of Australian tennis. His fighting spirit is exemplified by his very shortened grip. He always had his rackets loosely strung for greater control.

Tony Wilding, the greatest New Zealand player of all time, Champion 1910–13.

Maurice E. McLoughlin, American champion 1912–13 – the original 'Californian Comet' – delivering his cannonball.

people's possessions, which he often borrowed. Despite this rather cavalier attitude, he was a welcome guest anywhere.

Norman Brookes was totally different from Wilding. The most obvious difference was that he was left-handed. And he was self-reliant and self-taught, smaller of physique but as tough as they come both in body and in temperament. He was a fantastic competitor at any ball game. He had very nearly succeeded at his first attempt in 1905 when he won through to the Challenge Round, having beaten Riseley, Gore and S.H. Smith.

Laurie Doherty held him at bay there. At bay is right because Brookes loved to attack. He had a variety of services, some of them super googlies, all with apparently the same action, and his volleying was adroit and incisive. He soon earned the nickname 'the Wizard'. His brilliant footwork helped what seemed to be an uncanny anticipation. Laurie Doherty had been watching his play round by round and it was only because he studied the Wizard's tricks so closely that he found the answer just in time. Brookes was not abashed. He came off court feeling that next time he would beat Laurie easily.

But next time never came, for in Laurie's final year at Wimbledon, 1906 (69),
1907 Brookes did not play. On the Wizard's return in 1907 (85) he won through the All-Comers, beating A.W. Gore easily in the Final, which gave him the title (the first overseas men's winner), since Laurie Doherty, the holder, had retired. Indeed, it was largely due to the retirement of Big and Little Do that Australasia, for whom Brookes and Wilding played all five rubbers, were able to challenge the British Isles successfully in the 1907 Davis Cup at Wimbledon. Australasia held this famous cup for four more years before in 1912 losing once more to the British Isles, who next year ceded to the United States, from which Australasia, spearheaded again by Brookes and Wilding, won it back just as the First World War broke out.

In Brookes's first year as Champion, although he was fortunate in the absence of the four leading home players, the Dohertys, Smith and Riseley, who had all retired, there was still plenty of opposition. In the second round he met Tony Wilding, in one of his many stirring encounters with his Davis Cup partner, and beat him only 3/2. Danger was still there in the form of Karl Behr of America who, after being two sets down, squared the match but faded in the fifth set.

1908   1908 (70) saw the amazing persistence, courage and stamina of Arthur Wentworth Gore rewarded again. He first entered the Championships in 1888 and won the All-Comers Singles only after eleven years, there of course to be repulsed by Reggie Doherty. He gained his first title against a weakened Reggie two years later. His second was won at the age of forty, twenty years after his first attempt. He won, despite his weakness on the backhand. In the Final he beat Roper Barrett in five sets and was perhaps lucky that Barrett had beaten Wilding in the quarter-finals. With Brookes not defending in the Challenge Round, Gore automatically became Champion.

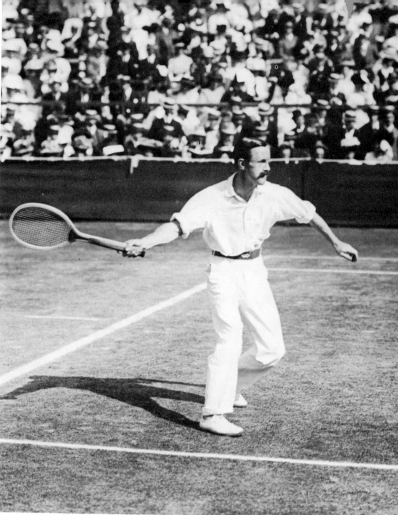

1909 (85) was to be remembered for two things. They were the abominable weather, which for the first time caused the Championships to go into the third week, and the defiant defence of his title by Gore. From a field which included many new faces, and had lost the seasoning of the old Champions, and also Brookes and Wilding, M.J.G. Ritchie came through to beat Roper Barrett in the All-Comers in four sets.

Ritchie was an ambassador for lawn tennis. He had spent many years playing the game, much of it abroad, and he had left a trail of inspiration across Europe. His game was known for its all-round steadiness, deploying a variety of strokes without great power. His defence was excellent and he loved the lob. It was this particular shot which had played a significant part in Ritchie and Wilding's win over Gore and Roper Barrett in the 1908 Doubles Final. Though largely defensive he was no slouch, for, adapting his game to a bit more speed of drive, he had twice beaten Laurie Doherty.

In the 1909 Challenge Round Ritchie is said to have been at his best. The steady qualities of the Challenger, and the long baseline rallies which ensued, provoked many a mistake in Gore's famous forehand, which began to break down. Ritchie led 8/6, 6/1 and then 2/0. At about this point there occurred an interesting incident, which is best told in the words of F.R. Burrow:

> 'I was taking a line in this match, and early in the third set I gave a decision, which was probably wrong, against Gore. Ritchie evidently thought it was wrong. Anyway, he "threw" the next point; and from that moment he was never really on top again. Perhaps it worried him; anyway he played a very different game in the last three sets from that which he had produced in the first two.'

Gore, sensing that his opponent had relaxed, for whatever reason, seized his chance, won the next six games for the set and the last two sets 6/2, 6/2. At forty-one Gore was the oldest champion there had been – a record that has not since been beaten.

1910 (92) had a strong foreign entry, including Beals Wright (USA), R.B. Powell (Canada), Otto Froitzheim and Otto Kreuzer of Germany, the two Fyzees of India, Max Decugis and his protégé André Gobert of France, from Australia Stanley Doust, by now a regular and a beautiful doubles player, and from Ireland J.C. Parke. To round off the strong overseas entry Tony Wilding was there.

Ritchie, winner of the All-Comers in 1909, was unlucky to meet Wilding in good form in the third round, and he lost in four sets. In the quarter-finals Parke took four sets to beat Beamish, as did A.H. Lowe to beat Doust. Easier wins went to Wilding over Froitzheim, and Wright over Powell, both in straight sets. In the semi-finals Wilding beat Parke 3/0, though Wright dropped a set to Lowe.

In the All-Comers Final Wilding and Wright played the classic encounter

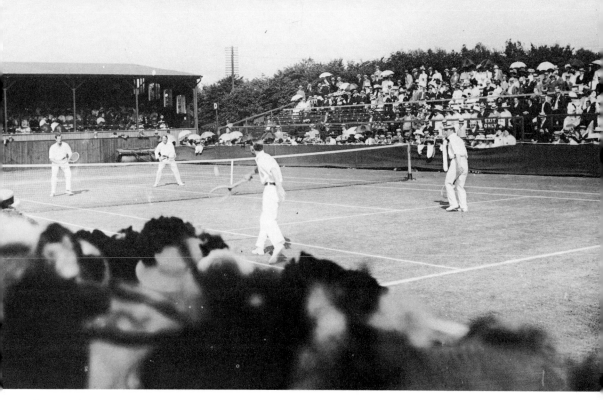

Pre-war doubles at Worple Road.
All-Comers' Final 1908: A.F. Wilding and M.J.G. Ritchie (far side) v. A.W. Gore and H. Roper Barrett.

Challenge Round 1911: André Gobert (serving) and Max Decugis v. Wilding and Ritchie.

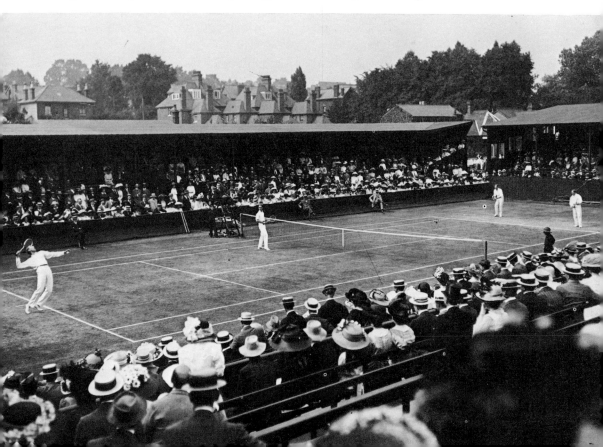

of baseliner versus volleyer. Not that Wilding scorned the volley. He realised the importance of gaining the net, once the ground had been properly prepared. To Wright, however, it was the natural place for him to be. Either following his rhythmic, left-handed service or a well-controlled chop, which kept the ball bouncing low, he would take the net and more often than not command it. This he did in the first two sets which he won 6/2, 6/2.

But Wilding, trained as always to a hair, and never turning one, knew very well that sooner or later the effort of continual serve–volley (it must be remembered that in those days there were few players who trained to modern standards) would take its toll, and good judgement of the right moment could bring the initiative into his grasp.

So it happened. More and more his extended opponent failed to be decisive and was driven back, whereupon Wilding himself came in and volleyed the winners, to win a rousing match in five sets. In the Challenge Round Wilding, now more mature and confident and certainly improved on his 1906 form, reversed his semi-final defeat by Gore in that year, taking the title from him now in four sets. This was the start of Wilding's four titles running, a distinguished reign.

1911   In 1911 (104) Dixon beat Decugis in a good semi-final match and Barrett beat F.G. Lowe. The All-Comers Final was another five-setter, with the winner Barrett this time coming from two sets to love down, to win the match. The Challenge Round between Wilding and Barrett was a strange affair. Wilding began well, as expected, and took the first set 6/4. Towards the end of that set Barrett changed his tactics and began to play half-court shots with no pace. Wilding found these hard to attack but they drew him to the net, whereupon Barrett lobbed him. The ploy succeeded so well that Wilding lost his touch and played like a man bemused. Leading now two sets to one, Barrett tired rapidly in the heat of the airless Centre Court. Having won the first game of the fourth set, he lost the next six for two sets all. His legs would now scarce bear him and he had to retire.

1912   The entry in 1912 dropped to eighty-one and that great campaigner, Gore, got through once again to challenge Wilding. He played well right through the draw, keeping on top of some tough matches and, in the All-Comers Final, he met a much-improved André Gobert and beat him in four sets. This was the more remarkable – and the crowd recognised this by the ovation they gave him – because at the age of forty-four he had beaten a man half his age, who had just won the tennis Gold Medal at the Stockholm Olympic Games.

In the Challenge Round Wilding, who would have preferred to play through the All-Comers, had too much youth (and now experience) on his side. Gore, fighting hard, did well to take the third set. Although this was Gore's final Challenge Round it was by no means his final appearance. He was still there, fifteen years later, still admired by the crowds, at the sixth Championship at New Wimbledon in 1927, by when he had competed in all but one Championship for 36 years. He had lived and played through the eras of the Renshaws, the Baddeleys, the Dohertys, Brookes and Wilding and the new stars of the Twenties, Tilden and the Four French Musketeers.

1913   Wimbledon had its highest pre-war entry in 1913 (116). The Championships were becoming more and more international, with overseas players regularly returning to try again. The exception was the 'Californian Comet', red-headed Maurice McLoughlin, whose tremendous service power first gave rise to the description 'cannonball'. His reputation having gone ahead, his first round match with Roper Barrett, still a force, drew tremendous first-day crowds and the gates had to be closed. The match lived up to its promise, for Roper Barrett had seldom played better and took the fiery American youngster all the way, losing only 6/8 in the final set. After that McLoughlin was irresistible, and anticipation of the Challenge Round meeting between Wilding and McLoughlin was so high that hundreds never got near the Centre Court. Ticket touts had the day of their lives, with stand seats reputedly fetching £10.

Wilding had not wasted his time. He had watched McLoughlin's service closely and, to the surprise of all, stood right in to take it, before its great break and jump took it too wide. Wilding also attacked relentlessly the American's weaker backhand. That first set was a battle and when McLoughlin got to 5/4 40/30 and set-point, he put everything he had into a super-fast service. Wilding not only blocked it but, making pace from pace, hit an outright winner. This was undoubtedly the turning point, for he went on to win the first set 8/6 and now had the initiative.

He won the second 6/3 and led 4/2 in the third. Here McLoughlin came again to lead 5/4. The battle swayed to 9/8 and Wilding had 40/30 matchpoint on his own service. The first was a fault. On the second he overstepped the line a long way and was foot-faulted. Many a player would have had his grip on the match loosened. But undismayed, he won the next two points for the title. The Comet had just failed and was not seen in the Wimbledon firmament again.

1914   In the last pre-war Championships (102) the 1907 Champion, left-hander Norman Brookes, entered again after a seven-year absence. He immediately showed himself to be in great form, searing through the opposition, winning seven love sets out of the fifteen needed. The All-Comers Final against the German, Otto Froitzheim, seemed to be going much the same way when Brookes won the first two sets 6/2, 6/1, and led 5/3 in the third. Froitzheim would not submit and, fighting furiously, took the set 7/5 and went on to win the fourth 6/4. 'Wimbledon Sensation'. The headlines were already being written. And indeed it very nearly was. Brookes never regained that early ascendancy and the final set was hard fought all the way. Many thought Brookes lucky since he had several net-cords at critical points. But he finally gained the day 8/6.

The Challenge Round was played between two men, each full of confidence.

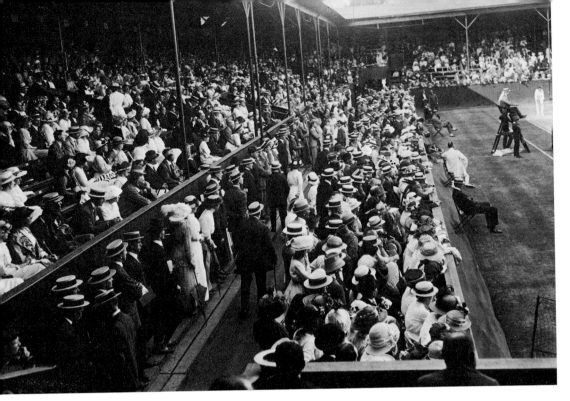

Worple Road before the world changed, July 1914.

Spotless attire for the umpire and the two great players from Australasia, Norman Brookes and Tony Wilding.

Brookes' came from an innate belief in his own competitive ability. Wilding's, fostered perhaps by two recent easy wins over Brookes on the Riviera, was a false confidence – an unusual complacency puffed further by his friends, all of whom told him that he would surely win. Having recently lost some of the keen edge of his interest in tennis, due to business involvement, Wilding had been most uncharacteristic and had not trained for this match. Perfect fitness was so much the complement to his tennis skill, that its absence may have tipped the issue on a particularly hot day. Brookes won his second title 6/4, 6/4, 7/5. Wimbledon was never to see Wilding again. Within a year he had been killed in France.

men The Women's Championship, during its first fifteen years, had been fought
1914 out between a few strong players. In 1898 (18) the entry was more than doubled. This was the start of a widening interest. Within three years the entry had almost doubled again until, by 1914, it reached fifty-one, still only half the men's field. Women's tennis had yet to be emancipated.

Chattie Cooper, who lost a set only to Miss Steedman in the third round, won through and took the title with a walk-over, Mrs Hillyard not defending. Mrs Hillyard was back next year (17), beating Miss Tulloch in three sets in the semi-finals and Mrs M. Durlacher 7/5, 6/8, 6/1 in the All Comers Final. Her challenge, though, was completely successful, as she beat Chattie 6/2, 6/3.

1900 (16) brought Chattie Cooper promptly back to the Challenge Round, but she failed to unseat Mrs Hillyard who won 4/6, 6/4, 6/4. It was the last of the Champion's six titles. She had deserved them all. She was a great competitor, whose chief asset was a powerful forehand drive. She sometimes wore gloves to improve her grip and followed through so far that the racket head often hit her left shoulder. Like so many of that era her backhand was poor, but she volleyed well and was quick about the court. Three times when she was holder, Mrs Hillyard did not defend. This was because, like any good Victorian lady, she put her duties as wife and mother first.

The girl who had been her main rival over the last five years, Chattie Cooper, now Mrs Sterry, beat her in 1901 (30). In 1902 (22) Chattie lost her title to Muriel Robb. Their match was stopped by rain at one set all and, uniquely, was replayed from the start the next day.

The name of Miss D.K. Douglass occurs for the first time in the 1902 draw. Dolly Douglass was beaten only in the semi-final by Muriel Robb 6/4, 2/6, 9/7. She had given notice that she was to be one of the great champions who, more renowned as Mrs Lambert Chambers, won the title seven times, the last in 1914. Dolly Douglass had her first two wins in 1903 (28) and 1904 (41). But an American girl was to intervene in her run of success. May Sutton, who in 1905 (45) made her first challenge, became the first overseas winner of any Wimbledon title. Dolly had been suffering from a strained wrist but she got her revenge in 1906 (48). The American again reversed things in 1907 (42).

Champions who fashioned the game. Chattie Cooper (Mrs Sterry), 1895–6, 1898, 1901, 1908.

Muriel Robb, 1902.

Dolly Douglass (Mrs Lambert Chambers), 1903–4, 1906, 1910–11, 1913–14.

May Sutton, 1905, 1907.

Dora Boothby, 1909.

Challenge Round 1905: May Sutton (far side), the first overseas winner, v. Dolly Douglass.

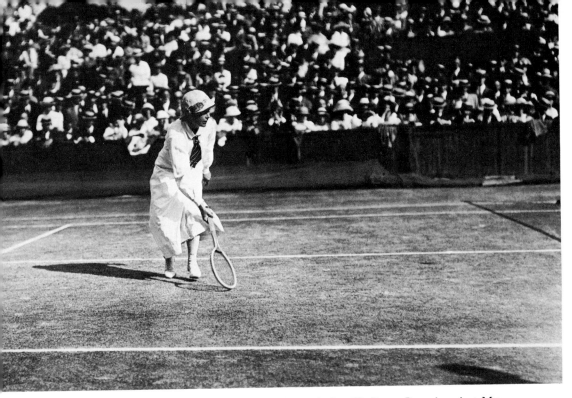

Mrs D.R. Larcombe, 1912 winner, makes a cool start in her Challenge Round against Mrs Lambert Chambers, July 1914.

But things seem to have hotted up.

Mrs Lambert Chambers – seven times Champion – in formidable mood.

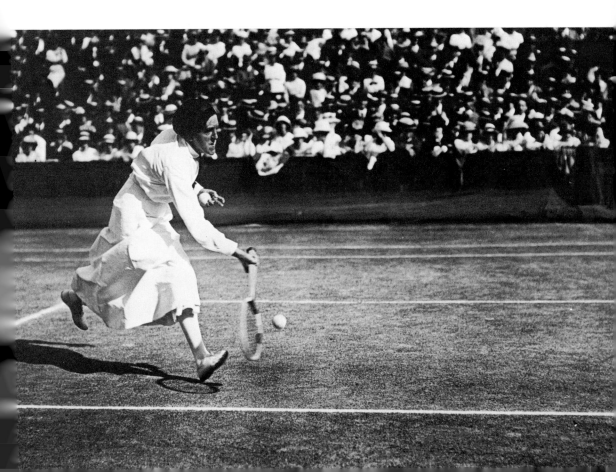

May Sutton developed her skills early in Pasadena by playing against her four elder sisters. Once she beat them she was on her way. When she was only sixteen her brother took her to the East Coast where she won the US title at her first attempt. She had a strong forehand and an effective service. She was a good volleyer but did not rely on it. Her main strength was that she had no nerves at all. Being so young, convention allowed her the freedom of shorter skirts which became the envy of the older players who were imprisoned in Edwardian attire. In 1908 (30) May Sutton did not defend and Mrs Sterry won the title without losing a set. Her hardest match was, as might have been expected, in the quarter-finals against Mrs Lambert Chambers, who took her to 6/3, 7/5. That was the last of Chattie Sterry's five titles.

Between now and the war there were only three winners: Dora Boothby in 1909 (37); Mrs Larcombe in 1912 (34); and in 1910 (31), 1911 (34), 1913 (42) and 1914 (51) the winner was Mrs Lambert Chambers, a player whose game had improved considerably since her losses to May Sutton and Chattie Sterry. Her speed and accuracy had increased and her forehand was formidable.

By 1914 Wimbledon had run more than a third of its centenary course. What had started as a game played by the few had developed, but only at the same pace as developments in other spheres of a still slow-moving life. The war was to bring revolutionary change. A hint of the shape of things to come had been provided. In the south of France tennis lovers marvelled at the precocious talent of a fifteen-year-old girl: her name was Suzanne Lenglen.

4

LENGLEN AND TILDEN

Just as the Second World War ushered in a new and exciting – if for some alarming – modern world, so the revival of the All England Championships in 1919 brought in a new era of lawn tennis and with it two superstars of such magnitude that each can lay strong claim to be the greatest player of their sex in the history of the game. Lenglen and Tilden are names which glitter through the record pages of almanacs and encyclopaedias, and the players themselves glittered at the time not only by the prowess of their performance but by the dramatic quality of their glamour. Today we would have called it charisma. Their charisma was all the more remarkable in that it was so immediately achieved, mainly by word of mouth reputation rather than by the instant impact of television.

Suzanne was the first on the scene. Her reputation as a precocious youngster from the Riviera was long known. Many were the stories which flew round about how her martinet coach, Papa Lenglen, had fashioned her accuracy with the light but unrelenting hammer of practice, always practice. He was never satisfied until perfection was reached in any stage, and that was only momentary, for a new mark would be set by placing an object on the far side of the net and telling Suzanne to aim at it repeatedly until she could hit it at will.

Papa soon realised that speed was fifty per cent of a champion's make-up. He made Suzanne skip, sprint and do other training exercises to build up and sharpen her physique. The result of his all-round training was that her perfection of stroke was balanced by her perfection of movement, which was that of a ballerina. This gave her economy, as well as speed, in her court coverage. As a superstar she dressed the part – both on and off court. When Diaghilev introduced shaded silk chiffons, Suzanne brought the fashion to the tennis court by using them for her famous bandeaux.

She made an immediate entrance on a stage which she was to command until her sad exit in 1926. The crowds were so thick round her court at her very first appearance that F. R. Burrow, the new Referee, such a strong personality at the Championships in the inter-war years, was unable to check on a report that she was being illegally coached by her father from the sidelines.

Winning through the All-Comers, Suzanne had arrived at the threshold of her ambition. The clash, which had so long loomed on the wartime tennis horizon, between the reigning and record-breaking seven times Champion, Mrs Lambert Chambers, and the rumoured exceptional player from France, had at last come. Their only previous meeting had no bearing. Mrs Lambert Chambers played Suzanne on the Riviera in 1914 and, although given a sur-prisingly good game, had managed to win in straight sets.

The Champion's pre-war record had been an outstanding one, and her long jaw and strong face proclaimed her a tenacious fighter. In telling her own story of this match, she said:

'In those days the Champion stood out. I used to practise on the Centre Court every morning, but it is not quite the same thing as playing before the crowded stands, and one knew one's Challenger had become accustomed to the court and the crowd after playing for a fortnight. I was giving Suzanne a good many years [Mrs Lambert Chambers was forty to Suzanne's twenty] and I had not played for five years; many people wondered if it was wise of me to defend my title. I argued to myself that if an English girl came through I would not bother to defend, but if the French girl won the All-Comers event and challenged me, it was up to me to give her a chance to beat the reigning Champion.'

The pre-match tension for both players must have been more than normal before any Final. Apart from the public build-up to it the weather took an unkind hand. The players had changed and were ready when down came the rain. It went on and on and, although the court was covered, the match had to be abandoned for the day. Mrs Lambert Chambers went on:

'The newspapers wondered why I was making such an unnecessary effort as my chance of winning was quite hopeless. I do not think they put me off; on the contrary they rather put my back up and I played the game of my life.'

This is how Mrs Lambert Chambers set the scene:

'In those days, to honour the finalists of the Ladies' Singles at Wimbledon, the Secretary of the All England Club always umpired the match and famous men players were on the lines. I think that this was a gallant gesture and wish it had not been given up. The crowd loved it and cheered the umpire and the linesmen as they took their places. King George v, Queen Mary and Princess Mary were present and received a tremendous ovation on their arrival. Lord Curzon, Admiral Beatty and Mr Hughes, the Australian Prime Minister, were some of the notable people I remember being in the Royal Box. There was also the biggest crowd I had ever seen at Wimbledon, many of them having slept out all night.

'It was a perfect day for lawn tennis. There was no wind (wind I dislike intensely) and, although it was hot, the sun was not too intense, there being quite a lot of cloud about. The court as usual was quite perfect.'

So to the match. Suzanne won the first set, in which every point was a
battle. Mrs Lambert Chambers, who said she felt on top of the world that
day, hit back to win the second. Suzanne, who had shown signs of wilting,
now asked for some brandy. Mrs Lambert Chambers tells the story of the
final set:

'I must admit I was beginning to feel that I had had enough exercise
for one day, and there was another set to be played. After an interval we
continued the game. I had become somewhat chilled and I played badly
at the beginning of the set. Suzanne quickly went to 4/1 for, as well as
my bad lapse, she had some net-cord strokes, which did not help my mood
of the moment. However, I tried hard to concentrate and get back my
game.

'I then regained my confidence and to my great delight and satisfaction
made the score 4 games all. Unfortunately I was getting terribly tired, foot-
sore and weary; I had run many miles and, as well as the physical, there
was mental tiredness, which perhaps for me was more upsetting. 4-all became
5-all and the crowd was now worked up to a pitch of the tensest excitement. A very long game of terrific rallies followed, which I won to reach
6/5. I then led 40/15 – two points for the game, set and match, and Suzanne
in my bag of victories! Alas, it was not to be. That winning point had
always been a nightmare to me (whether I was playing the best or merely
a rabbit). My arm felt like cottonwool. Also I am afraid that when the
umpire called 40/15 I lost my concentration and could not help thinking,
"Those newspapers will feel rather small now"; it was a dreadful moment
to think like that.

'Suzanne was evidently also feeling the strain, because she came up to
the net on a short return – a thing she would never do normally. I lobbed
her but not quite deep enough; she put her racket up and the ball touched
the tip of the wood and hit the top of the net, falling on my side! She
told me afterwards she never even saw the ball and if ever there was a
lucky shot it was that one. Score now 40/30. Suzanne again came up to the
net on a short return to my forehand. If I had been asked what I should
like her to give me in order for me to make the winning shot – it would
have been this one. I had scored over and over again in this match, as
in many others, with a short cross-court dipping forehand, which I now
played, but unluckily for me (it was, I am sure, because it was match-
point) the ball hit the top of the net and fell on my side; why, oh why,
could it not have dropped the other side?

'I do not remember anything about the rest of the match but I must
have won another game because Suzanne won that set at 9/7 and the match
10/8, 4/6, 9/7.'

(Forty-four games – the longest women's Final until another epic fifty-one years

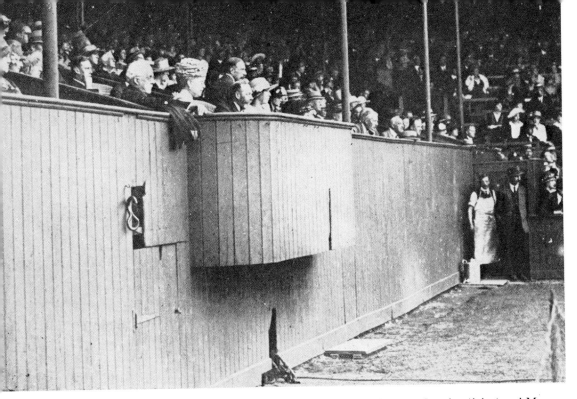

A long-anticipated confrontation: the Challenge Round of 1919 – Suzanne Lenglen (*below*) and Mrs Lambert Chambers (*opposite*), watched enthralled by Queen Mary, King George V and Princess Mary. Later the King told Mrs Lambert Chambers, 'I don't know how you were feeling but *I* felt quite ill.'

later between Margaret Court and Billie Jean King.) The King sent a message
to the players asking them to come to the Royal Box as he wished to congratulate them. This proved quite impossible as they were both 'laid out utterly
exhausted'. Suzanne's feet were actually bleeding. (Later the King did see
Mrs Lambert Chambers and said, 'I don't know how you were feeling but *I*
felt quite ill.')

Mrs Lambert Chambers and Suzanne became great friends –

'We frequently stayed together at country house parties and would
challenge any men's double – great fun, as we were often the winners. I think
perhaps it was a tragedy for her, as for me, that I did not win that first
1919 match, because after that she just could not bear the thought of ever
being beaten (which of course is absurd – we have to have our off days).
Consequently, her nerves went to pieces and in the end she did not enjoy
her tennis at all ...'

But for the moment Suzanne's horizons were boundless. She could do
nothing wrong. Her fame spread like a bushfire. The excitement she caused
and the arrival of Tilden on the scene next year clinched the argument
Commander Hillyard, Secretary of the All England Club, used in persuading
his committee that Worple Road could no longer contain the Championships.
Accordingly a new ground was found in Church Road – fortunately still
Wimbledon – where the venue as we now know it was ready just in time for
the 1922 Championships.

In the next seven years Suzanne Lenglen was truly invincible. The only
match she failed to win was in the 1921 US Championships, her first and last
match at Forest Hills. After losing the first set to the American champion,
Molla Mallory, and reaching 2-all in the second, she retired. Unsporting
though such an action seemed, there was cause for it. The Atlantic crossing
had been terrible, with Suzanne not only seasick for the whole voyage but
suffering also from chronic asthma.

She had not come to America to play in the Championships but to raise
funds for the devastated regions of France. However, the Americans had
entered her for them, with play due to start in two days' time. She was
persuaded that it was impossible to withdraw as her entry had caused thousands
of advance tickets to be sold. The vice-president of the French Association,
M. de Joannis, explained to Suzanne that she must play for the honour of
France. Unfortunately, since seeding had not yet been introduced, fate had
drawn her against the Champion in the second round. Her first round
opponent was asked to withdraw to give Suzanne an extra day's recovery
time – but it was not enough.

The only break in her further Wimbledon success came in 1924 when, after
an illness in the spring, although winning her first three rounds comfortably
enough, she lost a set to Bunny Ryan in the fourth – the second she had

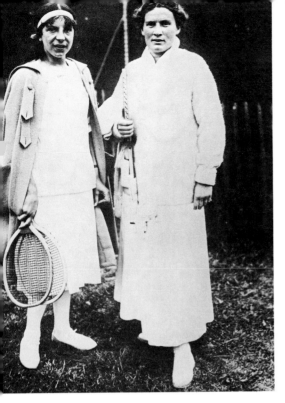

The start of a famous partnership. Suzanne Lenglen and Elizabeth Ryan in 1914.

Elizabeth Ryan in 1914.

Together they won the Doubles six times.

yielded since she first played at Wimbledon. With four days of the Championships left she felt unable to continue in all three events and so scratched from
the Mixed Doubles, thereby getting dispensation from the Referee for a day's
rest. But on the evening of the Thursday, still not feeling fit, she retired
altogether from the tournament.

This was extremely bad luck on Bunny Ryan, who was not only out of the
Singles to a conqueror who then retired but the same lady was also her
doubles partner. In the light of historic hindsight that would have meant
that Bunny's record tally of Wimbledon titles would undoubtedly have stood
not at nineteen but twenty–since she and Suzanne had won the Doubles
for the past five years.

In 1925 Suzanne resumed her normal sway over both her opponents and the
crowds. But then what promised to be a high-point, even in her career, the
Jubilee year of 1926, turned sour. She arrived at Wimbledon with her mind
unresolved* whether to accept a tempting American offer to turn professional,
thereby helping her parents in a difficult financial situation, or to remain an
amateur and continue to enjoy the glamorous life she knew.

These thoughts may well have exercised her as she stood in the opening
day Centre Court line-up to receive her commemorative medal from the
King. But who in the crowd there could possibly have foretold that the ill-
fated 'Lenglen incident' was about to happen – with Suzanne and F. R. Burrow,
the Referee, as the chief protagonists.

All aspects of the famous confrontation have been 'burrowed' into deeply by
tennis historians and it seems to have been a clear case of a strong and
volatile temperament clashing with an authoritarian personality. In the light
of Suzanne's unique standing both as a player and star attraction, a tradition had arisen whereby Suzanne, before leaving the Club at the end of each
day, would be escorted either by Commander Hillyard or a member of the
French team to the Referee's office, to find out what her programme for the
morrow would be. Due to some oversight on the first Tuesday, Ladies' Day,
no one appeared to escort her. She did not come by herself.

A busy Referee had other things to do besides worry about someone he
was known to regard as a *prima donna*. At the same time, knowing that Queen
Mary was coming next day to watch Mlle Lenglen, it would have seemed
prudent to make certain that she knew her programme, which was to play a
single at two o'clock and a double at 4.30. When she arrived at 3.30 and
was told tersely that she was late, she claimed only to have known about
her doubles and said that she would not play her single first and, if the
Referee insisted upon that, she would scratch from the Championships.

Discussion became hot argument and, reportedly, hysteria on Suzanne's
part. So excited did she get that she soon left the ground. The first official
reaction to such an ultimatum by a player would be immediately to scratch

* John Olliff, *The Romance of Wimbledon* (Hutchinson, 1944).

him or her. This was considered, even in the case of the great Suzanne, but it was felt that the crowd might react badly. Her opponents were unwilling to see her scratched and this face-saver allowed the Referee to postpone her two matches until Thursday and even to put the double on first.

The double was duly played, Suzanne and her partner, Didi Vlasto, lost to the Americans, Bunny Ryan and Mary Browne, after having twice been at match-point. Rain then prevented her playing the single which she won easily next day though, to quote Referee Burrow, 'complaining of pain in her arm and feeling ill'.

On Saturday her only match was a mixed double with Jean Borotra, the last on the Centre Court. When she and her partner came out for the match, some of the crowd appeared to resent the apparent discourtesy to the Queen when she had been kept waiting on Wednesday, and they made clear their displeasure. Borotra, the arch-improviser, responded by doing without a hit-up. He started the match with a grotesque game, in which he sent wild services all over the place, and even into the crowd. Miming his surprise and dismay, he soon had the crowd laughing and they forgot their bad humour. However, it had not gone unnoticed by Suzanne and such a highly strung nature was undoubtedly affected by it. The mantle of idolatry was slipping from her shoulders and she could not bear it.

In the Monday's programme the Referee's wording of 'Mlle Lenglen (if well enough to play) versus Miss C. Beckingham', intended, he wrote, as 'precaution', may perhaps have been taken by Suzanne as provocation. At any rate, an announcement was eventually made by the Club Secretary, Major Larcombe, that the Champion was retiring from the Singles altogether. Next day a second announcement said she had decided that she was too ill to take any further part in the tournament. She accepted the American professional offer and Wimbledon never saw her again.*

1919 The end of the war – a war which had caused such a violent break in the pattern of life – found the importance of Wimbledon as the peak of the tennis-playing world somewhat surprisingly undiminished, partly due to tradition and the desire on the part of everybody to get back to normal, and partly to the Wimbledon organisation which had really become strengthened in the immediate pre-war years to keep pace with the spreading interest – particularly in the men's game.

Widespread interest in the men's game was immediately shown by a record entry of 129 players – 129 because one player from South Africa telephoned the entry of his countrymen but forgot his own. Fortunately for him another entrant withdrew through injury, or the South African could not have been included in the draw. 128 was henceforward the accepted limit – with one exception in 1923, when for some obscure reason 133 appeared in the draw. The women's draw remained an unconstant number until fixed at 96 in 1929.

*She died in Paris on 4 July 1938 and thousands came to line her funeral route.

Suzanne Lenglen, magnetic personality – highly dramatic player.

In full swing, winning Wimbledon.

The international element in 1919 was increased by there being demobbed officers who had not yet gone home and so eight overseas countries were represented. Added to all of which there was the exciting prospect of Lenglen.

The men's event was undistinguished, for few had had opportunities to practise enough to get back to pre-war standards. One exception was Gerald Patterson, a twenty-three-year-old from Melbourne, who was the first Australian with a cannonball service and an all-round more powerful game than his countryman, Brookes, the 1914 title-holder. Algy Kingscote, who had been blooded at Wimbledon just before the war, had three very hard five-set matches against Max Decugis, Pat O'Hara-Wood and C. Garland from the fourth round on – for a total of 148 games.

In the All-Comers Final against Patterson he was very tired and Patterson won easily. In the first-ever all-Australian Final (All-Comers or Challenge Round) Brookes, at forty-one, was much slower than the Wizard of pre-war years and the storming young challenger won in straight sets.

1920   If the glamour in 1919 was all Lenglen's, 1920 saw the first challenge of another Tennis Great – William Tatem Tilden. It is curious that the careers of possibly the finest player of either sex should run such parallel courses. The mainsprings in Lenglen and Tilden were utter opposites. Suzanne was wound up by her father. Tilden had an inner coil which made him self-motivated. He won his first tournament as a boy of eight. All his early success came from natural flair and the ability to hit the ball hard. He did not then capitalise on his inborn qualities, playing only by instinct, though at an early date he advocated, 'never give your opponent the shot he likes to play'.

Unfortunately he did not live up to his own maxim, being more concerned with hitting forehand winners and, although very promising, he never seemed to fulfil his potential. Suddenly he realised that there was a 'Why' and a 'How' to tennis and that the mind was as important as the racket arm. Being single-minded he got down to studying the game and analysing it. Soon he had theories and he set about proving them. It was this capacity to think analytically and then perfect which above all made him a supreme champion.

In the 1919 American Championships his opponent in the final was the diminutive Bill Johnston, who had tamed the Californian Comet, Maurice McLoughlin, in the 1915 Final. Johnston had used the beautiful symmetry of his game to beat Tilden in three sets. In particular he had assailed Tilden's weak backhand with his own powerful forehand. When the match was over a bystander remarked, 'It took Little Bill to show up that big stiff' – Big Bill Tilden.

The lesson was well taken. Tilden, realising that he would remain only a finalist and No. 2 to Johnston while his backhand was ill-produced, spent the whole winter working on it, adjusting his grip, grooving it until he had an entirely new stroke. So often when a player does this the manufactured shot does not stand up to the anxieties of competitive play. Tilden had shaped a quality article. And the stroke survived. His game was now pragmatic and fully fashioned. He was ready for the big time.

At Wimbledon Big Bill sailed through his first three matches but then, in his sternest test, Kingscote took him to five sets, clear evidence that only Kingscote's great fatigue had prevented him from giving Patterson a far better match the previous year. In the All-Comers Final Shimizu of Japan, a player of very awkward strokes, led Tilden in each of the three sets, bringing out the best in Big Bill who won 6/4, 6/4, 13/11. In the Challenge Round, Patterson won a probing first set, after which Tilden, having discerned a weakness in his opponent's backhand, attacked it – and that was the end of the affair.

Tilden's exceptional height and reach gave him his famous cannonball service and added to a commanding presence. By his superb play and magnetic personality, he caught the enthusiasm of the crowd. But, like Nastase in later years, he could blaze with annoyance at inefficient linesmen and lazy ball-boys. The crowd thought these posturings were those of a *prima donna*, and they seemed more so in such a big man. This impatience was a symptom of his own perfectionist nature. He was certainly a sportsman, with a habit of shouting an engaging 'Peach' when an opponent made a good winning stroke.

Tilden, fortified by his Wimbledon win and the knowledge that his hard groundwork over the winter had made him a much more complete player, now started a run of success in the American Championships which was to give him a sequence of six titles, and seven in all before he turned professional. In 1920 he reversed the result of the previous year's Final against Johnston, who was to be his Final victim in five of those six consecutive years. Three of those matches were fantastic five-setters.

1921 In 1921 Tilden won the World Hard Court Championship and soon afterwards fell ill. He was in a London hospital until the second week of Wimbledon. This was the last Challenge Round year. He had four days' light practice but he was still a sick man when he faced Brian 'Boy' Norton, winner of the All-Comers. Norton was a twenty-one-year-old South African with real promise. He also happened to be a firm admirer of Big Bill.

Tilden started quite well but was soon tiring. Norton won the first set 6/4 and the second 6/2. At this point Tilden looked finished. But he always had great courage and he played on. Norton, thinking the match was in the bag, and possibly annoyed by a spectator shouting: 'Play the game, Tilden!' when the Champion used some drop-shots, allowed his opponent to win two sets easily. Tilden then launched himself into a despairing final effort, but Norton got to match-point at 5/4. Tilden's drive seemed to be going out and he was already on his way to the net to congratulate Norton when the ball just touched the sideline. It still presented Norton with a simple winner but, thinking Tilden was ready to volley, he tried a passing shot and failed. Tilden went on to win a match he thought he would not survive.

These last Championships at the old All England Club at Worple Road

W.T. Tilden, the Nijinsky of tennis – in the view of many the greatest player ever.

were both forward- and backward-looking. Records had been set. There were nearly 170 entries of whom some forty had to be refused. Manuel Alonzo, the Spanish Champion, was the first from his country to reach the All-Comers Final, as was Brian Norton of South Africa. Roper Barrett, born the year Wingfield took out his Sphairistike patent, made this his singles swansong. He was to become the most successful Davis Cup captain Britain ever had. In the early years of the century he had been one of the finest players, who often wove a spell around the best opponents, but lacked the killer instinct. He was at his best in doubles, winning three Wimbledon titles.

The old Club and ground had proved the vision of Henry Jones. It had taken lawn tennis from Victorian pat-ball to become what was already a twentieth-century international sport. It was a fitting moment for the abolition of the Challenge Round. All men would be equal when the stage was taken at New Wimbledon.

5

THE 'FOUR MUSKETEERS'
1922–31

The New Wimbledon was a triumph for tennis architecture and planning. Much was due to the foresight of Commander G.W. Hillyard, the Secretary and former player. The Centre Court, stark new concrete, looked like some vast fortification and it was the showpiece of fifteen courts available to the Referee. It retained the name Centre for old times' sake, though it was to one side, instead of as at Worple Road in the middle of the ground. And the name has always symbolised the highest examination in lawn tennis. No. 1 Court was built alongside it.

Lenglen and Tilden had already been put to the test and signalled their individual supremacy. A new *national* power was now to arise which was to conquer and reach world dominion. France already had her St Joan in Suzanne and now there came four French men who were immediately dubbed the Four Musketeers. Three of them, Borotra, Cochet and Lacoste – all future winners – were making their first appearance. Their various talents and characters so complemented each other that between them, starting in 1924, they won the Wimbledon Singles titles for six years and from 1925 to 1933 they won the Doubles five times. From 1925 when the French Championship was thrown open they won it for the first eight years. Two of them took the American title in 1926 and 1928 and France held the Davis Cup for six years from 1927 to 1932. All these successes were gained by these three men and a partner.

The partner was 'Toto' Brugnon, the only one of the four to play at old Wimbledon. Though a good singles player, he was superb in doubles, the catalyst of any combination he cared to make. His major partners were Borotra and Cochet, with whom he won four Wimbledon titles, five French titles and one Australian. His strokes were not forceful, but they were so well placed that they set up the kill for his partners.

Jean Borotra came from the Basque country where his first love had been pelota, that combination of a scintillating ball game and tumbling acrobatics. Small wonder that his eye and reflexes were hyper-fast. Perhaps the rhythm of the pelota swing prevented him from acquiring pure lawn tennis strokes, but his service, his overhead placements and his pugnacious volleys more than made up for this. Moreover, he was utterly determined, schemed cleverly on court and had an electric personality.

The Four Musketeers: the inspired unorthodoxy of Henri Cochet (*above and opposite below*); the drilled perfection of René Lacoste (in white cap, *below and top right*); the exuberance of the Bounding Basque, beretted Borotra (*below and top left opposite*); and the imperturbable generalship of Toto Brugnon (*opposite below*, in play).

His pelota experience also made him the most acrobatic of lawn tennis players the game had yet seen and the most fearless. He would chase the ball anywhere and throw himself at anything if there was a chance of returning it. He was known to end up in the crowd on a lady's lap and then gallantly kiss her hand before resuming the court. He always wore a beret and the crowd adored their 'Bounding Basque'. Borotra was quite aware that these antics did not always endear him to his opponents.

Henri Cochet was small, had a weak service and a very poor backhand, but he was a tennis genius. His game was even more unorthodox than Borotra's. It was built on his uncanny footwork and anticipation, triggered by his speed-of-light reflexes. He engendered despair in opponents, who found winners improvised off their best strokes as Cochet strolled nonchalantly to the net. As with many great players the ball seemed commanded to come to him. A disdainful stroke then dispatched it.

René Lacoste was the last to join this famous band of individuals. Like Tilden he perfected his game by studying his weaknesses, analysing them and eliminating them. For inspiration he watched the best players and learned from them, until he brought himself to a high state of efficiency. Although he lacked the exuberance of Borotra his unassuming and well-drilled game made him a most popular player with Wimbledon crowds.

1922   Whoever coined the expression 'Wimbledon weather' was not thinking of the first Championships at New Wimbledon. They were the wettest on record and fifteen days were needed to complete the meeting, in which there were entries from eighteen countries. The first round was not over until Thursday. If ever the Referee, F.R. Burrow, were called upon to use his crossword-compiling expertise, it was in 1922. However, the dauntless British, headed by their King and Queen, continued to show their increasing interest and support. On three days the gates had to be closed.

For this and the next year the Four French Musketeers were learning and perfecting the drill and tactics which were to make them such a force. Only Brugnon and Cochet got as far as the last sixteen. The title went again to Gerald Patterson, the 1919 winner, who beat his Australian compatriot, James Anderson, one of the biggest hitters the game had seen, in a five-set semi-final, before beating Randolph Lycett easily in the Final. Tilden was not defending and Suzanne Lenglen had said that she had no objection to the abolition of the Challenge Round.

She was nearing the peak of her great career. On the final Saturday, rain having caused postponements, the Referee was in doubt whether to start the Women's Final at such a late hour. Both wanted to play, so rather reluctantly he put the match on. The players went on court at one minute past seven. They were off again well before half past, Suzanne having allowed Molla Mallory only two games. She went on to win her second triple crown.

Leslie Godfree, a fine player and later husband of Kitty McKane, was alive to his chance when he was the first man to serve on the Centre Court at New Wimbledon. Kingscote having netted his return, Godfree was quick to pounce on the ball and pocket it for a unique souvenir.

1923   If New Wimbledon had been given a wet launching in 1922, the next year made up for it, the sun shining more brightly each day. For 'Little Bill' Johnston 1923 was a lucky year. No Big Bill was there but another American, Frank Hunter, got through to the Final where he gave Johnston no real fight. Little Bill was right on his game that day and with no pressure upon him made a succession of brilliant shots.

In the semi-finals Norton had run him closer, as had Richards in the quarter-finals. At nineteen, Richards was the new boy-wonder and a good volleyer. That Wimbledon was becoming more an entertainment spectacle every year was exemplified by Richards's filmstar entourage. He brought with him a secretary, a typist and a doctor.

In the Women's Championship Suzanne's name was drawn first. It did not really seem significant. She carried on in her royal progress, losing only eleven games in twelve sets. Four of those were in the Final against Britain's young Kitty McKane. And of course she won the Doubles with Bunny Ryan, although that 'of course' very nearly suffered when Joan Austin and Evelyn Colyer, the young pair British fans were taking to their hearts as 'the Babes', precociously reached the Final. Their tennis was as attractive as their personalities. Fine volleyers, their natural place was at the net where they leapt and danced like the most graceful ballerinas. John Olliff, later a Wimbledon player and distinguished lawn tennis correspondent for the *Daily Telegraph*, was entranced at the age of fourteen as he watched the Final:

> 'The champions went to 4/0 in the first and then 'the Babes' shook off their nerves and gave the wildly excited crowd a thrill for their money. They won the next three games and came within a point of making the score 4/4. That first set will not be forgotten by any who saw it. After that the champions drew ahead and lost only one game in the second set. 'The Babes' added something to the romance of Wimbledon, and left it more artistically charming than it would have been without them.'

1924   This was the year that the French stormed their Centre Court Bastille, and for the first time ever produced the two Finalists, Lacoste and Borotra. It was an extraordinary match which went the full five sets, but each lasted only a quarter of an hour. The average rally was less than four strokes and winners rather than losers abounded. Borotra was shooting all over the court, like a jack-in-the-box which Lacoste the marksman was aiming not to hit but pass by.

The first set was nearly all Borotra, his interception being uncanny. In the second the machine-like game of Lacoste gave him the edge. The Bounding Basque was back with a vengeance and won the third to lead 2-1. For Borotra it was always imperative to win two early sets, whereupon he would coast and

New Wimbledon. No. 2 Court before it became the graveyard of so many hopes. The cabby fares best.

Something to laugh about in the rain-affected first Championships at New Wimbledon. Gerald Patterson, the 1919 winner, and James Anderson before their semi-final. Patterson, a nephew of Dame Nellie Melba, went on to win his second title.

'Little Bill' Johnston, winner in 1923, runner-up so often in the US championships to 'Big Bill' Tilden.

Gerald Patterson and J.B. Hawkes (*behind*), runners-up to Cochet and Brugnon in 1928.

reserve himself for a final set assault. Everybody knew this, including Lacoste, and the suspense lay in whether Borotra could last with his uniquely forceful net attack. He volleyed the ball so early that, even if he did not make an outright winner, he often forced errors (or sitters for the next smash) from opponents hustled into uncontrolled strokes. So Lacoste got the fourth set 6/3 and Borotra stormed through in the fifth, 6/4.

The crowd were delighted with Borotra's win and even more so when the two Frenchmen left the court arm-in-arm, both happy that the day's glory belonged to France. Some glory went to veteran Norman Brookes who, in a third round match, showed, like Rosewall after him, that time did little to dim his fire. It was twenty years since his first appearance at Wimbledon. He was playing Frank Hunter, seventeen years his junior, and beat him in five sets.

When Suzanne Lenglen retired from the Championships before her semi-final because of the continuing effects of her attack of jaundice, it gave her opponent, Britain's Kitty McKane, her supreme chance. Helen Wills, the American girl who was to take over Suzanne's premier position, had quickly settled in at her first Wimbledon and won through to the Final quite easily. Facing her in the Final, Kitty started badly and Helen won the first set 6/4, led 4/1 in the second and had four points for 5/1. Kitty McKane was ever a fighter and desperately she saved those points, starting a run of five games to take the set. Her confidence mounting, she volleyed more and held the initiative to win the final set and the title 6/4. It was a great triumph for Kitty who was the only player to beat Helen Wills at Wimbledon. Her other unique record was of concurrently being the All England Badminton Champion (she also won in 1920–2). S.H. Smith had nearly achieved it when, as Badminton Champion, he won the Wimbledon All-Comers in 1900 but lost in the Challenge Round.

1925   The Qualifying Competition came into being in 1925. Ever since, to those condemned to earn their Wimbledon right by this tortured route, the Qualifying has seen more drama and felt more anguish than the main Championship ever has. The increased entry which made the Qualifying necessary had been matched by the increase in spectator interest, and the Committee had taken the decision to ration tickets for the first time. Centre Court season books were split into two. Later they were split further, into three and then six.

Whereas 1924 had seen a record seven overseas men in the quarter-finals, 1925 provided six – three of them Musketeers. Borotra then had the unhappy job of eliminating a Frenchman, Cochet, whom he beat 5/7, 8/6, 6/4, 6/1. This was a significant win for the Basque, who was normally beaten by Cochet. It was particularly so, since Borotra lost the first set and only just won the long second, in which Cochet was clearly put off by being foot-faulted. His hold on the match was relaxed a little and Borotra seized his chance. Once in charge, he stayed there. René Lacoste, runner-up to the Basque in 1924, beat three national champions on his way to the Final, Washer of Belgium, Jacob of India and Anderson of Australia.

A historic occasion. Helen Wills' first Wimbledon Final and her only defeat there, by Britain's Kitty McKane (Mrs Godfree), seen (*above*) in play.

The Centre Court was full to overflowing for this return of the last year's Final. It was quite a different affair. Whereas in 1924 there had been five sets, this was only four but the match lasted much longer. It was Borotra who was out of favour with the foot-fault judge and this seemed to disturb his normally brilliant attacking concentration. Lacoste won the first two sets 6/3, 6/3. The Bounding Basque, denied the early lead he loved to have, refused to submit in three. He had a point for 4/0 and got the set 6/4, going on to 4/1 in the fourth. Lacoste's lead was vanishing and he raised his game again just in time.

This, combined with some near-misses on the volley by Borotra, brought Lacoste to 5/4. The bobbing beret led again 6/5 but with his chance there Borotra sinned with double-faults and the lead was lost. Now with the Bounding Basque's energy – so vital to those net attacks – ebbing, Lacoste ruthlessly applied the *coup de grâce* and won his first title. Normally phlegmatic, he allowed himself a Gallic moment by hurling his white cap high into the air.

The luck of the still seedless draw found the Ladies' Champion, Kitty McKane, in the same half as the great Suzanne who had retired to her before the 1924 semi-final. Clearly the French girl thought that there was a score of honour to be settled for she played mercilessly to beat the Champion 6/0, 6/0. Her Final opponent, young Wimbledon débutante Joan Fry, who was the surprise of the Championships, did well to take two games in the first set. Suzanne again won the Doubles with Bunny Ryan and went on to her third triple crown, partnered by Borotra in the Mixed Doubles.

1926   When 'the tumult and the shouting' died and a tearful Suzanne Lenglen had departed the Jubilee Championships of 1926 and Wimbledon for ever, the way was open for lesser mortals. One of these, Kitty McKane (by now Mrs Godfree), had previously seized her unexpected chance, and now she did it again. In the Final she met Spanish champion Lili de Alvarez, who, at her first Wimbledon, was another to capture the crowd's admiration for her beauty and her magnetic style.

Lili was an all-out attacking player and used to winning her matches fairly quickly. But Kitty's dogged defence denied this and, having contained her opponent's attack, she counter-attacked and won the first set 6/2. Lili hit back to take the second 6/4 and reached a point for 4/1 in the final set. Taking courage no doubt from the memory of her come-back from a worse position against Helen Wills in the 1924 Final, Mrs Godfree drew on her unfailing resolution and won five games in succession for the match. Her two titles have since been equalled only once by a British girl – Dorothy Round. To add to her Singles title, she and her husband became the first and only married Mixed Doubles Champions.

The opening day of Jubilee year had been a gala occasion. The stage was set, the curtain was about to go up on the King's presentation of commemorative medals to past Champions, when who should make his entrance but the Bounding Basque, who had flown over and changed in the taxi from the airport. He had timed it to perfection.

In an exhibition match Suzanne Lenglen and Bunny Ryan played Kitty Godfree and Mlle K. Bouman. This was to be the last time that the famous partnership of Lenglen and Ryan was seen, for the French LTA had insisted on Suzanne teaming up with Didi Vlasto. The irony was that Suzanne and Didi were beaten by Bunny and Mary Browne, her new partner, in the first round and these two went on to take the title. Nobody was to know that within a few days Suzanne would be turning professional and the Lenglen/Ryan partnership would be dissolved for ever.

The interest of their Majesties, the King and Queen, in Wimbledon was already well established. It had begun through the friendship of Commander Hillyard with the then Prince George, with whom he had served in *Britannia*, and the Prince had first come to Old Wimbledon in 1907. Now, in Jubilee year, the King's second son, the Duke of York, became the first member of the Royal Family to take part in the Championships. He and his friend and partner, Wing Commander Louis Greig, had entered as reigning RAF champions. His Royal Highness wanted the match played on one of the remoter outside courts, but it was realised that the throng of those who wished to see him would be too great. So the match was played on No. 2 Court.

The RAF champions had drawn a one-time Wimbledon Champion pair, A. W. Gore and Roper Barrett. Duncan Macaulay, later an exceptional secretary to the All England Club, saw this match and wrote: 'The Duke, who was left-handed, was a good player but against such formidable opposition his partner tried to do too much and too often committed the sin of "poaching" rather than intercepting.' Gore and Barrett won in straight sets.

In the Men's Singles French dominance was still there, despite the absence of the holder, René Lacoste, who withdrew for health reasons. Again the quarter-finals had six foreign players in them. Colin Gregory, later the Club's chairman, took Cochet all the way and Charles Kingsley, with his unassuming game, did as well against Brugnon. Borotra beat the great Czech player, Jan Kozeluh, in four sets, while America's Howard Kinsey beat Pat Spence of South Africa. Kinsey was lucky that his semi-final opponent was Brugnon, the least powerful of the French trio in singles. Kinsey himself was a defensive player and he and Brugnon had a good fight, Brugnon having five match-points before Kinsey struggled home 9/7 in the final set.

In the other semi-final Borotra, always happiest on the fast Centre Court (or his favourite surface, wood), beat Cochet in a long vacillating match. He was nearly two sets to love down and, had he not stolen the second set from the fire, Cochet must have won. Borotra might have got home sooner, had his approach shots to Cochet's backhand been sounder. In the fourth set he did get them more under control and his volleying then became more effective. He won the fifth set 7/5. In the Final Borotra, playing for France, would have

Period piece: the lady champions at the Jubilee Championships lined up to receive their commemorative medals. *Left to right:* Maud Watson; Mrs Hillyard; Lottie Dod; Mrs Sterry; Mrs Lambert Chambers; Dora Boothby; Mrs Larcombe; Suzanne Lenglen; Mrs Godfree.

Period peace: Tilden (*left*) and Cochet during their remarkable semi-final in 1927.

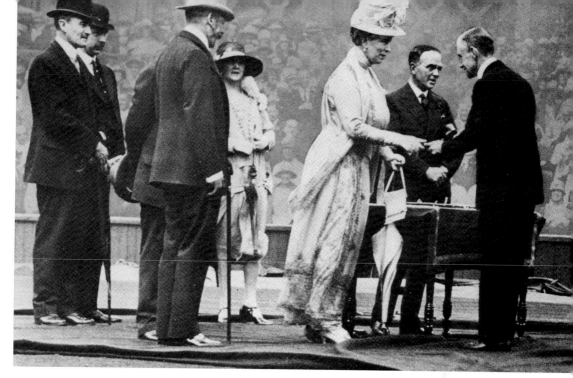

The Jubilee Championships. Queen Mary presents
A.W. Gore with his medal. Club Secretary D.R.
Larcombe stands between them, and King George V
looks on.

Tilden in play against Cochet.

Drawn together, René Lacoste, already a Wimbledon winner, gives future champion Sidney B. Wood, at 15.231 the youngest competitor ever in the men's events, his first Centre Court experience.

needed a more aggressive opponent than Kinsey to deny him. He mastered the American's defence in a tight first set 8/6 and then romped home 6/1, 6/3.

1927   It was a wet Wimbledon again in 1927 (play going into the third week) but drama was not lacking. At last good sense had prevailed and the leading players were seeded, so avoiding any danger of luck making the draw lopsided, as had happened so often. Because of the weather this was also the first time that play had started at one o'clock. As usual whatever the weather there were record attendances nearly every day.

Lenglen was lost to Wimbledon but Tilden was regained. Since defending his title successfully in 1921 he had been content to compete only at home where he had won every year, until beaten by Réné Lacoste in 1926. Réné had just regained his French title and so he had the honour to be seeded No. 1 at Wimbledon. Tilden on his great record had to be 2 while Borotra, the reigning Champion, was 3 with Cochet (4)* and Brugnon (7). What an honour for France – half the seeds – and well it was deserved.

The four top seeds swept to the semi-finals. Borotra beat Lacoste in his own favourite pattern, winning the first two sets 6/4, 6/3. He coasted in the next two, winning one game in each, and bounded through the final set 6/2. The other semi-final between Cochet, who had survived his quarter-final against Frank Hunter after losing the first two sets, and Tilden was to be one of the most talked-about matches ever – posing the eternal question, 'How could a champion of Tilden's mettle and experience allow his supremacy to be usurped when his position seemed to be impregnable?' He was leading 6/2, 6/4, 5/1 and seemed about to realize what he had set out to do – win in three sets, knowing that Cochet thrived on long matches.

Cochet was serving and Tilden, no doubt thinking it worthwhile to go for complete winners since he had two service breaks in hand, put three terrific drives out. 5/2. These three mistakes, tiny as they seemed, were the first breach in the dam through which the flood of Cochet's game was to pour. Tilden lost his service to love! Cochet held his to love. Then came the incredible. Tilden lost his service to love again! 5/5. Cochet's winning sequence of 17 points ran out at 30/0 on his own service, but he took the set 7/5.

F.R. Burrow thought that Tilden's conscious effort to make it a short match fizzled physically just too soon. This view is borne out by Brian Porter, Junior Champion of South Africa in 1926, who was the service-line judge on Tilden's side of the net at the start of that extraordinary turnabout. As Tilden changed over at 5/4 he paused at Porter's chair and said: 'You know I'm finished.' Later, in *My Story* (1938), Tilden wrote, 'Personally, I have no satisfactory explanation. All I know is my co-ordination cracked wide open and I couldn't put a ball in court.'

The crowd, not believing that this could be anything but a temporary setback for the American, watched Tilden struggling to regain his rhythm and

* From 1927 figures in brackets after the players' names indicate their seed numbers.

get back into the match. However, he could not reach the same high level, and was guilty of many double-faults. Cool Cochet went on his nonchalant way as if the result had never been anything but inevitably in his favour – as it turned out to be. The full score was 2/6, 4/6, 7/5, 6/4, 6/3.

In the Final Borotra must have felt that everything was going according to his plan when he took the first two sets 6/4, 6/4. But Cochet the comeback king did it again. True, Borotra took his normal two sets rest (though he still won seven games in them). In the fifth he came bounding back to lead 5/2 and match-point at 5/3 but netted a return of serve. Serving himself at 5/4 he double-faulted on his second match-point. On the third, in a close-volleying rally, Cochet seemed to play a double-hit on the backhand. Borotra claimed this, and had the support of most spectators, but the umpire decided against.* The Basque had three more match-points in the same game. Twice he volleyed out and once Cochet brought up chalk on a sideline. Cochet then got to advantage and Borotra again double-faulted. For once Borotra did not have to pretend dismay. Cochet the 'unflippable' won two games for the match.

Helen Wills (1) and Mrs Godfree (2) headed the Women's seeding list. Gwen Sterry, Chattie's daughter, had the honour in the first round of taking the only set which Helen Wills lost. In the semi-finals Helen beat Joan Fry, who in the quarters had put out Betty Nuthall. Lili de Alvarez reached the Final for the second successive year but could not stop Helen Wills from winning her first Wimbledon Singles title. This is an understatement. Lili's tremendous attacking game was at its exciting best. Helen more than matched it and the result was a superb display. At the height of the second-set battle one rally went to over forty scintillating strokes. Helen won it and, like the losing Boat Race crew, Lili was spent. She won only one more point in the match, which went to Helen 6/2, 6/4.

1928   1928 had five previous winners in the men's lists (Patterson (8), Tilden (3), Borotra (5), Lacoste (2) and Cochet (1)), two more than ever before. Tilden, in his comeback, was joined by three Frenchmen in the semi-finals, Cochet, Boussus and Lacoste. Frank Hunter (4) was a first-round casualty in a long battle with E. D. Andrews of New Zealand; while Borotra was Tilden's quarter-final victim – the big American's driving being so accurate that it discouraged even the 'Bounding Basque' from going to the net. Tilden then fell in five sets to Lacoste, who with his strong defence was always the most likely of his contemporaries to prove his undoing. Unseeded left-hander, Christien Boussus, eventually filled the semi-final vacuum left by Hunter. Cochet disposed of him easily enough but was lacklustre in the Final against Lacoste, who had revenge in four sets for his French Final defeat at Cochet's hands.

The Ladies' Final found the same opponents matched again. The Champion (1) had allowed only one game in either set to Bunny Ryan (4) in their semi-

---

* Brian Porter writes, 'I was in a perfect position to see what happened.... It was definitely a double-hit.'

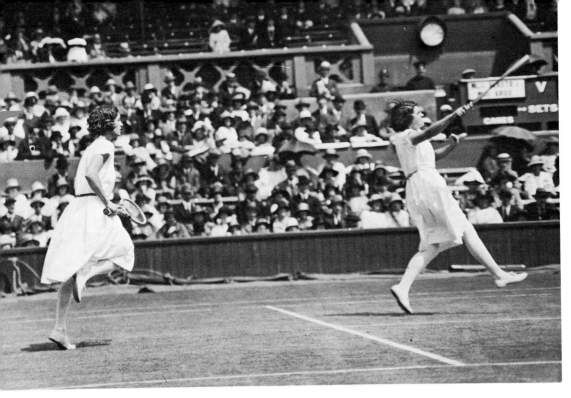

Ladies' Doubles at their best.
'The Babes', Evelyn Colyer and Joan Austin, who made a ballet of the game, unexpectedly reached the Final in 1923.

Helen Wills and Hazel Hotchkiss Wightman, donor of the Cup, winners in 1924.

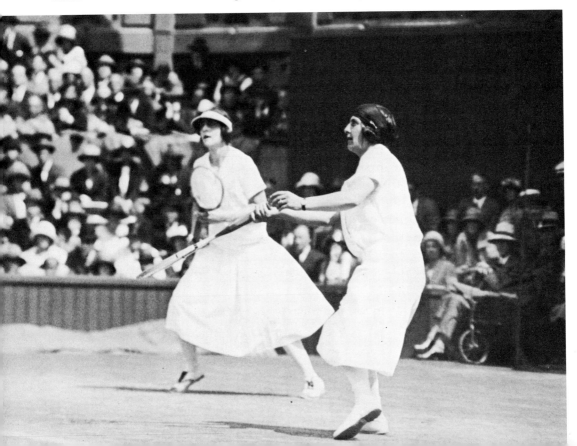

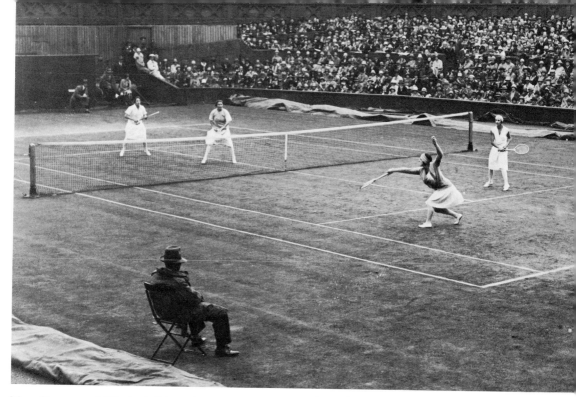

Mary Browne and Elizabeth Ryan of America (far side), the 1926 winners, in their first-round match against Suzanne Lenglen (her last doubles at Wimbledon) and Didi Vlasto, who had two match-points.

Bunny Ryan and her second great partner, Helen Wills Moody, winners in 1927 and 1930.

Prominent pre-war doubles pairs.
ABOVE John van Ryn and Wilmer Allison, American winners in 1929 and 1930.
OPPOSITE TOP Colin Gregory (later a distinguished chairman of the club) and Ian Collins, runners-up in 1929.
LEFT Another successful British pair, Raymond Tuckey and Pat Hughes, 1936 winners.
RIGHT Americans George Lott and John Doeg, runners-up in 1930 (Lott won in 1931 with van Ryn, and in 1934 with Lester Stoefen).

final and Lili de Alvarez (2) was as severe with the Australian Daphne Akhurst (due to win her National title for the third time later that year), who in reaching the semi-final unseeded had beaten Mrs Haylock, Helen Jacobs (8) and Eileen Bennett (3). The result and the manner of another fascinating duel were inevitably the same. Lili could only attack and some of her shots were breathtaking. Helen Wills was as patient and imperturbable as ever – except for three games at the start of the second set when the Spanish girl had her literally on the run. But the fireworks had to lose their brilliance and soon 'Little Pokerface' had resumed her mastery, though the stroke-making on both sides was still lovely to watch. Helen Wills won 6/2, 6/3. Lili had only the satisfaction that no one had ever made Helen run so much.

The Men's Doubles produced a brilliant semi-final performance by Hawkes of Australia, who with Patterson (4) beat Tilden and Hunter (1) in a five-set match of seventy games. In the Final he was not quite as good against Cochet and Brugnon (2), who won in straight sets. Cochet was denied a triple crown when he and Eileen Bennett (1), the new French Champions, were beaten by the unseeded Australians Crawford and Daphne Akhurst. The eventual winners were Spence and Elizabeth Ryan (2).

1929   Colin Gregory (8), the new Australian Champion, was the first Englishman to be seeded. Frank Hunter (4) again suffered almost the same fate as the year before, when he lost in the second round to Bunny Austin, who many felt should have been seeded. Austin did well to be the first Englishman for six years to reach the semi-final (unusually five got to the last sixteen), where he took a set from Borotra (2).

In the absence of the Champion Lacoste, who was unwell, Tilden (3) might have felt optimistic, but he was soundly beaten in straight sets by Cochet (1), who was at the top of his skill in taking an early ball. In the Final Cochet had learned how to play Borotra, keeping him from the net with accurate drives to the baseline and, when he did venture in, tangling him up with clever shots to his feet. The result gave Cochet his second title, 6/4, 6/3, 6/4. The French Musketeers – Cochet, Lacoste and Borotra – had now won six titles between them (two each) and there seemed to be no end in sight to their reign. But Fate enjoys her own statistics and none of the three even reached a Final again.

The two Helens – Wills (1) and Jacobs (5) – came through to contest the first of their four Finals, none of which Jacobs was destined to win. Neither had lost a set in getting there – nor did Helen Wills now, a feat she went on to achieve three times running and five times in all – and one that only four men (playing through) have achieved once each, two women (Mrs Lambert Chambers and Suzanne Lenglen) three times each and four twice each.

Lili de Alvarez (2), who should have provided another Final firework display, was outgunned herself by Mrs McIlquhan in her third match. The victor was one of those hard-serving and hitting players who on their day are sometimes unbeatable. Mrs Bundy, who as May Sutton had been the first Overseas

All but there. Runners-up who reached the Finals more than once but never won.

ABOVE Elizabeth Ryan, 1921, 1930.

ABOVE RIGHT Hilde Krahwinkel Sperling, 1931, 1936.

RIGHT Lili de Alvarez, 1926–8.

Centre Court appearance.
Betty Nuthall and Cilly Aussem, 1927.

Helen Wills Moody and Helen Jacobs, 1932.

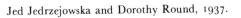
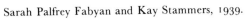

Jed Jedrzejowska and Dorothy Round, 1937.

Sarah Palfrey Fabyan and Kay Stammers, 1939.

Henri Cochet and Bill Tilden, 1929.

Jack Crawford and Ellsworth Vines, 1932.

Wilmer Allison and Vivian McGrath, 1935.

Gottfried von Cramm and Donald Budge, 1937.

Champion in 1905, now forty-one, made a doughty comeback, beating Eileen Bennett (4) to reach the quarter-finals.

Other points of interest in 1929 were the first appearances of Cilli Aussem, later the first German to win the title, and of Dorothy Round and Betty Nuthall, both of whom were to perform prodigies for Britain in 1934 – Dorothy as Wimbledon winner and Betty, as an even rara avis, US Champion. Fred Perry, too, made his first bow, playing through the qualifying and winning two rounds before losing to John Olliff. Perhaps even more 'interesting' was the first appearance on court of a bare-legged feminine competitor – a bold pioneer, Miss Billie Tapscott of South Africa, who reached the quarter-finals unseeded.

In the Doubles Collins and Gregory (4) had a magnificent run for Britain, beating Borotra and Boussus and Lott and Hennessy (2), the American Champions, before losing a stirring five-set Final to Allison and van Ryn who had the first unseeded win in this event. Phoebe Holcroft-Watson and Peggy Michell (2) retained their title; while in the Mixed Ian Collins and Joan Fry reached the Final unseeded through two valiant victories in the same day against Cochet and Eileen Bennett (1) and Gregory and Bunny Ryan (3). After that, though, they found Hunter and Helen Wills (2) too much for them.

1930   The rising German star, attractive Cilly Aussem (6), beat Helen Jacobs (3) in the quarters, only to have to retire at 4/4 in the final set against Bunny Ryan (8) when she fell, sprained an ankle and was carried from the court. So Bunny reached her second Wimbledon Singles Final, where any player it seemed was doomed to be beaten by Helen Wills, now Mrs Moody (1), who won 6/2, 6/2. In the quarter-finals Bunny had dropped the middle set to Betty Nuthall. Betty fired the public's imagination with her hard-hitting game and this year became the first* British girl ever to win the American title.

In the Men's Championship of 1930 Austin, on his fine performance of 1929, was seeded 6 but failed to get to the quarter-finals, though Colin Gregory did – after putting out Fred Perry in a long five-setter. Only Borotra (3) raised the French standard in the semi-finals and Tilden (2) beat him in a typically fluctuating match, 7/5 in the fifth. This was regarded by good judges as the best encounter between them at Wimbledon. Tilden's experience of Borotra's manner of attack enabled him to withstand the storm and take advantage of the lulls, edging ahead when it blew itself out, after Borotra had led 3/1 in the final set.

In the quarter-finals against Allison, Cochet (1) gave himself the usual handicap of losing the first two sets but, to the general surprise, the reigning Wimbledon and French champion lost the next set, too. Allison then had a long five-setter with his countryman, Johnny Doeg (4), but in the Final was tamed by his senior citizen Big Bill Tilden 6/3, 9/7, 6/4.

Allison had the consolation of being the first unseeded player to reach a Wimbledon Singles Final, a remarkable endorsement of his Doubles achieve-

* Virginia Wade was to win the first US Open in 1968.

The graceful German champion Cilly Aussem, 1931 Wimbledon winner.

The Final that never happened, between Frank Shields (*left*) and his doubles partner Sidney Wood, to whom he was forced to concede a walk-over.

ment the year before. Tilden had at last, after three previous attempts, won at New Wimbledon, gaining his third title at thirty-seven. He was now able as reigning Wimbledon and American champion to end his amateur career on the highest note, and become the first great tournament professional.

1931   Next year, 1931, was no *annus mirabilis*. Helen Moody was not defending and two Germans reached the Final for the first time. Cilly Aussem (1), who had just won the French title, beat Simone Mathieu (3) of France in the semi-finals. Meanwhile, Hilde Krahwinkel (4) just got the better of a grim battle with Helen Jacobs (6) – the conqueror of Betty Nuthall. The Final was a disappointing match for, in a baking fortnight, the courts had become so hard that both girls had blistered feet. Cilly Aussem won in two sets, the only German ever to win a Singles title.

In the Men's Singles, though it was no vintage year, a record was set in the fight for the men's title. The Final between Sidney Wood (7) and Frank Shields (3), both Americans, never took place. In his semi-final with Borotra, Shields fell heavily, injuring an ankle, when leading 4/3 in the fourth set. He managed to finish off the match but, with Davis Cup ties pending, his captain insisted that he should scratch from the Final.

Tilden had turned professional; the Musketeers had shot most of their bolts; but great players were waiting in the wings. In the fourth round Fred Perry (5) of Great Britain beat Germany's Gottfried von Cramm.

6

PERRY PREDOMINANT
1932–9

Fred Perry had started his charge but in 1932, before his peak years were reached, a second Californian Comet appeared. H. Ellsworth Vines (2) exploded onto the Wimbledon scene with the most ferocious service and forehand ever seen. Although he dropped a couple of sets in earlier rounds he became better and better as he got the feel of Wimbledon and the Centre Court. His service was getting grooved and the forehand was booming in. In the other half, Wood (5), the Champion, went out disappointingly to Satoh, who was stopped by Austin (6) in the semis in straight sets. The quarter-finals had seen sweet revenge for Austin against Shields (3) for his semi-final defeat the year before.

Perry (4) disappointed his fans when he was beaten in the quarter-finals by Australian, Jack Crawford (8), in four sets. They had hoped to see him play Vines in the semi-final, for the feeling was that he could beat the Californian. Instead, Vines ran through Crawford 6/2, 6/1, 6/3. It was a massacre. Many of his services Crawford could not touch. The same went for many of his service returns.

To reach his first Final Austin had produced his best form, but could have had little hope of winning against the power of Vines. The American hit his big serves and forehands nearly flat, which meant that he had to be right on form to keep them in. Apart from the first set, he was. Vines made enough mistakes to give Austin every chance, had he found his semi-final form. With the first set won 6/4, Vines attained his peak. His service and his forehand were both working to perfection and he blasted Austin out of his way.

The service ace he produced at match-point brought this comment from his victim: 'I did not know which side of me it had gone.'

The historic footnote to this year's Men's title was the defeat of Cochet (1) by Ian Collins in the second round. Quite unperturbed Henri entered for the Plate (the consolation tournament for first and second round losers). He won it, the second former Champion to do so, the first being A.W. Gore in 1903.

In any event in which Mrs Moody (1) was competing the result had become a foregone conclusion. In her six matches she lost only thirteen games, beating Kitty Godfree 6/3, 6/0, Dorothy Round (8) 6/0, 6/1, Mary Heeley 6/2, 6/0. At least the hapless Helen Jacobs (5), her Final victim, could rightfully claim that her four games were more than anyone else achieved. To get to the Final

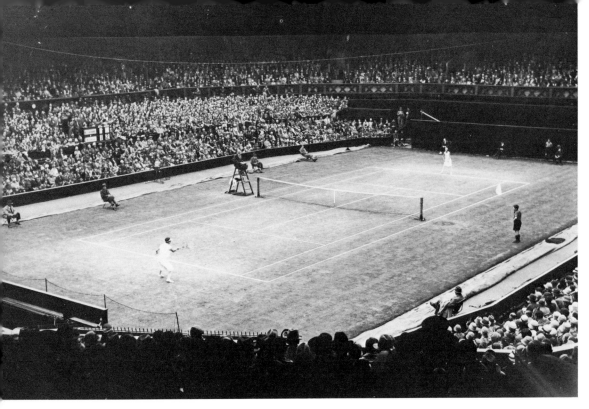

Where there's a Wills: 'la belle Hélène', holder of the record eight singles wins at Wimbledon – with (*above*) one of her loveliest Final victims, Lili de Alvarez.

she had beaten a string of good names, past and present, Mrs Covell, Mrs Shepherd-Barron, Hilde Krahwinkel (3), and Madame Mathieu (2).

Fred Perry and Pat Hughes (3), now the established British Davis Cup pair, who had reached the semi-finals the year before, led Borotra and Brugnon (4) 2–1 in the Men's Doubles Final, and the French pair won the last two sets only by 7/5, 7/5. For the first time more than 200,000 watched the Championships.

1933   Next year, 1933, Perry and Hughes (3) went out to the Japanese Nunoi and Satoh in a five-set quarter-final. Borotra and Brugnon (1) kept their title, though they were taken to four sets by the Australians, Crawford and Vivian McGrath (the first two-handed player of note, who had already beaten Vines in the Australian championships), in the quarters and five sets by South Africans, Farquharson and Kirby (4), in the semis.

After his devastating form in winning the title at his first attempt, few looked beyond Vines (1) for the winner of the 1933 Singles. But in the second round he dropped a set to a qualifier, A.T. England, and in the quarters lost the third to the huge Czech, Roderic Menzel. In the semi-finals Cochet (3), who appeared more in his old Champion's form than he had in the last two years, lost a close second set to Vines, 6/8, and won the third 6/3. So Vines was in the Final again but his results suggested that he might after all have toes of clay. Crawford (2) was given a tremendous first round match by Maier of Spain who took him the distance. He then had no real trouble reaching the Final.

The Vines–Crawford Final has always been remembered by those who saw it as one of the best matches ever played on the Centre Court. This was a different Cràwford to the previous year. Vines could huff and puff as he would, but Crawford was not going to let his house be blown down. There was no blasting off court this time. There was no ostentation about Crawford's game. He was good, he was accurate and he concentrated. He was of the old school of players. And he looked it, using a square-headed racket and playing with his sleeves rolled down. A positive sign with Crawford that things were getting to a crisis was the occasional rolling up of the sleeve of his racket arm.

Despite the power and reach of the tall Californian he was largely a baseline player, and there was little volleying between these two. It was a mighty battle, the hammer blows of Vines countered by the solid defence of Crawford. Vines won the first set 6/4. Crawford, with the advantage of serving first, led all the way during the crucial stage of the second. He was mainly attacking Vines's weaker backhand, but threw in some tempting high-bouncing balls to his forehand. On some of these Vines made mistakes but he was never fed enough to get his range. At 9/10 down Vines missed out on some of his big serves and Crawford punished the looser ones to break through and win the set.

Crawford's impetus carried him through the third set 6/2. Back came Vines to win the fourth by the same score. Two sets all, twenty-three games each. Crawford, though, in this final set still held the advantage of serving first. At

Ellsworth Vines – the second Californian comet – in his cap (*above*) and taking everything in his great forehand stride (*below*) to win in 1932 at his first attempt.

Immaculate as ever in his strokeplay and appearance, Jack Crawford, Vines' conqueror in 1933, one of Wimbledon's greatest finals.

4/4 Crawford's uncanny instinct told him to come to the net and Vines, now tiring, had not the accuracy to pass him with winners. Crawford won two games, the match and a famous victory.

Vines retained his American title and turned professional. So Wimbledon never saw this great player again. In only two visits he had left his mark, on his opponents, on the crowd and, one is tempted to say, on the court.

Reports that Helen Moody (1) was not playing quite up to her own supreme standards seemed unfounded when she lost only six games in her first three matches. But in the semi-final Hilde Krahwinkel (6) actually took seven games off her. Dorothy Round (2) lost no sets until she met Helen Jacobs (5) in the semi-final. She won 4/6, 6/4, 6/2 to reach her first Final. There was general expectation that she could give the Champion a good game. But to everybody's delight she did much more than that and, but for inexperience, might have won.

Mrs Moody began confidently and a close first set went to her 6/4. Miss Round then started playing alternately short and long, drawing her opponent in and sending her back. It must have been a new experience to the Champion to be given the run-around. The tactic succeeded and Dorothy Round won the second set 8/6, though a doubtful point went in her favour at a critical moment. This upset both players and jarred the tenor of the last set.

The Champion was tiring and, had Dorothy switched her attack from side to side and kept her on the run, she should have driven home her advantage. Instead she tried drop-shots but they were not good enough to be winners and became losers. Helen Moody, as ever Miss Poker Face, kept her head and won the set and the match 6/3. The title was still hers. The Moody legend remained but the invincibility of it had shown a crack.

1934 Fred Perry gave Britain back her tennis pride. He was remarkable by any yardstick. He was the first Englishman to win the Men's Singles since A.W. Gore in 1909, the year Fred was born, the son of a Labour Member of Parliament. Fred did not start tennis until fourteen – quite late for a future champion. His interest was triggered by chance when on an Eastbourne holiday with his parents he just had to see what was happening on the other side of a wall. The wall happened to be around Devonshire Park, venue for much top-class tennis. What he saw excited him and he rushed home to tell his parents that he wanted to play. When windows started being broken some of the Perry neighbours wished that he had not looked over that wall.

Fred's unfettered enthusiasm overcame all obstacles. Hearing that all school-boys could enter for the Queen's Club annual tournament, Fred arrived on the opening morning to enter himself. He so impressed the Secretary with his keenness that he was eventually allowed in, although the entry lists had officially closed. At this time, though, Fred lacked the inches he was to grow. Fred had gone to an elementary school and his father intended him to go into business. However, he was so impressed with his son's unremitting efforts to improve his tennis that he decided to give him a year to make good. One of the factors in this decision was the knowledge that Big Bill Tilden had played against his son in a covered courts doubles match at Queen's and had commented that he was a potential World Champion.

Not quite twenty-one, Fred was entered for the British Hard Courts Championships in Bournemouth. He got to match-point against Bunny Austin. Fred's friend and mentor, 'Pop' Summers, remarked, 'I felt like throwing my hat in the air for joy when Fred missed that match-point. It was too soon. Had Fred won, the public would have expected him to live up to it. Give him time.'

Fred came to rely on Pop Summers and has never forgotten the wisdom and kindness he distilled. One thing Pop said was 'Fred, you've got to take the ball early.' Fred did, in the manner of table tennis at which he had been World Champion. His famous forehand was directly derived from table tennis, where a wristy flick takes the ball on the rise. Only Fred could do it on a lawn tennis court off the wrong foot and with perfect timing. This early-hit ball put the pressure on his opponent. To the tennis purist Fred's strokes left much to be desired. But he did not play to please purists. He played to win, and there was nothing wrong with his ambition and determination. Duncan Macaulay recalls: 'Fred was always certain that he was going to win Wimbledon.'

Both Finalists at 1934 Wimbledon had tough matches on their way there. Crawford (1), the Champion, lost a set each to the talented German, Henner Henkel, to Britain's Ian Collins, Japan's Yamagishi, America's Stoefen (6), and against Frank Shields (5), who had beaten Austin (4) in five sets in the quarters, Crawford also took five sets. Perry (2) had been 1–2 down against the Czech Menzel in the third round, had beaten Lott (USA) 10/8 in the fourth and had needed five sets in the semi-finals to beat the 1931 Champion, Sidney Wood (7). Fred had an extra incentive to beat Wood, who had ousted him in the 1931 semi-finals. The form of many players had been affected by a mysterious bug called 'Wimbledon Throat'. It had even caused some to withdraw.

Perry was already American and Australian champion but Wimbledon was the one he really wanted. Both started well and Crawford led 3/1. Then Perry went berserk. He reached Arthur Ashe's 'serene high' and stayed there for twelve unforgettable games to lead two sets to love (in the second set Crawford won only eight points) and 1/0. Crawford, temporarily finding the eye of the storm, got back into the match and at one time looked like winning the third set when he served at 5/4. But Perry broke back and held his own for 6/5. Crawford, serving, reached 40/0. Perry pulled him back to deuce and then got to match-point. Crawford, determined to get to the net before Perry, foot-faulted on his first service. His second went into the net.

Fred Perry had achieved every tennis player's dream ambition. He could wake up and it would still be true. To him it meant more than to most. He had had to do more to get there. Inevitably he retained his US title.

Perry predominant. His famous forehand was derived from his skill at table tennis (he was world champion in 1929). It was taken on the rise, off the wrong foot, and hit with tremendous power.

Perry's great speed and athleticism, aptly illustrated below left, made it difficult to pass him.

Wimbledon had gone wild at the excitement of a British Champion at last. Was it possible, with Mrs Moody not defending, that Dorothy Round (2) might succeed in making it a double? Helen Jacobs (1) the American Champion hoped not. She had waited long enough in the wings. She had lost only one set on the way to the Final, against Britain's Joan Ingram in the third round. Dorothy lost two, one to Mrs M.R. King in the fourth and one to Madame Mathieu (8) in the semi-finals.

As in the Men's Final, but unlike so many finals, both players started well and Dorothy Round, getting the fast pace of the court first, took the lead and kept there to win the set 6/2. It was a swaying battle in the second set. Helen Jacobs led 5/3 but was pulled back. She got to 6/5 and then Dorothy Round had a fit of overhitting and lost the set. She managed to break Helen's service in the first game of the third set. Her length and accuracy then deserted her, so that Helen led 2/1 and had a point for 3/1. Helen Jacobs then hit what looked like a tremendous winner, but Dorothy just got her racket to it and had the bonus of a net-cord, which left her opponent helpless. It was the sort of incident which changes fortunes. She again broke Helen Jacobs's service in the important seventh game and then, scenting a win, attacked from the net. Three superb volleys gave her 5/3 and she won the next game at her second match-point to take her first title. Britain's Double had been achieved.

Bunny Ryan, that inveterate American competitor at Wimbledon since she arrived in Britain in 1912, won the Doubles with Madame Mathieu (1), making her bag of Wimbledon titles a record nineteen. Her total tally is reputed to have been 659 tournament wins, including the last women's championship of Imperial Russia. The amazing thing is that with her record she never won a major singles title. When she started at Wimbledon corsets were still the order of the day and she recalled them hanging up to dry, bloodstained from the wounds they had inflicted.

1935   To a man like Perry (1), who had a real Champion's make-up, once the goal had been achieved it should and would be done again. He was the Champion, he looked the Champion, and he made every opponent feel that he was going to stay the Champion. He dropped a set here and there in 1935, one in the semis to Crawford (3) who had wrested his Australian title from him, but there was no sense of danger about it. In the Final he met Gottfried von Cramm (2). Perry had just won the French title so had now won all four major honours, but not the grand slam in one year. In Paris he had beaten von Cramm on the slow surface of Roland Garros. He was quite certain he would beat him on the Centre Court, and told Duncan Macaulay before the match, 'I shall beat him 6/2, 6/3, 6/4.' The score was actually 6/2, 6/4, 6/4.

Austin had again reached the last eight by his fluent play, and there had been beaten by a nineteen-year-old American newcomer called Donald Budge, whose backhand alone already gave him the hallmark of greatness. He took a set in the semi-finals from von Cramm. For Australia Crawford and Quist (2)

Dorothy Round, winner in
1934 (a happy double with
Fred Perry) and 1937.

took the Doubles, and went on to win the American title. (Quist was to win again fifteen years later with John Bromwich, and again they went on to win the American. From 1937 to 1950 he won ten consecutive Australian doubles titles, eight of them with Bromwich.) Fred Perry won the Mixed Doubles with Dorothy Round (3) and a third British success came with the win in the Women's Doubles by Freda James and Kay Stammers (3).

This year Mrs Moody had returned for the Ladies' Singles but was seeded at No. 4. Joan Hartigan (8) from Australia was a fine and improving player, who beat the Champion, Dorothy Round (1), in the quarter-finals, so the prospect of another clash between Miss Round and Mrs Moody was unfulfilled. Helen Moody was not match-tight, having played little in the last year. She lost a set in the fourth round to the all-out attack of Miss Cepkova of Czechoslovakia, but beat Madame Mathieu (5) easily enough and overcame Joan Hartigan 6/3, 6/3. Helen Jacobs (3) had an easier draw and made reasonably light weather of reaching the Final. In the semi-finals she beat Hilde Krahwinkel, now Mrs Sperling (2), who had just won the first of her three French titles. In the quarter-finals the German had been too experienced for Britain's attractive and rising young star, left-handed Kay Stammers, winning 7/5, 7/5.

The Final was by far the best of the four Wimbledon Finals the two Helens were to play. There was much at stake. Helen Jacobs had lived in the shadow of Helen Wills Moody since they had grown up together, attending the same college in San Francisco. They had played each other eight times and Helen Moody had won seven of them. The eighth had been in the American Final two years before when, at 0/3 down in the last set, Mrs Moody retired with a back injury, later diagnosed as 'a slight displacement of a vertebra'.

Mrs Moody started the Final in high mettle. Her drives streamed to the lines and she was soon 3/0. Helen Jacobs then won twelve successive points to level at 3/3 and have Helen Moody at 0/40. She clawed back those three points, just salvaged the game and ran out for the set 6/3.

Helen Jacobs's length and passing shots were so good in the second set that, despite serving a double at set-point, she won it 6/3. The third set was tense. Nerves took their toll. Helen Jacobs was the first to recover and went to 4/2 and then 5/2. She had a match-point at 5/4. This she lost, then volleyed out twice. Helen Moody was level. Her calmness and resolution brought her the next two games for the set and match at 7/5. It had been a sustained and courageous fight by both girls, and they were cheered for several minutes. Helen Moody had now equalled the record of Mrs Lambert Chambers – seven times a Wimbledon champion.

1936   Fred Perry (1) joined the immortals in 1936 when he won the Singles title for the third year running, a feat not repeated since the Challenge Round was abolished until Borg equalled it in 1978 and, of course, went on to beat it. The consistent Austin (7) again reached the semi-finals, where the German cham-

Two of the finest strokemakers, both runners-up to great players.
ABOVE Bunny Austin (1932, 1938).   ABOVE & BELOW Gottfried von Cramm (1935–7).

pion, von Cramm (2), beat him in four sets, and Perry lost his only set at the same stage to Budge (5). These scores suggested that Perry was as confident as ever. But an accident during the year before, which had undoubtedly cost him the American title for the third year in succession, had kept him out of tennis for seven months. He had lost to von Cramm in the French Final and he was not match-tight. He needed reassurance from his friends at the beginning of the fortnight but his results soon re-established his own. By the Final it was the old Perry, certain of winning.

Except for the first game, the Final was a sad anticlimax. That first game lasted nearly eight minutes. There were ten deuces with three break-points to von Cramm. On each of these Perry served an ace. At the start of the next game von Cramm pulled a muscle in his right leg. Although in pain, he concealed it so well that it was some time before Perry realised it. Von Cramm insisted on playing on and limped through game after game, Perry winning 6/1, 6/1, 6/0. Perry then helped the British team to win the Davis Cup for the fourth successive year before turning professional.

Mrs Moody did not defend and at last Helen Jacobs (2) had her just reward, winning the Final 6/2, 4/6, 7/5 against Mrs Sperling (5). Although Dorothy Round (1) reached only the quarter-finals, as did Kay Stammers (4), it was a good year for Britain. Freda James and Kay Stammers again won the Doubles and Fred Perry and Dorothy Round the Mixed, and to cap it all, it was an all-British Men's Doubles Final with Pat Hughes and Raymond Tuckey (2) beating Charles Hare and Frank Wilde 6/4 in the final set.

This year was the last of the eighteen championships refereed by F.R. Burrow, whose skill at compiling crosswords enabled him to counter the inroads of weather very quickly. His firm but friendly approach to the players earned him great respect.

1937–8   The years 1937 and 1938 hang well together in Wimbledon history. With Perry gone, Donald Budge completed a double triple crown, and von Cramm as ever played beautifully to reach the Final for the third time running in 1937. Budge was the third Californian Comet. His immediate success was not as great as Vines's, who won at his first attempt. But he was the first player to complete the grand slam of the four major titles in one year (1938) and he was the major factor in the United States winning the Davis Cup in 1937 and 1938. Budge then turned professional in 1939 and beat both Vines and Perry in his début at Madison Square Garden. In winning his two Wimbledon singles titles he lost only one set. As well as his pre-eminent backhand he had a good forehand, a tremendous serve and a sure command of his volleys. To this natural display of talent he learned from Perry to add aggression. Here was another superstar.

In 1937 seven seeds reached the quarter-finals, where the unseeded Jack Crawford gave a classic exhibition to take von Cramm (2) to a fifth set, after being 0/2 down. This was the fighter, if past his very best, who had beaten Vines in 1933. Bunny Austin (4) was a fluent straight sets winner over Bitsy

Donald Budge, an all-time great and first winner of the grand slam, particularly noted for his potent backhand.

Budge in play against Gottfried von Cramm in the 1937 Final.

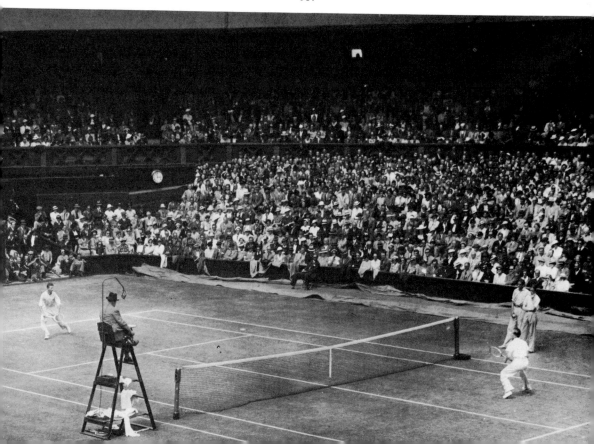

Grant (5); Frank Parker (8) outlasted Henner Henkel (3) in five; and Budge (1) outgunned Vivian McGrath (7).

In the semi-final strokemaking was displayed at its best when von Cramm beat Austin 8/6, 6/3, 12/14, 6/1 and Budge dropped the first set – his only loss in the Championships – to Parker. In the Final, though von Cramm performed well and there were many fine rallies, Budge was playing with awesome power and certainty and won 6/3, 6/4, 6/2. Gottfried von Cramm must have felt he was the unluckiest Wimbledon competitor ever. He was beginning to peak when Fred Perry was at the top and then immediately suffered Budge. In 1939 he would surely have won but was unable to play. He would have been at his best during the war years and was still to show fine form in post-war years. His was the most beautiful game of fluent and poised grace. A match between him and Austin was a feast of stroke-making.

It was Austin who was Budge's (1) Final victim in 1938. Bunny Austin (2) himself was a perpetual near-miss, twice in the Final, three times semi-finalist and four times a quarter-finalist between 1929 and 1938. With Perry he was a key man in Britain's successful quest for and holding of the Davis Cup 1933–6. All he needed to be a Champion was a more severe service and a killer instinct. His skills were of little avail against a Budge who was now at the peak of his prowess and allowed Austin only four games, two more than Vines had conceded to him in 1932. If it was any comfort to Austin, he had himself dropped only six games in his win over Henkel (4) in the semi-finals and five to Elwood Cooke in the quarters. It was not a vintage year.

But 1937 was for the British women. Dorothy Round (7) beat Helen Jacobs (1), the reigning Champion, in the quarters much more easily than in their 1934 Final, the score being 6/4, 6/2. Alice Marble (5) beat Hilde Sperling (2) 7/5, 2/6, 6/3; the popular Polish girl 'Jed' Jedzrejowska (4) beat left-hander Peggy Scriven, the first British girl to win the French title (1933 and 1934) 6/1, 6/2; and Simone Mathieu (6) beat the attractive Chilean girl, Anita Lizana (3), 6/3, 6/3. In the semi-finals, Dorothy's fine tennis was altogether too much for Simone's clay court game; and Jed had the marvellous satisfaction of beating Alice Marble 8/6, 6/2. This was almost as big a feather in her retrospective cap as reaching a Wimbledon Final. This proved to be a tremendous tussle, in which Dorothy just got home 6/2, 2/6, 7/5 and so became the last British player to win two Wimbledon singles titles. There was further British success when that talented doubles player, Billie Yorke, won the Women's Doubles with Simone Mathieu (2).

In 1938 Helen Moody (1) set up her record of eight Wimbledon Singles titles. She did it in her fourth Final against Helen Jacobs, the first woman to reach the Final unseeded (perhaps not significant since, owing to injury, her results were too few). This was a one-sided affair because Helen Jacobs injured an Achilles tendon when practising the day before with Tilden. Her ankle was bandaged and at 4/5 in the first set, finding the bandage too tight, she tried to

Helen Jacobs, four times Helen Wills Moody's Final victim, and 1936 winner in her absence.

The end of an era.
The 1939 Champions:
Alice Marble, combining
grace and power to bring a
new dimension to women's
tennis, and Bobby Riggs,
triple crown winner and
wily tactician who bet on
himself.

The runners-up:
Lovely Kay Stammers.

Elwood Cooke, who
went all the way with
Riggs in singles and
doubles.

loosen it. As the two players were at the umpire's chair she asked her opponent if she could stop to take it off. Helen Moody did not reply but, concentrating so intensely as she always did, she may well not have heard. The umpire gave his permission and, while it was being done, Helen Moody stood her own ground. However, she was known never to speak to opponents during a match.

In fact, after beating Kay Stammers (6) 6/1, 6/1 in the quarter-finals, Helen Moody had one of her few really hard Wimbledon matches – certainly the longest set – against Hilde Sperling (4), whom she only beat 12/10, 6/4 in the semis. By contrast Helen Jacobs beat 'Jed' Jedzrejowska (3) 6/2, 6/3 and Alice Marble (2) 6/4, 6/4.

Helen Moody was the most dedicated and single-minded player, the epitome of concentration, often not knowing the score, just playing for every point as if each mattered equally. Everything about her was tightly controlled and appearances were perfect. The effect was cold and when she bowed out it was as if the Snow Queen had gone, still wearing her crown – in her case an eyeshade.

1939 Helen Jacobs had not the strokes of Helen Moody – and her forehand was chopped – but she, too, had great dedication. She was back at Wimbledon in 1939 as No. 2 seed but this time could not capitalise on Mrs Moody's absence. Indeed, she was beaten with surprising ease by Kay Stammers (6) in the quarter-finals, 6/2, 6/2, and the British girl went on to beat Sarah Palfrey Fabyan (8) in a match which hinged on the first set which Kay took 7/5.

However, like everybody else who played her, Kay Stammers was no match in the Final for Alice Marble (1), who beat her 6/1, 6/1. Left-hander Kay, one of the most attractive British players ever, could take a crumb of comfort from the fact that Alice had whitewashed that redoubtable scrambler Hilde Sperling (3) 6/0, 6/0 in the semi-finals. She had already won the American title twice and was to win it twice more before turning professional. Alice Marble brought the men's power game to women's tennis. She was the complete champion and, in this last pre-war Wimbledon, won the triple crown, the Doubles with Sarah Fabyan and the Mixed with Bobby Riggs. Her coach was 'Teach' Tennant, who was later to nurture the game of Maureen Connolly.

The Men's Champion was Bobby Riggs (2), the only player to win the triple crown at a first Wimbledon appearance. It is significant, though, that von Cramm (who did not play at Wimbledon) beat Riggs with ease in the London Grass Courts semis at Queen's Club the Friday before the Championships. Riggs was a highly confident player with a good all-round game though he played mainly from the baseline. He had the temperament for the big occasion and is said to have made a lot of money from the bookmakers when, after his Queen's rout at the hands of von Cramm, he backed himself heavily to win the Wimbledon title. In the Final he beat his fellow countryman, Elwood Cooke (6), in five sets.

The curtain fell in 1939 on the Second Act of the Wimbledon drama. This time the interval was to last for seven years.

The sacred turf in October 1940.

Acting Secretary Norah Cleather and assistant Marie Bompas study the form of wartime acceptances.

7

AMERICAN TAKE-OVER
1946–50

1946 Wimbledon emerged from the war slightly bruised – there had been the odd bomb about – but all was very quickly put so nearly to rights that the 1939 fans coming back to their Mecca might well have thought that from a tennis point of view no Second World War had existed.

All this was largely due to the organisation for which Wimbledon has ever been justly famous. The Secretary, Lt-Col. Duncan Macaulay, who had been an assistant referee up until 1939, soon got a firm grip on the running of the Championships. Duncan Macaulay put his stamp on Wimbledon and he ran it all by what he called his black book. This was a harvesting of experience set out in one loose-leaf book, to which he constantly referred and added in the light of experience. Self-analysis has long been a characteristic of the All England Club which for fifty weeks a year is a private club, but which devotes ninety per cent of its effort and administration throughout the year to making the Championships the nearest thing to perfection in international sport.

There was evidence of the war in the 1946 programmes, still very much utility efforts with only eight pages and practically no advertisements. A notice on the inside of the back cover and outlined in black, headed 'Bomb Damage to Centre Court', told of the night of Friday 11 October 1940 when a 'stick' of five 500 lb bombs straddled the Club grounds. The first bomb demolished the tool-house. The second fell on the roof of the Centre Court, the third fell in Church Road at the north-east entrance, and the last two produced bunkers in the Wimbledon Park golf course. The damage to the Centre Court meant a loss of approximately 1200 seats.

After a gap of seven years the known form of the various entrants in many cases scarcely existed, and the Referee must have had an extremely hard job working out acceptances and seeding. However, some of the old guard needed no introduction. Among the men Tony Mottram, who was to serve Britain so well in the Davis Cup, had played as a youngster in 1939, since when the RAF had claimed him with so many others, including John Bromwich of Australia, who had lost their best years and their best chances. Jaroslav Drobny, a name unfamiliar to most people then, but who was to become a Wimbledon heart-throb, had surprised everybody in 1938 with a victory over his famous fellow Czech, Menzel.

But the name on everyone's lips as the seemingly inevitable winner was Jack

1946, the first post-war Final. Yvon Petra of France, the last champion to wear the trousers, shares his triumph with loser Geoff Brown of Australia. Left-hander Brown was better known for his two-handed backhand and his whirlwind *right-handed* service.

Kramer (2) of America. He and his compatriot, Tom Brown, were also favourites for the Doubles. Kramer was a tennis machine, superbly built, with the big American serve–volley game and, although seeded No. 2, he was most people's favourite.

Kramer's fourth-round match with Drobny soon had Number 1 Court bursting at the seams. Kramer took the first set 6/2. The second, a titanic struggle, eventually went to Drobny 17/15. This battle killed Kramer's hopes. During earlier matches he had aggravated a blister on his racket hand. This was further inflamed during the gruelling struggle with Drobny. Drobny took the third set for a 2–1 lead. Kramer equalised in the fourth, but the effort with his blister had been too much and, with the crowd by now firmly supporting Drobny, the Czech won the deciding set.

Drobny went on to beat Pellizza of France in straight sets in his quarter-final. In the semi-finals he himself was beaten in three by Geoff Brown (3) of Australia. Brown had previously beaten the graceful Lennart Bergelin (8) of Sweden 13/11, 11/9, 6/4. Bergelin, like Cochet before him and Krishnan a little after, was a marvellous player of the unorthodox shot – especially the half-volley which he would pick up and turn into an attacking stroke as he wandered seemingly quite casually to the net. Today Bergelin is the man who brought Bjorn Borg to his pinnacle as Wimbledon Champion and Swedish tennis therefore has a double debt to him.

Dinny Pails (1) of Australia floated comfortably through to the quarter-finals. There he met Yvon Petra (5), of France, who put out Pails in four sets. Poor Dinny. On the way to Wimbledon that day he missed a train on the London underground. What made things worse was that he was playing on the Centre Court. He finally got on court twenty minutes late. Having kept everybody waiting, including Queen Mary, he was sweating with nerves and at a tremendous psychological disadvantage when he faced up to the big serve game of Yvon Petra.

Petra did not so much play tennis as perform. He was something of a mixture of Tilden and Nastase. The effect was that of a one-man whirlwind. Nor did it help Pails that each time he was at the Roller end he could see the familiar sight of Queen Mary, straight-backed, awe-inspiring in her familiar toque hat. She was flanked by the Chairman of the All England Club, Sir Louis Greig – who had partnered her son on his Wimbledon appearance – and Lady Greig, who took it in turns to hold Her Majesty's sunshade, relieving each other when an anguished look indicated that the arm was tiring.

After disposing of Pails, Petra beat Tom Brown in five hard-hitting sets. Came the Final and Petra rushed to a two-set lead against Geoff Brown (3) and most of those present thought he was on his way to quick victory. Brown did not think so. There then unfolded a memorable David versus Goliath battle with Brown conceding at least seven inches to his giant opponent. Petra used his full height to unleash cannonball serves and thundering forehands.

But Geoff Brown, small as he was by comparison, yielded nothing to Petra for power. The wind-up and the arc of his right-handed service swing were short, but the resulting delivery was so fast that he reminded one of a spring, tightly coiled, being suddenly released. And, like David with his sling, Brown served with such accuracy that, despite a low trajectory which allowed little margin of error, he served many aces. He had a left-handed forehand and an explosive two-handed shot on his backhand.

Brown came back at Petra just as furiously as Petra had come at him and he rallied to win the third set. Petra seemed to have got clear again when he made it 5/3 in the fourth set and at 40–15 was serving for the match. Whereupon Brown hit two devastating two-handed returns of service straight through the incoming Frenchman, followed by yet a third which left the crowd – and Petra – stunned. Brown won the game and took the set. Petra hit back in the final set which he won 6/4 for the match and the title.

Petra had many distinctions. To start with he was born in Vietnam, then the French colonial possession Indo-China, learned to play tennis in his bare feet and also became a soccer goalkeeper of some repute. After his family returned to France, Yvon became a barman and spare-time tennis player. During the war he was badly wounded in the leg and taken prisoner. By one of the ironies of war, when it seemed that the leg would have to be amputated, it was saved by the skills of a German surgeon who operated on prisoner Petra.

The Ladies' Singles in 1946 produced more evidence of the old guard. Names like 'Jed' Jedrzejowska, who had conquered Centre Court hearts as a girl of sixteen, Kay Menzies (4) – Kay Stammers that was – one of the most beautiful stylists who must surely have won during the war years, the Woodgate sisters, Mme Mathieu, that persistent French Champion who was a Wimbledon semi-finalist in the years 1930–2 and again in 1937, Mrs Jean Bostock (6), Mrs Uber (winner of the All England Badminton title in 1935), Mrs Joan Strawson, one of the leading pre-war players, Joan Curry, Mrs Betty Hilton, and Betty Nuthall.

However, the favourites were clearly the Americans, who had come with a tremendous reputation which was fully justified when they provided all the semi-finalists. The No. 1 seed was Pauline Betz. She played like a ballerina. Her grace was matched with power and she never had a qualm in taking the title without dropping a set. Her opponent in the Final was Louise Brough (3), who had had a big semi-final battle with her great friend and doubles partner, Margaret Osborne (2) (later du Pont). These two were to dominate the women's game for some years to come with Doris Hart (7). What had been hinted at by the masculine effectiveness of Alice Marble's winning game in 1939 was now an established fact. Top American women played like men. They produced big serves and they could volley.

947   Jack Kramer (1) had come to Wimbledon in 1946 to win. He failed, probably because of his blistered hand (although he himself refused to use that

Pauline Betz, the 1946 Champion. She might have joined the greats but turned professional. Her forehand here speaks volumes.

The 1946 Men's Doubles Final, won by Americans Tom Brown and Jack Kramer (*right*) against Geoff Brown and Dinny Pails of Australia.

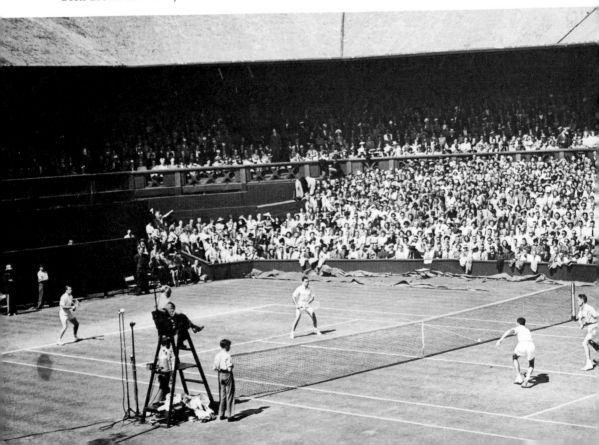

as an excuse). Kramer simply became more determined, if that were possible, when he came back in 1947. For it meant that he was now a year behind schedule. The Kramer plan was that he would win Wimbledon, turn professional and make his living from tennis. He had decided that he would make good in the world by doing what he was best at – playing tennis. So, from being an excellent player he turned himself through unrelenting practice into a great one.

With his crew-cut hairstyle and lean, keen looks, Jack Kramer appeared to have come straight from the Harvard Business School. That was how he played. He brought to tennis the percentage game. His tennis was intelligent, it was powerful, it was ruthless. His victory in the Final against fellow American, Tom Brown (3), saw him drop a mere six games and throughout the whole Men's Singles tournament he lost only thirty-seven. He must figure in any list of Greats.

Kramer, majestic and efficient on court, was to prove to be a businessman with the same flair, allied to shrewdness. After winning Wimbledon, which opened the golden door to professionalism as a player, he quickly became a promoter running an international 'circus', signing big cheques as readily as he had served and volleyed, but as ever with great thought behind the action.

The limitations of the Champion, Yvon Petra (7), were this time exposed by Tom Brown in the quarter-finals and Brown beat elegant Budge Patty fairly comfortably to reach the Final. In the fourth round Patty had put out John Bromwich (2). Bromwich, like Geoff Brown, double-handed on his right-hand side and left-handed on his forehand, showed just how ambidextrous he was by serving right-handed. He was a marvellous touch player and brilliant at doubles. Like his great compatriot, Norman Brookes, Bromwich used a loosely strung racket that gave him longer 'feel' of the ball. He deserved to win the Singles title, which he would surely have done but for the war. In 1947 we saw for the first time a tall American, all arms and legs which seemed to take time to unfold. His name was Bob Falkenburg (8). We were to see more of him and hear much more about him in 1948.

In the absence of Pauline Betz, who had left the amateur scene, Margaret Osborne (1) took the Women's title with a good win over Doris Hart (3). To get to the Final Doris had beaten Louise Brough (2) in a great three-setter while Margaret Osborne had outgunned the graceful South African, Sheila Summers (7). Many more battles royal were to be fought between these queens of the court.

1948   In 1948 John Bromwich (2) of Australia looked destined to achieve the crown which all who saw him knew he deserved. He was seeded No. 2 to America's Frankie Parker (1), a rather mechanical player who relied more on length and percentage shots than inspiration. Matters seemed set all the more fair for Bromwich when Parker was beaten in the fourth round by the graceful Swede Lennart Bergelin. Bergelin was then blasted out by Bob Falkenburg (7),

Margaret Osborne du Pont, with her all-round game, one of the great forces in women's tennis.

Jack Kramer, a precise exponent of the power game both on court and in tennis politics.

the gangling American with a cannonball serve, very reminiscent of Vines. Bromwich, with his soft wiles, bringing delicacy to the two-handed stroke, got through to the Final without dropping a set and must have felt in form enough to handle anything that Falkenburg would throw at him. But neither he, nor anybody else, knew what was in store.

Many names were being applied to the lanky Falkenburg – Daddy Longlegs or, when he sank to his knees, the Praying Mantis. Bromwich had set-points for the first set but lost them to his own nerves and fine passing shots by Falkenburg. The American then appeared wantonly to throw away the second to love and was already taking time out lying on the ground or stalling before service. Bromwich's concentration and confidence were disturbed, and his habit of shaking his head from side to side in a slow, rueful manner became even more noticeable. His game disintegrated in the third set which Falkenburg won 6/2. However, more 'throw-aways' by Falkenburg helped Bromwich to square the match at 2-all and the Australian got to 5/3 in the final set. At this point Falkenburg repeatedly held up play, sinking to his knees in Praying Mantis fashion. Clearly these delays took toll of Bromwich's nerves when he was at the brink of his ambition. He led 5/3 and 40/15 on his own service. Falkenburg saved the first match-point and a missed volley cost Bromwich the second. A brave passing shot saved yet a third. Bromwich was clearly over-anxious and, having missed these chances, he scarcely won another point.

After the match, Fred Perry said to 'Buzzer' Hadingham, later Chairman of Slazengers who always provide the equipment for the Championships, 'Well, I'd say Falkenburg won by thirty-four falls to thirty-one headshakes.' There was much controversy over Falkenburg's 'stalling' tactics. It did emerge subsequently that he suffered from a thyroid deficiency.

Bromwich gained some consolation when, in partnership with Frank Sedgman (3), he won the Doubles title, putting out top seeds Falkenburg and Parker in the semi-finals and winning the Final against Tom Brown and Mulloy (2).

Tony Mottram had the Centre Court crowd roaring for him in his fine third round win over Cucelli of Italy. It was a most exciting and exhausting match, the score being 6/8, 6/3, 10/12, 9/7, 6/2. When at the Roller end, where the Groundsman's friends have privileged seats on and in front of the roller itself, Cucelli was several times heard to say 'Basta! Basta!' meaning 'Enough! Enough!' To British ears it sounded rather different. The roller is the pony roller with long shafts that was brought from Old Wimbledon to prepare the new Centre Court. The stands were built round it before anyone realized that it could never be got out.

There was no question mark against the winner of the Ladies' Singles. The year 1948 saw the inauguration of a conspicuous reign by a tennis queen. After a Final in which points were fluently and fiercely contested, Louise Brough (2) beat Doris Hart (4) 6/3, 8/6 to win the first of her four singles titles. By her record alone Louise Brough has earned a special place in lawn tennis history. In all she was to win thirteen Wimbledon singles and doubles titles and in the Wightman Cup, playing for America between 1946 and 1957, she was unbeaten in twenty-two rubbers.

Her record is all the more incredible when it is remembered that she thrived among other fine players. That 1948 Wimbledon well illustrates this. No country has ever fielded four players of such quality as Louise, Margaret du Pont (1), Doris Hart and Pat Todd (3), who made up the semi-finals line-up in the Women's Singles. Louise and Margaret (1) then beat Doris and Pat (2) in a memorable Doubles Final 6/3, 3/6, 6/3. The partnership of Louise and Margaret was even greater than their combined singles talents. They were to win the American doubles title an unbelievable twelve times.

49   Wimbledon 1949 was a vintage year. It provided Drobny's first final; it saw the one appearance in his heyday of one of the all-time greats, Ricardo 'Pancho' Gonzales (2); and the year also marked the only appearance ever in the singles of F.R. 'Ted' Schroeder, the No. 1 seed, who quickly became known as 'Lucky' Ted.

A second-round match between Van Swol of Holland and Abdesselam of France provided the only occasion on which a squirrel has invaded and left its mark on the Centre Court, helping to change the course of at least a minor piece of tennis history. Van Swol, a big blond Dutchman, was 5/3 down in the final set and seemed to be sinking fast to the little Algerian, Robert Abdesselam. Suddenly the Centre Court was engulfed in roars of laughter. A squirrel was sitting pertly in possession of the court. Van Swol, quick to seek any relief, turned his racket head upwards and had a sit-down. A linesman made heroic but unavailing efforts to catch the offender. After an enthralling chase in which the squirrel jinked like a rugby three-quarter it was caught by a ball-boy, who promptly got bitten for his pains. The squirrel was removed, chattering unrepentantly while the ball-boy received attention from the St John Ambulance men. It was then back to the tennis. Van Swol, who had been able to enjoy a respite of some three minutes, rallied to win the set and the match 13/11. Next year Van Swol had a squirrel embroidered on his shirt.

After his great win over Kramer in 1946, Jaroslav Drobny (6) had become the Wimbledon crowd's 'favourite' favourite: So there was relief when the American champion, Gonzales (2), was removed from Drobny's path by little Geoff Brown of Australia. None of the tennis lovers who later came to idolise Gonzales could know that he would not be seen again at Wimbledon until the arrival of Open Tennis in 1968 – when he was still a giant but no longer a Colossus. It was a further tribute to Gonzales' ability and drawing power that he did not need the glamour of a Wimbledon Singles title to be the No. 1 target for Jack Kramer to sign for his professional circus. As it was he had slight consolation when with Frankie Parker (3) he won the Doubles, beating Mulloy and Schroeder (1) in the Final.

The 1948 Finalists.
ABOVE John Bromwich,
one of the closest near-
misses Wimbledon has
known, in typical two-
handed half-volley pick-up.
Although left-handed, like
Geoff Brown he served
right-handed; and like
Brookes, his rackets were
loosely strung for better
control.

LEFT & OPPOSITE Bob
Falkenburg, the 'praying – or
preying? – mantis', winner on a
Vines-like service and booming
forehand.

A wonderful competitor, Louise
Brough won the title four times.
She and her partner, Margaret du
Pont, played the same masterful,
all-round game.

In the semi-finals Drobny beat John Bromwich (5), losing only six games. Bromwich had previously got some revenge over his Final conqueror of the previous year, Bob Falkenburg (4). It had been another astonishing display. Falkenburg, when leading 2/0, threw twelve games to take a rest and Bromwich won the final set 6/4.

Lucky Ted Schroeder had almost gone out in the first round to unseeded Gardnar Mulloy, who took the first two sets. Schroeder with his chunky appearance and sailor's gait was just like Popeye and he did have a corn-cob pipe. You almost expected him to take a handful of spinach to sustain him through the next crisis. Not that he ever seemed to need sustaining. He was as cool as the refrigerators he sold – even in the tightest of situations. In the quarter-finals, against the speed and power of twenty-one-year-old Frank Sedgman, he found himself trailing two sets to love. He squared the match. In the final set he was called upon to save two match-points. On one of these he was foot-faulted on his first service. His nerve held and he went for a good and not just safe second serve, rushed the net to take the vital point and eventually the set at 9/7. In the semi-final he came from 2–1 behind to beat South African Eric Sturgess (7), who brought all the delights of the pre-war baseline game to his graceful strokeplay. In the Final against Drobny Schroeder dropped the first set, won an inspired second set to love, took the third but lost the fourth. He got to 5/4 in the final set and then clinched the title in the grand manner by serving out the last game to love.

The line-up for the Women's Final was Louise Brough (1) against Margaret du Pont (2). It produced a memorable three-set battle which went to forty-three games. Louise won the first four games and Margaret the next five, and it was not until the third break of service that the set went eventually to Louise at 10/8. Margaret, ever the fighter, came right back to take the second set 6/1. The final set was a survival battle. The first six games saw four service-breaks. At 8-all Louise found herself 0/40 on her own service, only to serve her way out of trouble and then hold on to win the match 10/8, 1/6, 10/8.

After a brief interval the two Finalists were back on court as a team (1) to retain their Doubles title against fellow Americans, Gussie Moran and Pat Todd (2), 8/6, 7/5. By now Louise had played sixty-nine games on that last Saturday. Her day was not yet done. She and John Bromwich (1), the holders of the Mixed Doubles, had again got to the Final where they were to meet South Africans Eric Sturgess and Sheila Summers (4). It became another marathon, going on so long and so late into the gathering dusk that it seemed it would overrun the traditional Wimbledon Ball. Sturgess and Summers won 9/7, 9/11, 7/5. On that day Louise had played a total of 117 games and had only just failed to win the triple crown for the second successive year.

It was not only serves, volleys and a squirrel which caught the eye that year. The lace around Gussie Moran's panties gave fashion designer Ted Tinling his first real imprint and brought an added alertness to many a male eye.

'Lucky' Ted Schroeder, a born survivor who smoked a corn-cob pipe and seemed to have the muscles of Popeye. Against Sedgman in the quarter-finals (*below*) he survived two match-points, and he lost eight sets in all – more than any other Champion.

The American invasion.
OPPOSITE Two of the finest women's fours of all time.
TOP The 1946 Finalists: Louise Brough, Margaret Osborne du Pont, Doris Hart and Pauline Betz.
BOTTOM The 1949 Finalists: Pat Todd, Gussie Moran, Louise Brough and Margaret du Pont.
Brough and du Pont won the first and third of their five titles.
ABOVE 'Gorgeous' Gussie Moran, with a quietly confident Pat Todd.

In 1950 sixteen men were seeded in the singles for the first time. This was due to the open nature of the field. The winners for the two previous years, Schroeder and Falkenburg, were absent. The No. 2 seed in 1949, Pancho Gonzales, had turned professional. The 1946 and 1947 champions, Petra and Kramer, were already in the professional ranks.

Frank Sedgman was No. 1 seed, mainly because, having twice won the Australian title, he had also just won the French Championship. He was given a close run by left-handed Art Larsen (7), and even super athlete Frank was drained after the battle, which went 8/10, 5/7, 7/5, 6/3, 7/5. Larsen was one of those great Wimbledon characters who have done so much to make the Championships. He was called Tappy because of his extraordinary compulsion to tap everything. The tapping had to be carried out to his own series of 'Enigma' Variations involving a prescribed number of taps for any one day. John Barrett illustrates this with a story from a particular French Championship. Coming into the dressing-room Barrett came across Larsen busily tapping. A shower and ten minutes later John found Tappy still tapping, this time rearranging his clothes in an obviously related sequence but unable it seemed to get the magic combination. 'Can I help you, Tappy?' asked John. 'It's OK,' replied Tappy. 'I'll get myself unhooked in a minute.' Tappy endeared himself to Wimbledon hearts not only for his quirks of behaviour but for his traditional style and fighting qualities. He was slightly built to the point of seeming frail.

Sedgman got through his semi-final, coming back from two sets down to Drobny (3). The man he faced on the other side of the net in the Final was Budge Patty (5), debonair as ever, nose tilted. Patty's tennis sparkled like the vintage champagne of his adopted France. It had carried him with fizz through a four-set quarter-final with Bill Talbert (2) and a four-set semi-final with Vic Seixas (12), who had beaten Eric Sturgess (4). Now it carried him zestfully to victory in the Final. This was a lovely match to watch, the incisive serve–volley game of Sedgman and his twinkling footwork against the elegance and artistry of the sophisticated Patty.

Bromwich and Quist (2), one of the greatest combinations ever, won the Doubles. The Doubles quarter-final between McGregor and Sedgman and Patty and Trabert, both unseeded pairs, played on a torrid No. 1 Court, produced a record second set won by the Americans 31/29.* Patty and Sedgman, on opposite sides of the net, seemed to be trying to conserve their energies for their Singles Final the following day.

The Ladies' Singles presented the usual American mixture, with a semi-final line-up of Louise Brough (1) v. Doris Hart (3) and Margaret du Pont (2) v. Pat Todd (4). Louise Brough won in straight sets against Doris Hart. Pat Todd, who was unlucky to be a contemporary of three great players, pushed Margaret

* Beaten in 1968 when Alex Olmedo and Pancho Segura won the first set 32/30 from Gordon Forbes and Abe Segal.

Winner takes all.
Tom Brown and Jack Kramer, 1947.

Pauline Betz and Louise Brough, 1946.

Budge Patty and Frank Sedgman, 1950.

Pancho Gonzales, Frank Parker, Ted Schroeder
and Gardnar Mulloy, 1949.

du Pont to the extent of her powers before losing 6/8, 6/4, 6/8. The Brough–
du Pont Final was a three-setter, but in the two sets which Louise won she
dropped only two games and so won her third successive title. She completed
her triple crown with Margaret (1) in the Doubles (again an all-American
affair against Doris Hart and Shirley Fry (2)) and Eric Sturgess (1) in the Mixed
Doubles against Geoff Brown and Pat Todd (4), playing this time a mere eighty-
nine games in the day.

8

MIGHTY LITTLE MO
1951–5

When Doris Hart (3) won match-point against Shirley Fry to gain the 1951 Ladies' Singles title, the Centre Court crowd and tennis fans everywhere experienced deep pleasure. For they knew that the road to victory, seldom easy, had been particularly hard for Doris. To start with, it was something of a miracle that she was playing tennis at all. As a baby in St Louis, Missouri, when taking her first faltering steps, she had fallen and hurt her knee. The tendons had been damaged and gradually the leg had been helplessly drawn up and all use of it lost.

With the help of friends, Doris's family by constant, tender massage brought life back to the leg. The family moved to Miami so that Doris could get the benefit of the sun. The next step was to provide exercise, so elder brother Bud took Doris to the local park to play tennis. It was a rare day when people using the park did not see them there.

In 1935 Doris and her brother had a particularly interested spectator – Slim Herbert, a tennis professional at a big Miami hotel. Doris was then ten. Slim began coaching her. Two years later she had won her first tournament. Within four years Doris was US Junior Doubles Champion and she caused a sensation when, still only sixteen, she beat Pauline Betz, second only to Alice Marble in the American rankings. At seventeen, Doris became American Junior Champion and was sixth in the senior rankings.

Having got to the top Doris had to live with two all-time greats, Louise Brough and Margaret Osborne du Pont. Doris made light of the impediment resulting from that childhood accident, for although her footwork looked affected her game was one of grace and flowing strides.

Doris Hart was at her fluent best in 1951. She was seeded No. 3, and to get to the Final she had to dispose of Jacqueline Marcellin, a young French player of promise, Maria Weiss of Argentina, Australia's Nancye Bolton, Britain's Jean Rinkel-Quertier and fellow Americans Nancy Chaffee (7) and, in the semi-finals, Beverly Baker (5).

Beverly, later Mrs Fleitz, at her first Wimbledon had become an immediate crowd favourite. With her pretty turned-up nose and happy smile she had a most engaging manner. Added to which she was a baseline driver of the old school – with the difference that her strokes were mirrored as she was ambidextrous. It was Beverly who had put out Margaret du Pont (2). Top seed

Doris Hart, another of the superb players America produced at this time. Despite her physical handicap, she was one of the most graceful strokemakers the game has seen. She won in 1951 but played perhaps her most glorious tennis in a losing Final against Maureen Connolly (*opposite below*) in 1953.

and reigning champion, Louise Brough, showing signs of elbow trouble, had been beaten in the semi-final by Shirley Fry (4).

Having got to her third Wimbledon Singles Final, Doris Hart seemed more than determined to win it and she beat Shirley Fry in just over half an hour. Then, with Shirley as her partner and seeded No. 2, she took the Ladies' Doubles title from the holders, Louise Brough and Margaret du Pont (1), in a hard-fought match 6/3, 13/11. Doris completed the triple crown when she and Frank Sedgman (2) won the Mixed Doubles.

As a result of the somewhat questionable long list of seeds in the previous year, 1951 saw the list for the men cut to ten. The main seeds were the holder, Budge Patty (4), the man he had defeated, Frank Sedgman (1), Drobny (2) and Larsen (3). Two American newcomers to Wimbledon were also seeded, Herbie Flam (5) and Dick Savitt (6).

Flam, the Paul Newman of tennis players, with hunched and self-deprecating look, got to the quarter-finals without dropping a set. There he met Sedgman. The Australian took the first two sets 6/2, 6/1. Flam then gave notice of his fine fighting qualities, took the third set 6/3 and, with two breaks of Sedgman's feared service, the fourth 6/4 to square the match. In the final set Flam, always a tenacious defender, broke Sedgman's service three more times to win an 'upset' victory. He then lost in the semi-final to another serve–volley specialist, Dick Savitt. Savitt was tall, dark and striking, both of looks and with his long sweeping forehand. In the Final, he outhit another big-game player, Australia's Ken McGregor (7), who had beaten Eric Sturgess (8) in the semi-finals.

The year provided the finest tennis hour for Britain's great favourite and loyal tennis servant, Tony Mottram, who in the third round beat the No. 2 seed Drobny. The match presented the Centre Court crowd with a dilemma. Drobny was an adopted favourite, Mottram was a home-born one. The crowd swayed Tony's way and finally urged him through an 8/6 final set. Mottram, like so many of the promising pre-war players, had lost his best years during the war, when he was a bomber pilot. He had a big game, particularly suited to Wimbledon's fast grass, and with full development of early promise could well have won the title.

1952   1952 was a significant year in tennis history. Three all-time greats made their first appearances at Wimbledon – Maureen Connolly (2) ('Little Mo'), Lew Hoad and Ken Rosewall. Little Mo was exceptional. She came, she saw, she conquered – three years running. She then had a tragic riding accident and never played at Wimbledon again.

She was primarily a baseline player, but her accuracy was so unerring and her drives so fierce as they sought out the lines, that she put her opponents under almost continual pressure. She had a huge competitive instinct and at the slightest sign of danger would raise her sights and lessen still further the margin of error. Her drives on either wing became withering and occasionally she put in a delicate surprise drop-shot. When she was in high mood, the crowd loved to watch her bobbing head, for as soon as a point was finished she immediately turned and marched briskly back to position, her head nodding like that of a foraging chicken. Most lovers of the game give her premier place since 1946 and many feel that she would have raised her game to beat any greats who came before or after her.

Maureen was the most sensational thing to happen to lawn tennis since Suzanne Lenglen. As an eleven-year-old she had been spotted playing on a public court in San Diego, California, by Wilbur Folson, who used to coach youngsters. Wilbur saw the potential in the girl with the curly hair and sparkling eyes and persuaded Mrs Connolly to let him coach Maureen. Almost immediately he made a radical change in her game, getting her to switch from left- to right-handed.

Maureen then came under the guidance of the top tennis coach in Southern California – Eleanor 'Teach' Tennant. Her progress was breathtaking. At thirteen she became the youngest girl to win the National Junior Championships; two years later she was ranked ten in the senior ratings; in August 1951, when only sixteen, she became America's youngest Wightman Cup player, beating Britain's No. 3, Kay Tuckey. The sensations continued, growing in size and in reaction. Nine days later, playing in the American Championships, Maureen knocked out Doris Hart. In the Final against Shirley Fry, sixteen-year-old Maureen took the first set 6/3, lost the second 1/6, and came back to win the decider.

At Wimbledon in her first match she beat Britain's Evelyn Moeller without needing to take off her cardigan. But she did have to struggle in a fourth-round match against attractive Sue Partridge. Here was a player with all the natural graces of beauty and stroke production, but lacking that essential killer instinct, a fault of so many British players. It was a lovely match, with the new phenomenon getting home only by 6/3, 5/7, 7/5. Little Mo also dropped a set in her quarter-final against Thelma Long (7) of Australia. These were the only two sets she was ever to lose at Wimbledon. She reached the Final by beating Shirley Fry (3).

Champion Doris Hart (1) looked vulnerable in her early matches, and was beaten in the quarter-finals in a long wavering match by Pat Todd (5), who in turn went out to Louise Brough (4).

The Final between seventeen-year-old Little Mo and the great Louise, who was conceding some twelve years, was eagerly awaited. Few thought that Maureen, even though she was reigning American champion, could sustain the high pitch she had reached at her first Wimbledon. She did. But how Louise fought to regain the crown she had worn so nobly. At one set down and 2/5 in the second, Louise was 0–40 facing three match-points. She saved them all and a fourth in the following game. But, at the fifth, after a thrilling rally, she was beaten by Little Mo's forehand which flashed across court, past

Mighty 'Little Mo' – Maureen Connolly – had the accuracy and determination to give her a perfect singles record at Wimbledon.

ABOVE Dick Savitt sweeps
all before him, 1951.
LEFT Vic Seixas, 1953
Champion, said, 'A true
Champion comes back to
win it twice.' Like many,
he failed in the attempt.
OPPOSITE Ken
McGregor and Frank
Sedgman, winners in 1951
– their doubles grand slam
year – and 1952, when
Sedgman (*below*), one of the
fastest reflex players at the
net, also won the triple
crown.

her own. So Maureen, who had been given the nickname 'Little Mo' after the American battleship *Mighty Mo*, had found the range with her big guns to sink all opposition.

Lew Hoad and Ken Rosewall had been heralded as prodigies and, under the firm management of Harry Hopman, they quickly made their marks. Rosewall lost in the second round, but Hoad survived to give Drobny (2) a real fright in the fourth before going down in a match of big serves and ricocheting volleys.

In the doubles, Hoad and Rosewall had the Centre Court in a roaring fervour of delight when, in a five-set third-round match, they fought off a match-point to go on and beat the highly experienced pair, Mulloy and Savitt (2). In a match of many memories, that tense final set produced one shot which was unforgettable. Hoad was serving at 6/5. On the first point – vital at that stage – Rosewall, lobbed by one of his tall opponents with a perfect pitch to the baseline and with the ball running away from him, sprinted after the ball, and caught up with it just before the stop-netting. His nimbly adjustable footwork placed him at the nth millisecond in perfect position to swivel and bring all the contra-rotating force of his body into a scintillating top-spin backhand which flew dipping at around shoulder height straight down the middle, splitting Mulloy and Savitt as if they had been straw figures. Like the audience, they could only stand, stare, wonder and laugh outright. The youngsters got through another round before falling to Seixas and Sturgess (4). They had not been able to emulate the feat of Little Mo. But they had served full warning of what was to come.

In the Singles Drobny, having survived Hoad's challenge, had two gruelling wins – each in five sets – over McGregor (5) and Flam (6) to reach his second Final. Mervyn Rose (3), that gifted left-hander and fine doubles player from Australia, beat an unconvincing Savitt (4), the holder, in five sets and then fell to Sedgman (1).

Sedgman v. Drobny in the Final. Both were previously defeated finalists. Both were determined that this would be their year. Drobny had beaten Sedgman a few weeks before in the Final of the French Championships. But at Wimbledon Sedgman emerged victorious because, in yet another battle of services, he had the more commanding net-play for support. This was the last time that Wimbledon crowds were to see Sedgman at his best for, with the title to his name, he could no longer deny the beckoning sirens of the professional game.

1953   Sedgman's win interrupted a long run of American success, which was renewed in 1953 when Vic Seixas (2) won from a field in which Ken Rosewall (1), on the strength of having won the Australian and French titles, had the signal honour of being seeded No. 1 when only eighteen and at only his second Wimbledon. However, in the quarter-finals he became the second in a row of three seeded players (the others were Mulloy (5) and Drobny (4)) to be beaten by the sensation of the Championships – Kurt Nielsen of Denmark, who reached the Final unseeded, to equal the feat of Wilmer Allison.

Hoad (6) also reached the quarter-finals where he took Seixas to a 9/7 final set – here we saw the boy out of sorts, looking a little sulky while some of the corners were rubbed off him. The semi-final in which Seixas beat Rose (8) was a marathon of seventy-one games but was overshadowed by *the* marathon.

Drobny (2), having failed in two Finals and with the years slipping by, was determined that 1953 should be *his*. His great friend Patty (12), the 1950 Champion, stood in his way in the third round. The resulting clash was not only the match of the year, but till then probably the best ever played at Wimbledon, setting up a new record of ninety-three games lasting four hours twenty minutes. It began at five o'clock and ended in the twilight at 9.20pm.

The drama – which developed quickly and was sustained on an impossible note for an impossible length of time – was a truly titanic struggle, such as was waged by the heroes of ancient legends. The final score, 8/6, 16/18, 3/6, 8/6, 12/10, indicates the level of the battle. The match was played to the fullest powers of both men. It was all a question of who was at the extreme elastic stretch of his ability and stamina at any one moment. Three times in the fourth set and again three times in the fifth, Patty held match-points. Each time Drobny countered him.

The winning effort probably cost Drobny the Championship for, although he survived two more rounds, he was ripe with leg weariness (he was hampered by a damaged blood vessel and by blisters on hands and feet) to fall to the bludgeoning of Nielsen's big game. In the Final the limited talent, and perhaps the nerve, of the great Dane were exposed by the more flexible and polished play of Vic Seixas who, after a tough first set, won in three.

Hoad and Rosewall, already Australian and French Doubles Champions, deservedly won the Wimbledon title and only just failed to complete the Doubles grand slam when they were beaten in the Final of the American Championships. On their way to the Wimbledon title they had a hectic time against two men who made up the most unusual ingredient of the Wimbledon scene at that time – the Austrian doubles combination of Huber and Redl. Huber was the Danny Kaye of tennis – a red-headed clown with similar features. His playing distinction was his fantastic acrobatic agility, particularly at the net, where his headlong dives brought off spectacular coups and compensated for his partner's slight lack of mobility. His favourite crowd-pleasing trick was to bite the ball which had offended. Redl was fair, balding and getting on in tennis maturity. His distinction was that he dismissed completely the loss of his left arm. He served by throwing up the ball from his racket and still managed to provide a most effective delivery. His balance was remarkable.

Between 1949 and 1953 Huber and Redl regularly won through a round or two and then in 1953 they reached the quarter-finals and gave a most lively display before going down in four sets to Hoad and Rosewall. The

The marathon friends and foes. Jaroslav Drobny (Champion at last in 1954) and Budge Patty (*opposite*, Champion 1950) battle it out. Their 1953 third-round score was 8/6, 16/18, 3/6, 8/6, 12/10 to Drobny – 93 games lasting 4 hours 20 minutes, a record until the Gonzales/Pasarell match of 1969.

austere Redl gave the impression that he regarded Huber's antics, which in response to the crowd had become more exaggerated, as distasteful. Whether true or not, although both continued to come to Wimbledon, they did not again play as a pair.

Women's Champion, Maureen Connolly (1), looked the part all the way. Her final with Doris Hart (2) goes down as a Wimbledon classic. She won it 8/6, 7/5. Both players were at their peak and both felt afterwards that it was probably the best game of their lives. In the first set Maureen led 5/3, but nervously double-faulted twice. However, at 7/6 she had Doris Hart 0–40. Doris saved two set-points but at the third put her forehand out.

Connolly dropped the opening game of the second set, uncharacteristically making three mistakes, a reaction to that thrilling first set. However, she quickly took two services from Doris to lead 3/1, then dropped her own and games went with service to 5/5. At 4/4 Doris had a heaven-sent chance to break when she had two advantages in a game of six deuces on Maureen's service. But Little Mo, as always when danger reared, hit her way out of trouble. She went to 6/5 and then won Doris's service to love. Little Mo went on to win the US title and became the first woman to win the grand slam in the same year.

The calibre of Doris Hart's performance in this match is measured by her winning eleven games from the Champion. Up to the Final Maureen had lost only eight in five matches. Doris then shared in two Doubles titles, retaining the Women's with Shirley Fry (1) and the Mixed, this time with Vic Seixas (1).

1954   The following year Maureen (1) emphasised what a great Champion she was, retaining her title again with the loss of only nineteen games. She beat Margaret du Pont (5) 6/1, 6/1 in the quarter-finals, Betty Pratt (8) by the same score in the semis and yielded only seven games to Louise Brough (4) in the Final which she won 6/2, 7/5. That persistent British player, Angela Mortimer (6), was a-peeping through the green for the first time, reaching the quarter-finals, where Louise beat her, 6/1, 6/3, and then Doris Hart (2) 2/6, 6/2, 6/3.

The other outstanding event of the year was the success of Jaroslav Drobny in his third Final and after eleven attempts in sixteen years. Stung by being seeded only 11 out of 12, Drob blasted his way through Arkinstall, Torben Ulrich, Lennart Bergelin, Phillipe Washer and, sensationally, Lew Hoad (2) – all in straight sets. He then met Budge Patty (7), and hearts bled for them after the epic marathon of the previous year and the toll it had taken of them. This time, Drobny won in four sets.

In the other half Rosewall (3) ran into no difficulty until the semi-finals where he met US Marine Tony Trabert (1), the American Champion and lately victor in Paris. Tony was following in the steps of many recent American champions, establishing himself before making a Wimbledon bid. Against Rosewall, Trabert had the slight edge after three sets, but then in the last two 'the Little Master' romped away 6/1, 6/1.

So to the Final and to the drama. Rosewall's genius was slightly subdued and his backhand was not the superb, reliable weapon everyone had come to expect. Drobny, too, made mistakes. But he also hit many glorious winners. His big serve and smash were much in evidence, so too was the delicate drop-shot touch he delighted in. Against this attack Rosewall deployed his full defensive dexterity, using spin and float in a varied mixture of shots. When Drobny led 2/1 he broke for 5/3 in the fourth, served for the match at 5/4 but was broken back, and games went with service to 7/7. At 30-30 on Rosewall's service Ken netted a *backhand*.

At this crucial break-point the gods finally came down on Drobny's side. He played a backhand and got a dead net-cord. Rosewall's response was to play like a man possessed. With Drobny serving for the match, but at 15-30, Ken hit a marvellous running forehand cross-court drive, falling over in doing so, and forced 15-40. Drobny saved one break-back point with a smash and was lucky on the second with a questionable line call. He followed with an ace and took the title at his first match-point.

Wimbledon euphoria that day was complete. Everybody, but everybody, had wanted Drob to win. He had tried for so long. He was obviously such a nice guy and the women adored him. Seldom has a player so had the crowd on his side. A Rosewall error would bring applause which at times would spatter out shamefacedly. Little did anyone there that day think that years later they would twice be willing Rosewall to do the same thing and in the same situation. Then it seemed that a Wimbledon title was coming fast towards him.

After Drobny's triumph in 1954, his peak had been reached and he was seeded only sixth in 1955. He got through to the quarter-finals where he went out to Tony Trabert (1). Trabert then won in straight sets against Patty (7), conqueror of young terror Hoad (4). Rosewall (2) came serenely through to the semi-final. Here he met Kurt Nielsen, victor in a five-set quarter-final over the gifted Nikki Pietrangeli. Pietrangeli was a delightful stroke-player with considerable tactical guile. His face and figure brought to mind a medieval cherub. But many an opponent who fell to his particular genius saw him in a different light. For Italy he was to achieve a Davis Cup record unlikely ever to be beaten – 119 victories in 164 rubbers.

Playing Rosewall, Nielsen clearly remembered his success against the Little Master in 1953, when he hit his approach shots down the middle and came to the net, making it difficult for Rosewall to play his favourite passing shots decisively. He pursued the same tactics and with the same result; for the *second* time he had reached the Final unseeded – a record which could stand for ever.

Finalists Trabert and Nielsen had similar games, the big serve followed by the clinching volley. But Trabert's had more depth, with a serious repertoire of strokes. He was moulded on the same pattern as Jack Kramer. Both were tennis machines with Trabert at his best almost Kramer's equal. His weakness was a long backswing on his forehand, which could be hurried into error. On

Tony Trabert, the all-American college boy, whose powerful game was too much for reigning champion Drobny (*above right*) in the 1955 quarter-finals. Trabert took the title.

Split image. Beverly Baker Fleitz,
Finalist in 1955, the most
graceful ambidextrine
Wimbledon has seen.

the day Nielsen lacked the inspiration he had found in beating Rosewall. Trabert won 6/3, 7/5, 6/1 at his second Wimbledon attempt and equalled the record of Hadow and Budge in winning the title without losing a set. He was one of the few players to possess a top-spin lob on forehand and backhand – an invaluable asset. His winning shot against Nielsen was a backhand cross-court top-spin lob which landed right on the line.

With Little Mo so sadly removed by her riding accident from her rightful place on the Centre Court, Doris Hart was the natural No. 1 seed, with thrice champion Louise Brough at No. 2. In the semi-finals Louise met Darlene Hard (6). Darlene brought something new to Wimbledon. The crowd had mixed views on her extrovert manner on court but most people were taken with her vivacity. She was always making gestures, slapping her thigh, talking, and was a natural reactor to any given situation, such as shaking hands with a linesman she had crashed into – in the manner of a Borotra. She played a strong, masculine-type game, occasionally rent by a gale of errors. Louise Brough beat her only 6/3, 8/6 to reach her seventh final.

In the other semi-final, ambidextrous Beverly Fleitz (3) gave a superb display to beat Doris Hart. With her shots speeding on either wing and to such length, she stood comparison with Maureen Connolly at her best. Indeed, she had been the only player to beat Maureen in 1954. Doris Hart, the reigning US Champion, did not win one game in the second set. Beverly's pace withered her game. Beverly Fleitz not only looked the complete player on the day, she was lovely with it. She was one of the most attractive movers in the ladies' game.

The Final presented the free-hitting Beverly Fleitz against Louise Brough, the majestic ex-Champion. Louise was always prone to tighten up at important points but had a greater breadth of stroke and experience at her command, which just saw her through a keenly fought struggle. In the sixth game of the second set, for example, it was only after nine deuces and five advantages to Fleitz that Brough wrong-footed her near-exhausted opponent with a backhand slice down the line to lead 4/2. This was a major turning point and Louise went on to win her fourth Singles title, 7/5, 8/6.

The year was also memorable for the performances of the British girls in the doubles. In the first round Jennifer Middleton and Doreen Spiers knocked out No. 1 seeds, Doris Hart and Barbara Davidson. They lost in the third round to Fay Muller and Jenny Hoad, but the Final was an all-British affair, the first time since 1929. In it Angela Mortimer and Anne Shilcock (4) beat Shirley Bloomer and Pat Ward (3), 7/5, 6/1.

For many, even more memorable was the grace in form and in dress of Italy's Lea Pericoli. Ted Tinling must have been delighted with her as a model for his frilly creations.

Austrian exHuberance – Alfred Huber.

Nikki Pietrangeli, a Wimbledon favourite, played in more Davis Cup matches than any other player – 164 – and won 120 of them.

'Why didn't you take both hands to it?' Adrian Quist and the prostrate John Bromwich, Doubles Champions in 1950, 15 years after Quist won the title with Jack Crawford. Quist won the Australian doubles title ten times, eight of them with Bromwich.

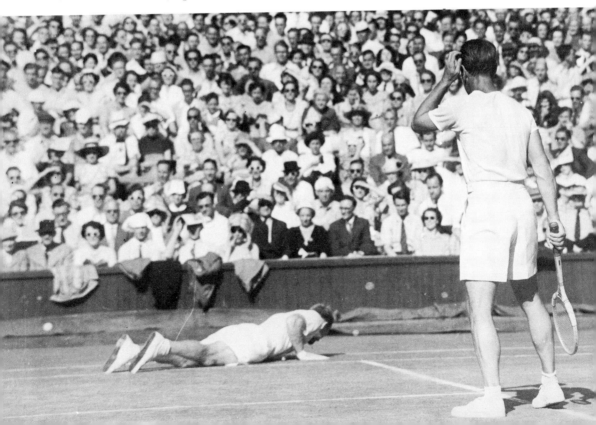

9

WALTZING MATILDA AND QUEEN MARIA 1956–60

In 1956 the Australian 'tennis twins', Lew Hoad and Ken Rosewall, who had threatened so much since their arrival as seventeen-year-olds in 1952, fulfilled that threat when they justified their first and second seeding by reaching the Final. Hoad had straight set wins until his quarter-final with Mal Anderson. Anderson, a rangy player from Queensland, had a big game and gave Hoad a good four-set fight, after which he had to receive treatment for sunstroke. Anderson next year caused a big surprise by being the first man to win the American title unseeded.

Hoad looked in ominously good form in disposing of Ham Richardson (6), who had caused a sensation at his first Wimbledon in 1951 by beating reigning champion, Budge Patty, but had then faded. This year Patty (4) had fallen in the second round to a brilliant No. 1 Court display by Britain's Bobby Wilson, one of the finest classic stroke-makers tennis has known. Wilson had a habit of springing good wins like this at Wimbledon but then going out next round, in this case to Neale Fraser. If Wilson had had the will-to-win of Fred Perry he would surely have been the first Englishman to follow in his footsteps. There was more cheer for Britain when John Barrett, who has done so much for home tennis, had the distinction in his first-round match of being the only man to take a set from Rosewall on his way to the Final.

So the twins at last met in their only Wimbledon Final, with Hoad, having won the Australian and French titles, going for the grand slam. Each knew the other's game well and they were almost perfect examples of complete opposites. Hoad was strongly built, chunky with a mighty forearm and a wrist of steel which allowed him to play almost any shot from any position with maximum force and control. On his day, when in a mood of high concentration, nobody could live with him. But he was a lazy player, as so many of the supremely gifted are, and he needed the spur of danger on an important occasion to bring out the best in him.

In contrast to Hoad's blond, forceful good looks, Rosewall, older by three weeks, was dark and always tended to look shy and self-deprecating, with a curious habit between rallies of appearing to droop suddenly. But he had a steely resolution, superb strokes, particularly his famous backhand, and his return of service was renowned. An aspiring Wimbledon player, an admirer of Rosewall's, seeking advice, asked the 'Little Master': 'What do you do when

Lew Hoad, Champion in 1956 and 1957 before turning professional, could play every shot, and play it with awesome power and precision.

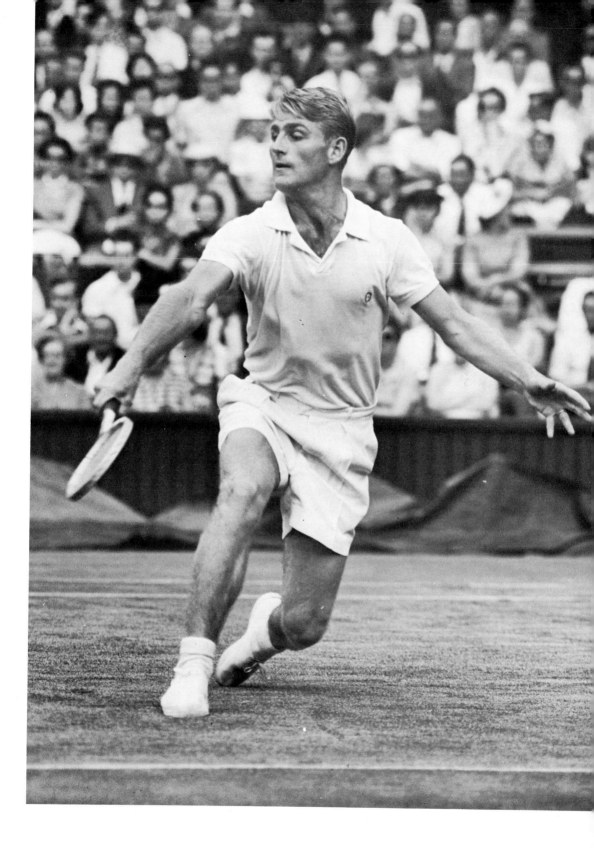

Men's Doubles.
As she should be: Vic Seixas and Tony Trabert, Wimbledon Finalists and US and French champions in 1954.

Lew Hoad and Ken Rosewall, winners in 1953 and 1956, when they also took the US and Australian titles.

And as she shouldn't: Nikki Pietrangeli and Orlando Sirola, Finalists in 1956 to Hoad and Rosewall (*below*).

you are having trouble with your service returns?' Muscles, scratching his head, replied, 'I wouldn't know about that.'

His one real weakness was his lack of power in service and overhead. He partly overcame this by his length and accuracy and in later years as a professional added more power. The weakness was always surprising in one who otherwise was so perfect, and was the most mercurial and quickest reacting volleyer the game has seen. But in his autobiography with Peter Rowley, Rosewall revealed that as a boy he was a natural left-handed thrower. What a player Rosewall might have been had he started serving left-handed; for the service is the action of throwing the racket head at the ball.

On that Final day of 1956 it was just Hoad, but only just, in four richly entertaining sets and *because* it was a Wimbledon Final. Hoad was the supreme player for the supreme occasion. Rosewall subsequently reversed the Wimbledon result when he beat Hoad in the American Final, so denying him an epic grand slam. It was inevitable, and fitting, that Hoad and Rosewall (1) won the Doubles, against Pietrangeli and Sirola. It was Rosewall's last Centre Court appearance for eleven years, for he turned professional after his US success.

In the Women's Championship 1956 goes down as the year Shirley Fry (5) came good and Angela Buxton (6) combined fortune with persistent courage to become the first Briton to reach a Singles Final since 1939. Beverly Fleitz (2) reached the quarter-finals but withdrew, in the words of the *Daily Telegraph*, 'for delicate and happy reasons'. This gave Pat Ward, who had been at the top of her form in beating Angela Mortimer (3), a semi-final against Angela Buxton who won well.

Angela Buxton had reached match-point against Shirley Fry only a week or two before in a Wightman Cup match. But in the Final Shirley Fry, of the big grin, would not be denied. She had had to live in the shadows of the great American tennis queens, Louise Brough, Margaret du Pont and Doris Hart, and so was all the more determined to make the most of this opportunity.

This then was the end of an era and the strain of great American champions had passed its peak. But Shirley Fry well deserved her honour, even though it was an interim year. On her way to the Final she beat Louise Brough (1), the reigning title-holder, and Althea Gibson (4), the Champion-to-be. Angela Buxton completed a fine Wimbledon when, partnered by Althea Gibson (3), she won the Women's Doubles.

1957   The following year Althea Gibson became a Wimbledon Champion in her own right, the first black player to win any Wimbledon title, and well she deserved it. The sixteen-year-old Christine Truman blazed a British comet's trail whose startling light lit the Wimbledon scene, especially the Centre Court, with a patriotic glow. As a result she was chosen for the Wightman Cup team – the youngest ever on either side.

The Queen came to Wimbledon on the final Saturday to pay her first visit as monarch. It was a scorchingly hot day and the luncheon room was stifling.

Shirley Fry, living in the shadow of the great American tennis queens, always gave it a try and came good in 1956 – at the expense of Britain's Angela Buxton (*below right*).

As ever the Wimbledon organisation was equal to the problem. Ice blocks were put in front of the fans and a cool lunch was enjoyed by all.

On court, Althea Gibson (1), in the Final at her second Wimbledon attempt, kept *her* cool to beat Darlene Hard (5) 6/3, 6/2. She was a good Champion, having the now accepted typical American big serve–volley game. Reminiscent of Doris Hart in her movements but without Doris's full range of strokes, Althea was tough and athletic and this was how she played her tennis. Her style and her competitive instinct were born of a background which had seen her as a thirteen-year-old playing street baseball and paddle ball (a form of small court tennis) in Harlem. How different from the home life of other tennis queens. With so little going for her it is not surprising that Althea took longer than most to make her way in the tennis world. It is a great testimony to her that she kept fighting, to make her breakthrough in her thirtieth year and win both Wimbledon and the US title.

Louise Brough (2), despite her lapse the previous year, was given second seeding but lost to Darlene Hard in the quarter-finals. This was her last Singles appearance, the end of twelve glorious years which left grateful memories. Angela Mortimer (7) unexpectedly fell in the third round to America's Karol Fageros, 'the golden girl of tennis', at her first Wimbledon. She became famous for her golden panties, outglittering even Gussie Moran.

Christine Truman quickly made herself the darling of the Centre Court. Still only a schoolgirl, she had a Diana the Huntress look as she swept into the net in her serve–volley game. There was something so fresh and appealingly English about her, and the crowd took her to their hearts as the Joan of Arc of British tennis. For she was succeeding when little success came Britain's way. Her first two wins were excusable temerity, but in the fourth round she met Shirley Bloomer (3), one of Britain's most experienced players, and disposed of her in straight sets. By now all Britain was in her triumphant wake and at times overtaking her, expecting miracles. They were granted one in the quarter-finals when Christine beat Mrs Betty Pratt, a highly experienced American. Christine won a long match 9/7, 5/7, 6/4. The fairy story ended when Althea Gibson doused Christine's tempestuous attack to the tune of 6/1, 6/1. But Britain now had a heroine and one whom they felt could grasp the prize. Christine's appearance was innocent, but behind it lay a strong determination.

1957 was unquestionably Hoad (1) again and Hoad all the way. The challenge to him was not as strong as before. Rosewall had gone to the professional ranks, Seixas (6) was declining, and Richardson (3), who might have provided a tough Final opponent, went out in a sensational first-round defeat to workmanlike Luis Ayala of Chile. Herbie Flam (7), finalist in Paris, was beaten by a new star from Australia, Ashley Cooper (2), who also disposed of the rising Neale Fraser (5) in the semi-finals. This was further illustration of what was for many years an almost invariable rule for the top American and Australian players, that when two of the same country met the senior ranker

Althea Gibson, a
determined Champion in
1957 and 1958.

nearly always won. In this instance Cooper, having lost the first set, needed a 14/12 second set to affirm his superior ranking.

Two leading British players, left-hander Bill Knight, more at home on the hard court with his heavy top-spin forehand and chipped backhand, and Bobby Wilson both reached the last sixteen. Knight fell to Flam, and Wilson to Sven Davidson (4), who was reaching his peak. Another British hope, Mike Davies, the Welsh boy who started playing tennis to prove that he could do anything better than his brother and hitch-hiked from tournament to tournament in his early days, had a good Wimbledon, defeating Arkinstall and Owen before going out in five sets to Neale Fraser.

The Final saw Hoad at his devastating best. His power, ferocious yet controlled, was awesome. Cooper was dismissed 6/2, 6/1, 6/2 in fifty-seven minutes. Hoad's mastery was so complete, not only over his opponent but over his own skills, that he was simply irresistible. In terms of skating or diving he would have gained maximum points. Hoad was again supreme on the supreme occasion. He was not consistent, because of his innate laziness, but had the depth of skill and stamina to see him through any ordinary encounter without great effort. However, when his own pride was at stake, as in a Wimbledon Final, he went into overdrive and stayed there. Hoad then joined Rosewall in the professional ranks, his last appearance being in the Doubles Final, when, with Fraser, he lost to the unseeded Budge Patty and Gardnar Mulloy, then at forty-three years and 226 days the oldest player to win a Wimbledon title.

1958 The following year Ashley Cooper (1) was again in the Final. This time he was the Australian No. 1 and his victim the luckless Neale Fraser (4), in a four-set repeat of their 1957 semi-final. It was a big serve–volley match, very like Cooper's battle against another Australian left-hander, Mervyn Rose (3), in the semi-finals.

Cooper had to work hard for his title. He was in difficulties in the first round against Britain's Geoff Owen, struggled through a fourth-round marathon against hard-hitting South African left-hander, Abe Segal, and was taken to five sets in the quarter-finals by Bobby Wilson. Fraser had a very hard quarter-final against Sweden's Sven Davidson (7), a handsome, dark player who would surely have gone further if he had not turned aside to concentrate on his studies. Against the battling Dane, Kurt Nielsen (6), in the semi-finals, Fraser had won in four sets, losing a mammoth third 17/19. Mal Anderson (2) was forced by an injured ankle to retire against Nielsen.

Althea Gibson (1) had stormy seas to weather in retaining her title. In a third round match against vivacious Mexican, Yola Ramirez, she won the first set only 9/7. Althea was more commanding in beating Lorraine Coghlan of Australia 6/0, 6/2. She then met Shirley Bloomer (5) in a replay of their Wightman Cup match of two weeks earlier when Althea had won comfortably 6/3, 6/4.

To digress, in her Wightman Cup double, partnered by Christine Truman, Miss Bloomer had surprised herself and the crowd when her petticoat slid to the ground. With the greatest aplomb, she stepped gracefully out of it, picked it up, carried it to the umpire's chair and resumed playing. It was in this same Wightman Cup tie that Christine played the greatest game of her life, to beat the Champion, Althea Gibson, and gain revenge for her semi-final defeat at Wimbledon the previous year. This unlocked the heavily barred door to a famous British victory. Christine relates how sportingly Althea took defeat.

In the Championships Althea Gibson was given a fight by Shirley Bloomer before winning 6/3, 6/8, 6/2 to get to the semi-finals. There she conquered unseeded Ann Haydon. Christine Truman (2) went out in the fourth round to a petite but determined Mimi Arnold, who won 10/8, 6/3. This, allied to Dorothy Knode's (3) failure in the second round, gave Suzy Kormoczi (6) a run to the semis, where she met Angela Mortimer, who had put paid to the old champion Mrs du Pont in a stirring three-set quarter-final. Angela crushed Suzy 6/0, 6/1 in thirty-one minutes, and so reached the Final unseeded, the second woman to do so. The foundation of her victory was her impeccable driving length and a relentless capacity of return, which were too much for Suzy.

Two British players in the semi-finals and one in the Final was a post-war record. In that Final Angela Mortimer brought the fighting best out of Althea Gibson. At 5/4 in the first set Angela had set point at 40–30, when Althea played a fine forehand deep into the backhand corner to save it. She eventually won 8/6, 6/3 with a run of six successive games, her sustained attack finally breaking down the pinpoint accuracy and length of Angela's driving. Althea Gibson took the Doubles with Maria Bueno (1) and just missed the triple crown when she and Kurt Nielsen (2) were beaten in the final of the Mixed Doubles, by Bob Howe and Lorraine Coghlan, 6/2, 13/11, in one of the most exciting matches of the tournament.

In her Wimbledon début Maria Bueno (4), although beaten by Ann Haydon in the quarter-finals, had caught the crowd's imagination and admiration with her catlike grace and majestic strokes.

1959 Wimbledon 1959 provided good weather and the first Russian entry. There had been concern over who should be accepted since the Russians had not played internationally and their form was not known. Fortunately their officials (and there were always some of those around) had no objections to their playing through the Qualifying Tournament. A. Potatnin and Tomas Lejus qualified in the Men's Singles but did not survive the first round. Nor did Anna Dmitrieva in the Women's. But they did enough to show that Russia meant tennis business.

It was also unique as the year in which South America won both singles titles. Maria Bueno (6) fulfilled the tremendous potential she had shown the year before and, although she dropped the first set to Margot Dittmeyer in the second round – a lapse she repeated against Mimi Arnold in the third round – in her last three matches against Edda Buding, Sally Moore (7) and, in the Final, Darlene Hard (4) she looked every bit the peerless Champion. Rarely, if ever, has such physical beauty of movement been combined with such marvellous strokes, to which timing gave ferocious power, allied usually to impeccable length. She looked like a panther hunting for the kill. At peak form her game was imperious; all she lacked was Little Mo's consistency.

Maria came from a well-to-do family, who lived opposite the Sao Paulo club. In her pram she could hear the sound of tennis balls. Later, qualifying to be a teacher, her schedule for the month before her first tennis tour was so severe that, although not overweight, she lost seventeen pounds. She was not just an inspired and beautiful player. She had a champion's mettle. She also made sure she knew what to expect by close study of her likely opponents.

Darlene had won through, 1/6, 6/4, 7/5, at the expense of Ann Haydon (8) in the quarters and Sandra Reynolds (5), 6/4, 6/4, in the semis. Before that Sandra's fine forehand had flailed Angela Mortimer (2), 7/5, 8/6. In the bottom half Christine Truman (1), the new and – at eighteen – youngest-ever French Champion, found the favourite's burden too much and, after an uneasy win over Pat Ward, lost to unseeded Yola Ramirez. When Beverly Fleitz (3) also fell to a non-seed, Edda Buding, Maria's way had been opened up to the Final.

The first round of the Men's Singles produced three sensations when 1950 champion, Budge Patty, was beaten by John Douglas of USA; Pietrangeli (3) went out to another American, Butch Buchholz, who was at his first Wimbledon; and heart-throb Drobny, the 1954 winner, was beaten in a marathon by that stylist from Great Britain, Alan Mills, 14/12, 3/6, 10/8, 8/6. Mills was playing excellent tennis at this time and, had he been of sterner temperament, might well have gone far in the game. As it was he progressed this year to the last sixteen, where he met a tough little redhead called Laver, who became the third man in Wimbledon history to reach the Final unseeded.

Laver had a terrific match in the semi-finals with Barry MacKay (5) of the USA, winning 11/13, 11/9, 10/8, 7/9, 6/3 (87 games), then second only in length to the Drobny/Patty marathon of 1953. Being a warm, dry year, long matches were the order of the day, with the fast, true surface favouring the serve–volleyers. Another long-winded match was Fraser's (2) fourth-round clash with the giant Italian, Orlando Sirola, which went to seventy-one games. This year was also significant for Roy Emerson (8), seeded for the first time, who reached the semis with a fine quarter-final win over Bobby Wilson (4).

However, Olmedo (1) put an end to Emerson's charge with a semi-final victory of three sets to love. Olmedo, Peruvian-born but playing for the United States, was rising rocket-like into the tennis stratosphere. Almost single-handed he had won the Davis Cup for the United States in Australia, and had gone on to take the Australian title. For the present he had more boost than the man known as the Rocket – Rod Laver.

Credit for originating Laver's nickname goes to Harry Hopman, the famed

Darlene Hard, Finalist in 1957 and 1959 and winner of seven doubles titles.

Sandra Reynolds, the South African gazelle and 1960 runner-up, had one of the most feared forehands in the game.

Australian coach and team manager. When the skinny, freckled redhead from Rockhampton, Queensland, was first presented to him, Harry said: 'Well, Rocket, let's see what you can do.' In the Final Rocket gave a good account of himself, and a warning for the future, but could not take a set from Olmedo. Olmedo followed this by getting to the Final of the American Championship, where he lost to Fraser and then turned professional. He had the unusual satisfaction, for a new boy in the pro ranks, of winning his first match – against Gonzales at that.

A sad note in an otherwise happy Wimbledon year was the sudden death in January of the All England Club's popular chairman, Dr Colin Gregory, who had succeeded King George VI's friend, Sir Louis Greig. Dr Gregory had been a notable player, who not only reached the Wimbledon Doubles Final in 1929 but in the same year had won the Australian Singles. In 1952 he made Davis Cup history when, in a tie with Yugoslavia, he forsook his captain's role to help win the important doubles.

1960   With Olmedo in the professional ranks, 1960 saw Fraser given the top seeding, although Laver had reached the Final in 1959. There were good reasons. Fraser was American Champion and, although beaten by Laver in the Australian Final, was still the official Australian No. 1, with Roy Emerson No. 2. At Wimbledon Laver was made third seed and Emerson sixth. Rod proved the Seeding Committee right when in the quarter-finals he beat Roy in four sets. Indeed, the Seeding Committee could congratulate itself. All the men's seeds reached their appointed quarter-final places (for the first time since 1936) and only two of the women's failed.

Krishnan (7) was the first Indian to reach a semi-final (beating Ayala (4) in a five-set quarter-final) and did so again the following year. Barry MacKay (2) was unfortunate that it was a wet year, for he depended so much on fast courts for his big game. In the quarter-finals he met Pietrangeli (5) in a match probably decided by the first set, which went to the Italian 16/14. Pietrangeli charmed the Centre Court further with his delightful free game and took Laver to five sets in the semi-finals. Neale Fraser had few worries in reaching the Final, except in the quarter-finals where he met Butch Buchholz (8), who had made such a mark the year before. In a marathon fourth set, the American, leading 2/1 and 15/14, twisted his left ankle as the result of a sudden thigh cramp, and had to retire at 15/15. At this point Fraser had remarkably fought off six match-points.

The Final was a battle of left-handers, the first in Wimbledon history. Fraser's big serve and senior status gave him the edge over Laver but not without a hard fight 6/4, 3/6, 9/7, 7/5. It was not going to be long before the Rocket powered into orbit. '

The Men's Doubles produced one particularly fine match, in which the unseeded Osuna and Ralston, having beaten the fourth seeds Pietrangeli and Sirola in five sets, played an inspired game in the semi-finals to beat the No. 2

ABOVE Ashley Cooper, in Hoad's shadow in 1957, finds the sun in 1958.
ABOVE RIGHT Alex Olmedo, the puma of Peru, 1959 Champion.
RIGHT Neale Fraser follows after and through, to take the title in 1960.

Maria Bueno. Olé!
At her best she was unequalled in her
majesty of stroke and imperious power.

BELOW Rafael Osuna (volleying) and Dennis
Ralston, winners in 1960 in the first unseeded
Men's Doubles Final against Britain's Mike
Davies and Bobby Wilson. Ralston is still the
youngest male winner of any title. Osuna won
the doubles again in 1963 with Antonio Palafox,
also unseeded.

seeds, Laver and Mark, 4/6, 10/8, 15/13, 4/6, 11/9 (eighty-six games). In the Final they met Britain's first pair, Davies and Wilson, who in the quarter-finals had beaten Emerson and Fraser (1), the Champions, in five sets. So the first Doubles Final between two unseeded pairs came about and, on the day, Osuna and Ralston were the sharper, winning 7/5, 6/3, 10/8. Rafael Osuna, at twenty-one, was playing at his first full Wimbledon, having failed to qualify two years before, while seventeen-year-old Dennis Ralston was USA Junior Champion and making his first-ever Wimbledon visit.

In the Women's Championship Maria Bueno (1) was already riding high. She had won the previous American title, defeating Christine Truman in the Final. She cruised through her early rounds, beating as good a player as Angela Mortimer (5) 6/1, 6/1 to get to the semi-finals, where yet again she met the lance of St Joan Truman (3) tilting for Britain. Bueno was at her majestic best, producing a stream of classic strokes to take the first set 6/0. It says much for Christine's fighting spirit that she could come back to win the second set 7/5. Thereupon La Bueno reasserted her authority to win the third set 6/1.

A new name had appeared in the women's line-up, Karen Hantze of America, whose looks caught the eye and who, despite deceptively slow movements between points, had a sound all-court American game. In the quarter-finals she had taken Christine to three sets. Ann Haydon (4) reached her ordained semi-final for the second time, where she met the attractive South African, Sandra Reynolds (8), conqueror of Darlene Hard (2). Sandra got the better of Ann in three sets and so reached the Final.

In the Final, Champion Maria was given a searching examination, especially by Sandra's famous forehand. Nor was the challenger's backhand as defensive as usual, for it seemed to have been sharpened by the pressure put upon it. Sandra did not use her renowned backhand drop-shot as she had with such success against Ann Haydon. Probably wisely, for Maria Bueno was a fast mover to the net where her volleys were very forceful. Indeed, she finished the first set 8/6 with three such superb shots. The second set score of 6/0 was cruelly unjust to Sandra. The third game, for example, went to nine deuces and five game-points on either side. When Maria won it after twelve minutes the South African's resistance crumbled and she won only three more points. That game underlined what a fighter Maria was. Even when on top she would never yield a point. Her first great triumph in 1959 had enshrined her in the hearts of all Brazilians, and her successful defence of the title prompted the Sao Paulo authorities to honour her with a statue and a postage stamp.

Two greats of the past died in 1960. Dolly Lambert Chambers, seven times Champion, died on 7 January, aged eighty-one. On 27 June, the second Monday of the Championships, Lottie Dod died at the age of eighty-eight. Lottie, five times Champion before retiring unbeaten at twenty-one, went on to conquer in other sporting arenas. She was, in the judgement of many, the greatest woman all-rounder of all time.

10

MORTIMER, SMITH AND TRUMAN TOO 1961–5

1961 Rod Laver comes from a hardy background on the family cattle farm in Queensland. Living in the seaside town of Rockhampton he grew up in a tennis atmosphere. Family outings were normally in the form of taking part in tennis tournaments, with the Lavers collecting most of the prizes. Being short and wiry, Rod decided that he must master top-spin. He did this to such effect that he became one of the few players able to control any stroke at will and he possessed those two deadly weapons, the forehand and backhand top-spin lobs.

Like Lew Hoad, he had the ability to play any shot from any part of the court, and play it with force and penetration. He had a wrist of steel and the muscles on his racket forearm looked almost twice the size of those on his right arm. Like Ken Rosewall he flourished under the coaching and team management of Harry Hopman, the man who guided, shaped and commanded the Australian squad. Stories of Hopman's strict routine and discipline were retailed with awe, stories of rigid curfews and spartan training. Certainly when it came to winning Hopman was single-minded. He could not have had better disciples than Rosewall and Laver, both dedicated to perfect fitness which allowed untrammelled expression of their genius. In Hoad, with his great natural strength and stamina, as well as brilliant inspiration, Hopman found a less compliant spirit.

Laver (2) had his worries on the way to the 1961 Final. That excellent French player, Pierre Darmon, later a respected voice on the Professional Council, had an on day and took the Rocket all the way, as did Wilhelm Bungert, that skilful German touch player. Thereafter Laver fired on full power and easily beat Krishnan (7), who had reached the semi-final for the second year running, taking out Emerson (4) to do so, and displaying all the delicate deftness and improvisation which – like Cochet and Bergelin before him – he had made his hallmark.

In the Final against Chuck McKinley (8) Rod brought to bear all the authority of his experience of two previous Finals, winning 6/3, 6/1, 6/4. Chuck ran down the baseline like a mechanical hare in his efforts to retrieve, throwing himself all over the place, falling, rolling over and still getting the ball back.

With four Britons, Knight, Sangster, Wilson and Taylor, in the last sixteen, home fans had more to cheer about from the men than at any time since the

Rod Laver, the Rocket, rivals Lew Hoad as the greatest Australian player ever.

war. Sangster and Wilson survived to the quarter-finals. Wilson again produced one of his Wimbledon conjuring tricks (alas he was never able to perform a repeat in the same year) when he put out the Champion, Fraser (1), in four sets. He then fell to McKinley. Sangster, with his big serve, started a gush of British optimism by sweeping aside Segal (who in the second round had beaten Santana (5) in straight sets) and Venezuela's Pimentel, to reach the semi-final for the first time, where McKinley, too, was his downfall. The cherubic Pietrangeli (3) had gone in the third round, his fluent strokemaking bludgeoned by the fierce serve–volley game of Chris Crawford (USA).

But it was the girls who in 1961 really delivered the goods for Britain. In the absence through illness of Maria Bueno, which cost her a possible hat-trick of titles, Angela Mortimer (7) and Christine Truman (6) made it an all-British Final. This was the first time such a thing had happened since those long-skirted days of 1914 when Mrs Lambert Chambers beat Mrs Larcombe, and Britain was sure of her first Singles title since Dorothy Round's in 1937.

Both Angela and Christine had earned their places in the sun on that final Wimbledon Saturday by right of conquest over highly rated players. Angela (7), full of stern resolve and purpose, the edge of her concentration at its absolute peak and enhanced, she felt, by a temporary deafness, beat Sandra Reynolds (1) to reach her second Final, coming from behind in both sets.

Christine Truman (6) caused the main shock in the quarter-finals when she beat Margaret Smith (2), the reigning Australian and French Champion. Still just eighteen, this was Margaret's first Wimbledon and her powerful all-round game, based on her fine physique, had made a big impression. In the deciding set Christine had to survive two match-points before winning 3/6, 6/3, 9/7. In the semis she beat unseeded South African Renée Schuurman, who had put out Ann Haydon (3) in the quarters.

With two home players in the Final, the crowd had a rare dilemma. Who to favour? Angela Mortimer was well liked and admired for her patience, persistence and sheer resolution, qualities which had helped her turn comparatively weak strokes into commanding weapons. But, and it was a big but, Christine Truman, for the last four years, had been seen as Britain's leading standard-bearer, going forward to meet the foreign invader. So it was Christine who had most of the crowd with her.

Truman served first, but at 30/40 dropped her service and gave Angela Mortimer an immediate advantage which she held to 4/2, both players repeatedly saving break-points. Then Truman stormed into one of her famous attacks to take four games in a row for the set. At this point rain interrupted play for half an hour. On the restart both players dropped their first service games. At 4/3, Christine had a break-point which Angela saved with a backhand passing shot down the line. A double-fault by Angela gave Christine a second chance. Coming to the net to seize it she fell awkwardly and hurt her left thigh. Her natural sportsmanship saw her jump up and carry on. She had

Angela Mortimer, Champion 1961. Hers was the reward for patience, perseverance and practice.

Christine Truman, runner-up in 1961, in her most famous victory, 1958, against Althea Gibson, the reigning Wimbledon Champion. It turned the key for Britain's Wightman Cup win.

two more break-points. On the first she put a backhand out and on the second her forehand return of serve bounced once on top of the net before skipping sideways and out.

She was clearly affected by the fall, becoming sluggish and slow on the turn, and dropped the next two games for the set. Angela got off to a good start to lead 2/0 in the deciding set. Christine's fighting spirit gradually pulled back to somewhere near her best and in a see-saw finish six games in a row went against service. Then, at 6/5, Angela held her service to win the coveted title.

The gods had dealt both players difficult hands that day. To most of those watching it seemed certain that Christine, at the moment she fell, was on the way to a straight sets win and the title which her adoring fans wanted her so much to have. If she had got one of the two break-points after her fall she would probably have succeeded in holding her service for the match. To lose that game then, with the memory of the fall so fresh and still physically affecting her, took the keen edge off her game.

Equally Angela found herself suddenly with a chance to retrieve what had looked like a lost cause. But she still had the difficulty of playing a handicapped opponent, and of playing the right game which was not to ignore the injury but to dwell on it. The opportunity was there to stretch Christine. The situation demanded that she should. Being a fine match player she did. In the outcome she was a good Champion.

Billy Jean Moffitt at her début gave notice of things to come. She very nearly beat Yola Ramirez (5) in the first round (11/9, 1/6, 6/2) and then, unseeded, won the Doubles with Karen Hantze.

1962   Billy Jean did even better next year, defeating Margaret Smith (1) in her opening match 1/6, 6/3, 7/5. It was to be the first of many Wimbledon battles between the two. Defeat for Margaret was all the more surprising as she came to Wimbledon as holder of the Australian, Italian and French titles. Billie Jean herself went down in the quarters to Ann Haydon (5), who reached the semi-finals for the third time, losing there to Karen Hantze, now Mrs Susman (8), recently married and playing with such conviction that she did not lose a set, her most doughty opponent being Britain's Liz Starkie (7/5, 10/8).

Karen's opponent in the Final was the Czech, Vera Sukova, who was the third woman to reach the Final unseeded, winning many friends on the way with her modestly endearing personality and determined game. In successive rounds she beat both Darlene Hard (2) and Maria Bueno (3), who were making their Wimbledon returns. In the Final nerves and a suspect ankle prevented the Czech girl from getting the best out of herself and she fell to the power of Karen Susman.

By now the Rocket had established his fame in his own name of Rod Laver. He was intent on equalling Donald Budge's 1938 record of winning the grand slam. He had already won the Australian and French titles. At Wimbledon in the fifth round he met Manuel Santana (6), whose inspiration was maturing

Karen Susman, attractive and provocative winner in 1962, and twice doubles champion.

with experience. The Spaniard gave the Champion a fright and the spectators marvellous entertainment, winning the first set 16/14 and leading 5/1 in the second. Up to that point Laver (1) had lacked his Champion's authority, due largely to the magical play of the Spaniard, with his adroit lob-volleys – the most difficult stroke to play with precision. With his title in danger Laver's Champion spark flared and he raised his game. He took four games in a row and eventually the set at 9/7, to level the match, and then continued his surge to win it. He saved his title and the grand slam by a narrow margin.

Laver's opponent in the Final was seeded to be Roy Emerson (2), who had a fine second-round match against Bungert, losing the first two sets 13/15, 4/6 but, fit as ever, cantering through the next three. In the fourth round Emerson had to retire with an injured toe when 1/1 to Marty Mulligan who, beating Hewitt (8) in the quarters, went on to be the fourth unseeded man to reach the Final. There Marty found Laver at his ruthless best, Champion again by 6/2, 6/2, 6/1.

Overall the Men's Championship had borne a distinctly Australian accent, with six of their players in the eight quarter-final places. Credit was due both to individual ability and its harnessing by Harry Hopman. Laver had been in four successive Wimbledon Finals, winning the last two. Had he remained an amateur there seemed to be nobody around to end his reign.

Three footnotes on 1962: Bob Hewitt, the balding, swarthy doubles magician, originally Australian but who adopted South African nationality after marrying his beautiful Delaille, won the first of his five Men's Doubles titles. The second note records that great champion, Margaret du Pont, winner of three American and one Wimbledon singles titles, partnering Neale Fraser to win the Mixed Doubles – sixteen years after her first Wimbledon victory in the Women's Doubles, and so gaining the record of being (at 44.124) the oldest winner of a Wimbledon title. Thirdly, Colonel Legg retired as Referee, having carried out this exacting duty with quiet and friendly firmness for twelve years. Perhaps the Colonel's most difficult assignment was in 1957 to remove the lady who decided to stage a one-woman peace demonstration on the Centre Court. This was just after the Ladies' Singles Final and when the Queen was in the Royal Box. There was momentary silence as many wondered if this was all part of the show. Then the short figure of Colonel Legg came to the rescue, advancing with long, jerky strides on the 'local disturbance'. Valiantly he tried to pull her off court. Weight for weight he was no match, but his resolution prevailed.

1963   For Colonel Legg's successor, son-in-law Captain Mike Gibson, 1963 was a difficult blooding, as it was for David Mills who succeeded Duncan Macaulay as Secretary. It was a year of disastrous weather. Through adroit rearrangement the programme had caught up by the second Friday. However, on Saturday it rained all day and so all but the Men's Final (decided on Friday) were postponed until the Monday. This was the first time in thirty-six years that this had happened because of rain.

Margaret Smith (1) was deservedly top women's seed and, despite attacks of her Centre Court nerves, she got through to the Final. Here she met Billie Jean Moffitt, who again provided upsets in beating Lesley Turner (2) and Ann Haydon (3), now Mrs Pip Jones, who had won through to her fourth semi-final. In the Final Billie Jean lost the first set. Audibly urging herself on, she rallied from 0/4 down in the second to lose it and the match 6/4. But she had done more than enough in getting through to the Final unseeded (the fourth woman to do so), and against Margaret, to establish her credentials for the future. It was Margaret's first title and timely revenge for 1962's defeat.

In the Men's draw it was a year of upsets, due partly to the wet weather and slower courts. Only three seeds reached the Men's quarter-finals: Emerson (1), beaten there by Bungert; McKinley (4), who took out Bungert to reach his second Final; and Santana (2), who beat Christian Kuhnke but fell to the tall, fair, gangling Australian, Fred Stolle (holder with Hewitt of the Doubles title), who became the fifth man to reach the Final unseeded. In the Final McKinley found the slower court suited to his fantastic retrieving game. In typical all-American fashion he grabbed his chance and the match 9/7, 6/1, 6/4. He had the distinction of joining Budge and Trabert as the only men, since the Challenge Round was abolished, to win the title without losing a set. He was also a rare Champion in having no lady Champion to lead out for the first dance at the Wimbledon Ball. Instead, his wife, Wylita, had that honour.

The weather and erratic form played havoc with the Doubles seedings. Only Emerson and Santana (2) reached the quarter-finals unscathed and they went out in the semi-finals to France's Barclay and Darmon. Both the other semi-final pairs were unseeded, the Mexicans, Osuna and Palafox, coming through to win the title against the Frenchmen. This was the second Final between two unseeded pairs.

In 1964 Fred Stolle (6) was seeded. The Committee would have been challenging fate to have left him out. Fred was set on this being his year and he more than justified his status by again getting to the Final. In the semi-final he had revenge over Chuck McKinley (2) 4/6, 10/8, 9/7, 6/4. Roy Emerson (1) reached his ordained Final place, suffering a 15/13 second set in his semi-final against Bungert, always an unseeded thruster, who had beaten Osuna (4). In the quarters Emerson crushed Hewitt, who had wasted Mulligan (8) in the second round.

A rain-interrupted Final saw a 12/10 second set which Emerson won to lead 2/0. Stolle rallied to take the third. But Emerson, who always seemed to carry too many big guns, won the fourth and the match to repeat his Australian Final win over Stolle, the eternal runner-up. Fred's day came at last when he won the French title the following year and the American in 1966. This time he won both Doubles and came so near the triple crown.

The Women's Championship saw the next encounter in the Billie Jean Moffitt (3)–Margaret Smith (1) saga, a saga to be related in many enthralling

The all-Court game. Margaret is perhaps the
finest athlete women's tennis has known.

and dramatic chapters. Billie Jean got to the semi-finals only after surviving shocks against Roberta Beltrame of Italy whom she beat 7/5, 4/6, 6/3, and Margaret Lee, daughter of a pre-war British Davis Cup player, Harry Lee. In her semi-final against Billie Jean, Margaret Smith won the first set 6/3 and with a run of five games came from 4/1 behind in the second set to take the match.

In the Final she came up against Maria Bueno (2), a great Champion showing some signs of recapturing her old form. A classic was in prospect, presenting two big names and two contrasting styles. In the American championships of 1963, the first time they had met in an important Final, Maria Bueno had won 7/5, 6/4. In the recent French Championships Margaret Smith had triumphed 5/7, 6/1, 6/2.

A classic it proved to be, with jittery nerves showing raw edges to make a brilliant pattern cross-threaded with commonplace errors, forgivable only in the high tension and drama. Maria, all feline grace, took the first set 6/4 when, at the pinch, Margaret was again beset by Centre Court nerves. Margaret hit back in the second, winning four games in a row, but Maria squared at 4-all. The ninth was a very big game and full of fire and mettle, the advantage like a swinging pendulum. There were eight deuces and five break-points to Maria before Margaret at last hauled the game in. But it was only after sixteen exhausting games that she took the set 9/7.

At 3/3 in the third set came the final crisis of the match, and of the crowd's fever. Maria took Margaret's service for the loss of only one point and, the initiative seized, dropped just two more points in the next two games to win the match. Maria had regained her title and dethroned the reigning Champion to do so. The evenness of the struggle is shown by the fact that at match-point each player had won the same number of points throughout their duel. Maria took that match-point when a lucky bounce turned her despairing half-volley into an unreturnable drop-shot. It was a cruel way for the guillotine to fall. Margaret, like Fred, was in three Finals, but only won the Women's Doubles, with Lesley Turner (1).

1965   Fred Stolle (2), who often gave the false impression of a wraith on court, was now armed anew with the French title, his first major singles' success. He tried hard but unsuccessfully in 1965 to lay his Wimbledon ghost. It was a case of third time plucky for stalwart Stolle, beaten again in the Final by his compatriot, Roy Emerson (1). This time Emerson won in straight sets. Stolle often suffered from being underestimated. Hopman said in 1963 that he was too old at twenty-five to play in the Davis Cup. But within a year he was helping Australia to win back the trophy from America.

Seldom can a player have felt so baffled by his Wimbledon bogey as Stolle. With Ken Rosewall and Gottfried von Cramm he shared rare records of frustration. Stolle equalled von Cramm in reaching the Final three years running, but unlike him did it the first time unseeded. Stolle had to cope with Emerson twice and McKinley, whereas von Cramm was up against the major

ABOVE Easy come for once
to Chuck McKinley,
winner 1963, one of the
quickest runners down of
his opponent's wide shots.

RIGHT Emmo rises to the
occasion. Roy was
Champion in 1964–5.

forces of Perry (twice) and Donald Budge, two of the candidates for the all-time top five. Furthermore, von Cramm had fourteen years, during at least five of which he would have been at his best, denied him. Von Cramm had, with Rosewall and Gonzales, the best claim to be the greatest player who never won Wimbledon.

The year 1965 did not quite present the same Men's mixture as before. John Newcombe (6) was beginning to show himself as a thruster and failed only in the fourth round to Cliff Drysdale of South Africa, who won 9/7, 6/4, 11/13, 11/9. Jan-Erik Lundquist (3), perhaps lucky to be seeded so high again, after early failures in previous years, was beaten by Allen Fox in the quarter-finals. Having achieved semi-final eminence, Drysdale bowed out gracefully to Stolle. Drysdale was elegant in all he did. He even made two-handed strokes look polished.

Osuna (8) never lived up to the distinction of his 1963 American title, but he reached the quarter-finals and took the first set 13/11 from Stolle. Bungert (5) was comprehensively beaten in the third round by Marty Riessen, who was to prove a doughty competitor for years to come. Riessen, a typical American serve–volley merchant, was always difficult to beat, especially on fast grass courts, and to do so usually meant a long and exhausting encounter.

Tony Roche (7), in his third Wimbledon, fell to the soft guile of fellow Australian, Marty Mulligan. Roche, with his short, scything, left-handed service-swing, was regarded in the Australian camp as the natural successor to Laver. He certainly looked the part but, like Hoad some years before, he was dogged by injury, and in his case it happened before he reached the heights which his potential predicted.

South African Keith Diepraam reached the quarter-finals in Roche's place. He was also a big serve–volleyer and took the first set from Emerson. But after that first set he was a spent force and Emerson took three sets in a row. Diepraam had played Provincial cricket in South Africa and was a ferocious bowler – at least at the standard of the Wimbledon Press v. Players match, which took place annually on the middle Sunday. George Worthington, that solid Australian player who became the very popular All England coach, was the unrelenting captain of the Players. He gloried in Diepraam's bouncers and the discomfort of the Press's batsmen.

In one of these matches came the ultimate in cricket history. The Australian No. 3 Test batsman, Bob Cowper, was caught by Okker at mid-on, off the bowling of Pietrangeli. 'White-flannelled fools' that they were, this was the first time that either had played cricket and the joy of this Dutch–Italian combination was such that you would have thought that they had just won the Wimbledon Doubles title. But this was won by Newcombe and Roche, the first of the five they jointly took.

Maria Bueno (1) reached the semi-final of the Women's Singles where she met Billie Jean Moffitt (5). The two had clashed in the 1963 quarter-finals

So near and yet so far.
Kurt Nielsen, unseeded Finalist in 1953
and 1955.

Wilhelm Bungert, 1967 unseeded.

Tony Roche, 1968.

Fred Stolle, 1963 unseeded, 1964, 1965.

and then Billie Jean had won comfortably. This time Maria raced away to a 5/1 lead. The fighting Billie Jean pulled back the score to 4/5 but Maria served out to take the first set 6/4. Again in the second set the Champion broke first to lead 2/1, but this time Little Miss Moffitt started her revival earlier and with a run of four games went to 5/2 and on to take the set 7/5. Into the deciding set and again Maria began well, twice breaking Billie Jean's service for a 4/1 lead. Billie Jean tried desperately to stem the flood and at 5/3 held off four match-points. But the fifth beat her and Maria was through to the Final.

Her opponent was Margaret Smith (2), who was in majestic form when she beat Christine Truman in the semi-finals. And so the Final battle of the previous year was rejoined, but there was a difference. Margaret had for once conquered her Centre Court nerves. She played her usual commanding game, but this time it was not to be upset by jittery moments. Maria did establish an early 2/1 lead in the first set. However, Margaret, playing a powerful game which allowed little argument, swept to a 5/2 lead and took the set 6/4. In the second set a run of three games saw Maria go 5/3 ahead. Margaret pulled her back to square the set at 5/5 and then, controlling those disloyal nerves well, she held her service for 6/5 and took the Champion's to love. So Margaret Smith grasped her second Wimbledon title.

Her achievement was the reward for consistent effort. Of the three great tennis queens of the time, Maria Bueno, Billie Jean King and Margaret, she was slightly below the other two as far as natural talent was concerned, but she made up for this with dedication and application. She was a fine all-round athlete. She did weight-training to build up her arms, and running to develop her legs and stamina. She could have been an international sprinter. Her determination was always fired by a fierce competitive spirit. Christine Truman, who played her often and knew her well, says of her: 'She did not let up for any day of the year and she just never seemed happy with herself unless she had played – and won – a game of tennis.'

It was the end of a Wimbledon era in women's tennis, an era in which Maria Bueno had mainly occupied the throne, with Margaret Smith a claimant come good. At her height, Maria had been a queen whose grace and power were without compare. Now a King would be Queen.

II

KING HIGH
1966–8

Billie Jean King has been one of the more controversial characters on the Wimbledon stage. Her record tells its own story – six times Champion, three times runner-up, four American singles titles, one Australian and one French. Moreover she won her titles in the second great era of women's tennis since 1946. Maria Bueno, though past her zenith, was still a Wimbledon Champion in 1964 after Little Miss Moffitt had made a considerable mark. Margaret Smith, the girl who really put women's tennis on the map in Australia and won more major titles than any other player, was Billie Jean's main opponent in her heyday. Then, at the end of her reign she had to contend with the merciless precision of Chris Evert and the instinctive skill and ball-sense of Evonne Goolagong. Even so Billie Jean won her last title as recently as 1975.

On court she always had a love–hate relationship with the crowd. To begin with, spectators were intrigued by this tomboyish American with the Hussars' busby haircut, who chattered ferociously to herself as she came back to the baseline between points. They sensed in her a new giant, and new heroines are the lifeblood of spectator sports.

But then discord came into their feelings, as people saw in Billie Jean an apparent conceit rather than mere coltish cockiness. Now she was being pressured by her new double status, that of Champion and that of wife and breadwinner for her student husband. So whereas before she had wanted to win, now she *had* to. As far as spectators were concerned they were asking whether her extrovert mannerisms were to psyche herself – or her opponent.

Toughness in champions is essential and is normally applauded but it does not always sit prettily on a woman's countenance. Billie Jean underlined her resolution in the way in which she dedicated herself to what might be called a suffragette movement in women's tennis which, in a short time, took them to near parity in earning power with men. Her playing skills and the accelerating rewards of winning made her the first woman athlete to earn over 100,000 dollars in one year from sport.

What made Billie Jean such a great Champion was not just the technical excellence of her American serve-volley game. Her seemingly unlimited determination made her above all a match-player rather than an exponent of her craft. And although she discarded her Hussars' busby hairstyle her court generalship increased. She hungered for victory and did everything possible to achieve it. Many Wimbledon spectators did not like what they felt to be her gamesmanship of upsetting the concentration of her opponents. What did opponents think of Billie Jean? Christine Truman, who often played and occasionally beat her, says: 'She definitely did not like losing but she took it all right. Off court she was very good-hearted and when I had my appendix out when I was in America she sent me flowers at the hospital.'

1966   The newly-wed Billie Jean brought her husband to the 1966 Wimbledon, where she was seeded four. Margaret Smith (1), already Australian Champion, looked in good enough form to retain her title, but as always there was the question mark against her of her Centre Court nerves. These showed in her opening set against Liz Starkie, which she won only 8/6. Margaret then sailed comfortably through to the semi-finals, where she came up against Billie Jean. At times Billie Jean had not looked too impressive in reaching the semi-finals. But like some great champions – particularly Hoad – she needed the stimulus of the big occasion or a crisis to bring out the best in her.

Against minor opponents she tended to give away more than did Maria Bueno and Margaret Smith. For example, that year in the quarter-finals Billie Jean beat Annette van Zyl (6), 1/6, 6/2, 6/4. Annette not only won the first set but broke to lead 2/1 in the second, before Billie Jean took five games in a row. Again a little relaxation endangered her in the third set, when she lost her first two service games to be 3/0 down. Once more the crisis was met with a run of four winning games and the set and match were soon won.

In the semi-final against the Champion, Billie Jean immediately put the pressure on Margaret's service and on her nerves. One forehand cross-court return of service and a backhand lob were executed with such command that the most confident opponent might have been shaken. Margaret lost that opening game and Billie Jean went on to win the set 6/3. Margaret rallied to take a 3/0 lead in the second set, but Billie Jean's match-play instinct rose to the occasion. She took the match by the throat and six successive games to win.

The other semi-final, between Maria Bueno (2) and Ann Jones (3), was a classical study in contrasts. Maria's game could be imperious or it could be fallible. The left-handed Ann was a steady, determined and persistent fighter. Her game, more suited to the clay of Paris's Roland Garros, had prevailed against Maria in the French semi-finals and Ann had gone on to win the French title for the second time.

In many ways it was surprising that Ann's lawn tennis was so defensive, for as a great table tennis player, who had reached the world title Final in 1957, she had possessed a fierce attacking forehand and it was table tennis which had inspired world champion Fred Perry's renowned forehand. Against Maria that day Ann had determined that her best chance lay in attack. Her backhand, normally a defensive chip, was played far more firmly and to a fuller length. Maria took the first set 6/3 and led 3/1 in the second. Here Anne gritted her teeth and fought for every point, even for every stroke. She twice broke

Maria's service and hung on and fought on, to take a gruelling second set 11/9, saving two match-points on the way.

Maria Bueno's answer was to win five games in a row at the start of the final set. Ann pulled back to 3/5, but when Maria got to 40–0 on her own service she seemed certain to take one of the three match-points. Ann saved them all, the third (the fifth of the match) with a stunning cross-court passing return of service which left Maria stranded.

The crowd was by now almost too tense to applaud, especially when in the next game Ann was 0–40 on her own service. Three more match-points to Maria. Again all of them were saved, and the set was square at 5/5. Maria went to 6/5 and then, with Ann serving, at 30–40, came the ninth match-point to the Brazilian. That, for Ann, was the fatal one. After two hours, during which spectators had been alternately on the edges of their seats and rising to their feet, Maria won a match which ranks as one of the most exciting in all Wimbledon's one hundred years.

Maria's Final with Billie Jean was a total contrast to her high-level match with Ann Jones. Maria reacted badly and made many mistakes, the first set going to Billie Jean 6/3 in seventeen minutes. Maria managed to win the second with imperious dismissal of her own imperfections, but when it mattered in the deciding third set, Billie Jean turned on full power, taking five games in a row, and came through with a long run to the winning post. Against this surge of power, Maria's game was again littered with errors. Afterwards, she declared that she had never played an important match so badly.

It was a horrible Wimbledon for weather – wet and cold for most of the fortnight. The conditions were almost certainly the cause of reigning Champion Roy Emerson failing to equal Fred Perry's achievement of winning the title in three successive years. Emerson (1), going for the hat-trick, was powerfully on course until his quarter-final match with fellow countryman, left-hander Owen Davidson. Then, when chasing a wide ball at full speed (he was an international class sprinter) the slippery surface caused him to crash into the umpire's chair. He lay on the ground, his left shoulder hurt. He got up to carry on with the match, but with his movement restricted he lost.

Roy Emerson was not one of the great champions but he came very near to it. He was not as powerful as John Newcombe, whose star was now ascending, but each used his limited repertoire of strokes to maximum effect. Newcombe pulverised his opponents into submission, Emerson ground them down.

Roy's game, if it looked a bit mechanical, was efficiency itself and his greatest weapons were his fitness and speed of foot. He and McKinley were the outstanding men athletes of post-war years. His service, which was always dependable, had a flourishing wind-up all his own. He was neat to watch and very likeable, being unobtrusive and with perfect court manners. It was a mean stroke that fate played against him when he was in full flight for his third Championship.

Emerson's defeat let in Santana (4), who beat Davidson in five sets to reach the Final. Dennis Ralston (6) achieved the high status of Finalist in the lower half of the draw by beating Drysdale (7) in the semi-finals, the South African having surprisingly beaten Roche (2) in straight sets.

Neither Santana nor Ralston had been in the Final before. Once again the crowd were able to look forward to a fascinating clash of styles, the touch artistry of Santana against the thundering power of Ralston. Artistry emerged triumphant and Santana won 6/4, 11/9, 6/4. It was artistry allied to determination. In the second set Santana was 4/1 down. He came back to 5/6, but still Ralston was serving for the set. This crucial game was the longest of the match and went to five deuces and it was Santana who won it and eventually the set and match.

The Spaniard will go down in the memories and hearts of tennis enthusiasts as one of the most delightful players to watch for his toreador grace and ease of stroke, both heightened by his superb anticipation. In Spain he became a national hero, rivalling top matadors and top footballers. After winning Wimbledon, he was awarded the high national honour of the Cross of Isabel la Catolica. His birthplace, Madrid, awarded him its Gold Medal.

Santana was a tennis wizard. His racket was a conjuror's wand, with which he would disguise the intended direction of a shot. He could use top-spin on backhand or forehand, so that the ball dipped maddeningly at his opponent's feet or cleared him with a perfect lob that raced tauntingly on, uncatchable. And he could slice and chop with such spin that the ball seemed to hang in the air. He would admit to having a little temperament and getting mad with himself. But he was a most likeable and modest man with the broadest of smiles ('I smile a lot because I love tennis for itself and for what it has done for me'). When congratulated after winning, he said: 'Emerson is the real winner.'

1967   Within a year, Santana's sporting approach was having to survive a tougher test. Opening on the Centre Court, as is the Champion's right on the first day, he was beaten in the first round of the 1967 Championship by Charlie Pasarell. Pasarell had already established himself as a most difficult customer for any player at any stage of the Championship. In that opening round Santana found the drizzle, which occurred at times during the match, restricted the footwork which was the basis of his touch shots. Pasarell fell several times but refused to be inhibited and maintained his all-out attacking style. In the deciding fourth set at 6/6 he hit four clean forehand winners to break Santana's service and then held his own to love for the match. It was the first time that the Champion, and for that matter the No. 1 seed, had been beaten in the first round.

The match between Bungert and Wilson was a highlight. Bungert played with the ramrod back of a Prussian guardsman and the wrist of a swordsman. His touch was delicate and his game inspired. When two players of this calibre are both hitting top form each raises the other's game. So the spectators were

Manuel Santana waves the wand.

John Newcombe and Tony Roche on the way to the first of their five Wimbledon Doubles titles, 1965.

treated to fine rally after fine rally, full of dazzling strokes and exquisite ploys. The finesses, the wrong-footing, the whispered drop-shots had the crowd applauding and purring. Wilson's flair fired brightly and quickly and he won the first set 6/1 and the second 7/5. Bungert took the third and fourth 6/1, 7/5 and had just that much more strength in reserve to win the final set 9/7, at the end putting Wilson to the sword with fierce forehand winners.

In the semi-final Bungert dashed further British hopes when he beat Roger Taylor in a tough five-set battle. This made him the sixth unseeded man to reach the Final. When Roy Emerson (2) succumbed to the big serve and sharp volleying of Nikki Pilic, it meant that of the semi-finalists only John Newcombe (3) had a seed to his name. He exerted his authority by first out-hitting Pilic and then in the Final overwhelming a disappointing Bungert. None could deny, however, the compelling way in which Newcombe settled his account to win the title. It was a masterful progress. The Doubles title saw the names of Hewitt and McMillan (2) inscribed together for the first time on the Roll of Honour.

The field in the Women's Singles was weakened by the absence of Margaret Smith. Billie Jean King (1) blitzed through to the Final, beating on the way Virginia Wade (8), seeded for the first time. Maria Bueno (2) went out in the fourth round to the little but lively Rosie Casals. Rosie, who looked like a gym-slipped schoolgirl, then beat Judy Tegart to meet Ann Jones (3) for the second successive year, this time for a place in the Final.

Rosie, with her all-court game functioning well, began with a precocious burst, winning the first set in twenty minutes 6/2. She seemed unstoppable, playing every kind of shot, and all of them coming off. But Ann Jones is not one to be swept aside that easily, or at all. She kept her nerve, saw that for her to stand a chance the pace of the match had to be changed, and so set about waging a war of attrition. At Ann's nagging dictate the rallies began to lengthen and suddenly Rosie was no longer dominating the game. Ann pursued the wearing-down process until the very end, hitting many fine passing shots past an at times bewildered Rosie, and winning by two sets to one.

So at her twelfth Wimbledon challenge, and after being five times a semi-finalist, Ann Jones got to the Final. The main difference in that Final between Ann and Billie Jean King was the way in which they played the big points. Here the Champion's match temperament shone through. In the opening game, for example, Billie Jean needed to save three break-points. She did so and then followed by capturing Ann's service.

But Ann could look back with satisfaction on a year which not only brought her her first Final but which signalled her as a better player, particularly on the backhand which was no longer purely defensive. This new-look Ann Jones confirmed the strengthened belief in herself by reaching the Final of the American Championships at Forest Hills later that year, where she again lost to Billie Jean, whose belief in herself already seemed total. Billie Jean completed the triple crown with Rosie Casals in the Women's Doubles and with Owen Davidson in the Mixed. This was the first triple crown since Frank Sedgman's in 1952 and the first women's since Doris Hart's in 1951.

The All England Club, a sanctuary of tradition, has always been ready to create new ones and to experiment. So it was not altogether surprising when, with the war of words, resolutions and attitudes over the question of Open tennis at its height and seemingly unending, the far-sighted Chairman, Herman David (who back in 1935 had advocated Open tennis) and the Committee took the initiative. In August 1967 Wimbledon opened its Doherty Gates to professionals and staged an all-professional tournament. This was the first and probably the last as, spurred on by Britain, other countries accepted the principle of Open tournaments and the following year the Wimbledon Championships were open to amateurs and professionals alike.

That pioneering first all-professional event saw the return to Wimbledon of previous amateur giants and favourites like Hoad, Gonzales and Rosewall. It was won by one of the most recent favourites and great champions of all – Rod Laver.

1968   The crowds flocked joyously to Wimbledon for the return of Laver and company for the 1968 Championships. For over the last few years the Women's Championship had contained more star names than the Men's. Some of the professionals themselves were a shade apprehensive about their return. Their fears were founded on a shortage of real five-set championship play in the professional ranks and the lack of variety in the opposition they met. These fears had been underscored at the British Hard Courts Championship at Bournemouth that year – the first Open tournament in the world. There, Mark Cox had beaten Pancho Gonzales in a five-set second-round match and then put out Roy Emerson in straight sets in the quarters. Laver had put a stop to the rot and salvaged professional pride when he won the title, but doubts remained.

The weather at Wimbledon that year was capricious and, for the first few days, downright appalling, which of course produced smaller gates. Because of the mixed amateur/professional entry, with in many cases little previous comparative form, sixteen men were seeded for the first time since the experiment of 1950. How glorious it was to see the mighty Hoad again and Gonzales and Rosewall and all the top names in tennis. Wimbledon was revitalized. It had never lost its position of being the world's pre-eminent tournament. Now greatness had returned.

The professional career of Hoad (10) had been a short one, brought to an early end by persistent back trouble, and with his wife Jenny he had started a tennis ranch in Spain. There were enough reminders of his once all-conquering power to bring back memories and it took the deftness, resilience and good service return of Bob Hewitt to beat him in five sets in the third round. Gonzales (8) reached the same barrier where Alex Metreveli of Russia beat him in four.

No fingers crossed for Billie Jean King, six times crowned queen and overall record-holder with twenty titles ...

... but alarm ball for Rosie Casals.

Rod Laver (1) was still the outstanding professional player, so that his number one seeding was unquestionable. Compared to his 1962 performance, when he dropped only one set to Santana, his results made him seem more vulnerable. He lost a set in the first round to Eugene Scott, one to Riessen in the third and another to Cox in the fourth. In the quarter-finals he dropped two sets to Ralston (9). But hoeing this hard row had honed his game into top shape. In the semi-finals he showed masterful form to beat Arthur Ashe (13) 7/5, 6/2, 6/4.

So Laver got to the Final, where Rosewall (2) was seeded to meet him in what everybody hoped would be the Final to end all Finals and so mark this important year. Alas for hopes and Ken's many admirers, for in the fourth round he went down to the big serve of Tony Roche (15). Roche went on to dispose of big-game specialists Buchholz (10) and Graebner (who had eliminated two seeds in Santana (6) and Stolle (11)) to meet Laver in the second left-handers' final. In it Roche showed his power; but Laver had more and could control it to play any shot. It took him sixty-seven minutes to win his third title.

Although other famous names had looked vulnerable and some had fallen before they should, Laver had never looked a loser. His dominance had not always been obvious but, aware of the demands of seven rounds of possibly five sets each, he paced himself with rare judgement and his play always had the mark of authority. He was truly now World Champion. Newcombe and Roche (4) could consider themselves so, too, for they won the Doubles for the second time in a stirring five-set Final against Rosewall and Stolle (2), 3/6, 8/6, 5/7, 14/12, 6/3 – the longest Wimbledon Final of any kind, 70 games in all.

Billie Jean King (1), who with Ann Jones (4) had turned professional in 1967, maintained her position as Wimbledon queen. She had to fight in the semi-final against long-standing rival Ann, but Billie Jean never minded a fight. Ann took the first set 6/4 and went to a 5/3 lead in the second. Then Billie Jean, raising her game to the heights to meet the crisis, got back on level terms and was never headed again.

Billie Jean's final opponent was Judy Tegart (7), surprise winner over Margaret Court (2), now married after a year away, and in the semis Nancy Richey (3). Judy had suddenly scaled a new peak, but could not quite make the highest. After a testing struggle Billie Jean won 9/7, 7/5. With her extrovert good humour Judy was a great favourite of the crowd. She was also a doughty fighter and came back strongly after losing the first three games of the match. Once again Billie Jean showed that when it was most needed, her temperament had a finer edge and she could find the right shot in her locker. At 4/4 in the second set she was 30-40. She saved the break-point with a forehand volley down the line which left her opponent helpless. She went on to retain her Doubles title with Rosie Casals (1).

King was still Queen and riding high.

12

TWILIGHT OF THE GODS 1969–72

1969 In 1969, Rod Laver (1) marked himself down as a candidate for the title of the greatest player of all time and certainly proved that he was the supreme player of the decade when he retained his Wimbledon title.

Laver's progress was punctuated by moments when certainty was not always apparent. In the second round, for instance, against India's Premjit Lall he lost the first two sets. Lall won three games in the third set but was not permitted to win any in the fourth and fifth. In the semi-final Rod met the rising star Arthur Ashe (5) and the two of them combined to put on a breath-taking display of searing pace – so fluently controlled. In the Final, Rod dropped a set to John Newcombe (6) but he never looked like losing.

What an outstanding Champion! Before 1977 he came to Wimbledon ten times, won the title on four of them, and in two of the other six was a losing Finalist. The fact that he came back and won twice more after a five-year absence, with all his main rivals in the field, suggests that he could have won eight times to beat the record of Willie Renshaw – and in a much tougher competitive era. In this year he won the title at the five major meetings in which he competed. This gave him his second grand slam. Only one other man had ever done it once – the great Donald Budge.

Greatness, in the vintage year of 1969, was not confined to Laver. It was revealed as early as the first round. Pancho Gonzales (12) was drawn against Charlie Pasarell, who two years before had written himself into the record books when he beat Santana and became the first player to oust the reigning Champion in the first round.

The Gonzales–Pasarell match, for all who experienced it, transcended anything that had gone before. It was longer and more dramatic even than the legendary Drobny–Patty marathon of 1953. That had lasted ninety-three games and four hours twenty minutes. This ended only after 112 games and five hours twelve minutes of broken time, broken temper and finally broken spirit. It was a match of heroic proportions which belonged in soul to an earlier age, when it would have come down in song and mime and have passed into folklore.

Gonzales, serving second, was struggling from behind throughout the first set. He had set-point against him at 12/13, two more at 14/15, two more at 17/18 and a further three at 20/21. Altogether Pasarell failed to clinch eleven

Pancho Gonzales (*opposite*) goes for bust ...

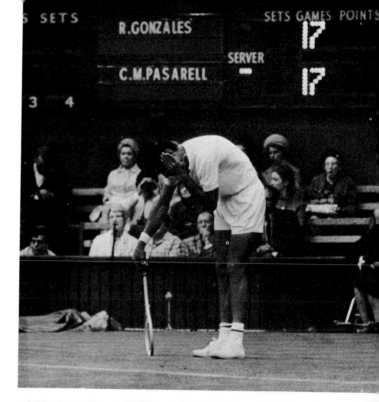

... after a hard day's night ...

... with Charlie Pasarell.
This outstanding contest will stand for all time as a record. The final score was 22/24, 1/6, 16/14, 6/3, 11/9 – a total of 112 games.

set-points in that record-equalling set of forty-six games. At last he got home on the twelfth.

The light was already poor and the umpires would certainly have called the players in at Lord's. Gonzales appealed. The umpire telephoned the Referee for a ruling. The answer was 'play on'. Gonzales did not take it with good grace and at forty-one he could not be blamed. He so far forgot his professionalism as to make scarcely more than a pretence of playing and lost the second set 6/1. His gesticulations to the umpire and to the Referee, who was now on the sidelines, brought boos from the crowd. At last, after two hours and twenty minutes the Referee, Captain Gibson, called it a day. Gonzales stalked off in fury, the whites of his eyes gleaming against his swarthy face and the gathering gloom.

The match was resumed the next day at 2.42. It seemed unlikely that, after the stresses of the previous evening, grandfather Gonzales could give fifteen years and two sets to as tough a character as Charlie Pasarell. But, having left in dudgeon the night before, Gonzales had returned full of consuming purpose. This was evident from his whole bearing and from every shot he played. For it was Gonzales who was always putting the pressure on Pasarell. The games mounted. So did the set-points, two at 6/5, four more at 11/10, the seventh at 14/13 and the eighth at 15/14 when Pasarell, having served a double-fault for 0–15, could win only one more point. The set had lasted an hour and twenty-eight minutes.

The fourth set was in minor key. Pasarell had one point to break service but could not take it, whereas at 3/4 and 30–40 he double-faulted. The set was there for Gonzales to take and he served out to 15. The match had now lasted four hours sixteen minutes with the overnight break. No match had received more coverage nor aroused more feeling than this conflict of such unparalleled magnitude. Where Gonzales had been booed off court the night before by a slightly misunderstanding crowd, today they cheered and cheered him on.

The final set provided a fitting climax to even what had gone before. All those present at the drama's dénouement sensed the prize at risk – the huge pride of this truly great player – Gonzales. Pasarell went to 5/4 and suddenly, after the hours of struggle Gonzales was 0–40. It seemed that only a thunderbolt from Jove could save him. After Pasarell had lobbed out to lose the first match-point, the thunderbolt came through a Gonzales service which crash-saved the second and Pasarell lost the third when he failed with another lob.

At 5/6, Gonzales was again in a morass of trouble at 0–40. All three match-points were tossed aside – with a smash, a glancing forehand volley and yet another cannonball serve. If hearts had been thumping earlier, they were now at danger level. 6/6, 7/7, 7/8 and Gonzales, after two deuces, had the seventh match-point against him. Again Pasarell tried the lob. Again it went out.

9/9 and at last Pasarell was spent. He lost his service to love and Gonzales went out to love on his own.

The final score was 22/24, 1/6, 16/14, 6/3, 11/9–112 games. An exhausted BBC radio commentator returned listeners to the studio with, 'That's all – believe me *all* – from Wimbledon.'

The euphoria made the crowds feel that Gonzales was almost superhuman, that nothing was beyond him and that even at forty-one he could win the title, for which he had been the favourite twenty years before. He won two more rounds comfortably enough, but then in the fourth round went out to Arthur Ashe.

What a superlative champion Gonzales could have been. This Colossus, who bestrode the Centre Court with such magnificence, was never seen at Wimbledon when at his best, having turned professional at twenty-one in 1949. Just before that he had made his one Wimbledon appearance as an amateur, when as No. 2 seed he was beaten by Geoff Brown in the fourth round, but he had won the Doubles title with Frankie Parker. His best years were in the professional ranks where for nine years between 1951 and 1960 he was the world No. 1.

He was born in California of Mexican parents. In the back streets around his home tennis was regarded as a cissy game and young Ric's most burning ambition was to own a bicycle. Instead, when he was twelve, his mother bought him a loosely-strung tennis racket. At first it was scorned, but after one game it became treasured. He took it to bed. He talked to it. Every morning he would get up at three o'clock to do a paper round to pay for balls and court fees. He played truant from school once too often and his angry father broke the precious racket over his knee.

Ann Jones (4) had not had to follow quite that path, but she kept up her resolve and determination over years of getting to within reach of the title but without managing to grasp it. Her victory in 1969 came at her fourteenth attempt after being six times a semi-finalist and once getting to the Final. On the clay courts of Stade Roland Garros, more suited to her game, she had twice won the French title. To win Wimbledon, Ann had to account for two of the all-time greats of women's tennis. In the semi-final she beat Margaret Court (1) 10/12, 6/3, 6/2. In this match she again showed the new style, revealed the previous year, when she gave Billie Jean King such a fight in the semi-final. Having lost the first set against the powerful Australian, Ann moved onto the attack and outplayed her opponent.

In the Final Ann was again a set down to Billie Jean (2), but again she grew in strength to win 3/6, 6/3, 6/2. This was the culmination of her tennis career. There was no shrewder tactician than Ann Jones. Year by year she had attacked the inner citadel, always seeking to strengthen her weapons, and had finally captured it by singleminded resolution.

Ken Rosewall (5) was a hero of different proportions to Gonzales. His

It shall not pass: Ann Jones,
Britain's best since the war,
overcoming Margaret Court in the
semi-finals, before beating Billie Jean
King to win the 1969 title.

immaculate tennis and demeanour had long made him a Wimbledon favourite. This had been enhanced by his 'little boy lost' look when he turned with drooping shoulder and seemingly reluctant step back to the baseline, pulling at an eyelash and apparently about to burst into tears. He looked like this so often that those who knew him were not deceived. It was merely Ken concentrating.

In the 1954 Final he had been beaten by Drobny. He and Hoad had played a memorable Final in 1956, after which Ken had turned professional. On his return with the professionals, for the first Open in 1968, Tony Roche had shut the gate on him, while the following year he had fallen unexpectedly to Bob Lutz. As far as Wimbledon titles were concerned he had been written off. But he had other ideas.

Rod Laver (1) came to the 1970 Wimbledon, aiming to complete a hat-trick of successes. There seemed to be no reason why he should not but his hopes were ended by Roger Taylor (16) when, in a fourth round battle of left-handers, Taylor won in four sets. Roger had never played better and, on a day when the temperature touched ninety, it was Laver who wilted under the pressure. It was his last challenge but one before the centenary year.

Taylor, in a battle of the big servers, then beat Clark Graebner (9) 6/3, 11/9, 12/10 to reach his second semi-final. His Yorkshire resolution and fighting quality had brought him a long way but he went down now to the perennial skills of Ken Rosewall, who beat him 6/3, 4/6, 6/3, 6/3 and earned his third bite at the Champion's cherry.

In the Final Rosewall met big John Newcombe (2), who had been using his bludgeoning serve–volley game to powerful effect. Rosewall saved a set-point at 4/5 and, capturing Newcombe's service, went out 7/5 on his own. Newcombe took the second set 6/3 to square the match and with a run of five games took the third to lead 2 sets to 1. Back came the ageless 'Little Master' in the fourth set with a run of five games to make it two sets all. Now, though, he was spent and his familiar dejected look this time reflected reality. At 1/1 in the final set Newcombe started another run of five games to win the match. Rosewall was given a lasting ovation, partly because spectators felt they were saying goodbye to such an old favourite, who must surely realise that he could not 'come again'. But Ken still had another surprise up his short sleeve.

In 1970, both Billie Jean (1) and Margaret Court (2) were back and both got through to the Final. They produced the match of the Championship – certainly the best women's match since the war. Both players were at their peak, both utterly determined to regain the title. Nearly every rally was a minor master-piece. Up to 8-all in the 14/12 first set (won by Margaret Court), half the games went against the server, and this in a match involving two of the most effective serves in women's tennis.

In the first half of that set there were twenty-two deuces and eighteen break-points, eight against Billie Jean and ten against Margaret. In the second half there were no deuces until the twelfth and thirteenth games. There were five break-points and two set-points. The twenty-six games of the set made it the longest played in a Wimbledon singles Final by men or women.

The second set, though shorter, was even more pulsating. At 7/6, Margaret Court had match-point which Billie Jean saved with a forehand volley down the line which even Margaret could not reach. In the next game Billie Jean had two break-points, but could not convert them. It was 8/8, 9/9, 10/9, with Margaret Court leading. Suddenly Billie Jean, at 15–40, faced her second match-point.

That final game alone was worth the admission money. From 15–40 Billie Jean drew on the dregs of her stamina and spirit to play like a demon. She saved four match-points. The fifth (the sixth in all) was too much and settled the issue of this superb duel. Margaret Court had won 14/12, 11/9, forty-six games played over two hours twenty-six minutes, beating the previous record of forty-four games set in 1919 in the famous Challenge Round between Suzanne Lenglen and Mrs Lambert Chambers.

Margaret Court's triumph was all the more incredible as she had been suffering from a tendon injury in her ankle and had been given pain-killing injections both for her semi-final and for the Final. Perhaps the ultimate spur to her fight was the knowledge that this might be her last chance to win the grand slam. This she achieved at Forest Hills a few weeks later, to equal the record of Maureen Connolly.

In the aftermath of that fantastic Final few people took much notice of the arrival and the first-round dismissal of an eighteen-year-old Australian girl. Her coach, Vic Edwards, said, 'By 1973 she could win Wimbledon' but for most the girl came to mind only because of her strange name – Evonne Goolagong.

1971   The following year Evonne was to bring a breath of fresh Antipodean air to the Centre Court. Evonne's grandfather was an aborigine and her name means 'tall trees by still water'. She entirely lives up to the onomatopoeia of her name. Her game is happy grace, as instinctive and natural as a gazelle. At first she had three apparent weaknesses in an otherwise complete game, her forehand was sliced and could break down, her second service was soft and inclined to be short, and every now and then she appeared 'to go walk-about' as the media soon dubbed it. When she did, a flawless performance could fall to pieces. She would continue to play through her part while her mind and spirit were evidently elsewhere.

Still just nineteen, but already heralded as the new French champion, Evonne was seeded 3 to Billie Jean King (2) and Champion Margaret Court (1). She got through to the semi-finals, there to be confronted with the redoubtable Billie Jean. She started by taking on the former Champion at her own serve–volley game. Strangely Billie Jean's play lacked its usual bite and accuracy and Evonne won the first set 6/4. She became slightly more defensive in the second set but managed to remain in command to win that and the match.

Hoad and Rosewall.
Muscles ageing . . .

, . . . ageless Muscles.

In the quarter-finals Margaret Court had beaten Winnie Shaw, the only Briton to get as far, which she did unseeded. This sunny Scot played a most attractive game. In her semi-final Margaret met fellow Australian Judy Dalton, unseeded conqueror of Virginia Wade (5) and Kerry Melville who, also unseeded, had beaten Rosie Casals (4). She dropped the first set to Judy but allowed her opponent to take only one more game. It must have been very satisfying to Margaret to see Australians taking three semi-final places, since her own amazing success had largely stimulated women's tennis at home.

In the Final Margaret soon showed her Centre Court nerves by losing the first four games. She rallied to win three games but Evonne held her off like a veteran to take the set 6/4. In the second set Evonne took five games running to lead 5/1 and 0–40 on Margaret's service. Margaret found the desperate courage of the mortally wounded to save three match-points but lost a fourth when nerves twitched at her serving arm for a double-fault. Evonne Goolagong had done it two years before Vic Edwards had said she might.

Rod Laver (1) was again the top men's seed, with reigning Champion John Newcombe (2). Newcombe justified his selection by winning a five-set Final against Stan Smith (4) to take his third Singles title. He will go down as a rugged champion, whose fighting spirit always enabled him to make the best of his talents.

Ken Rosewall (3) did not let his fans down. He played the match of the tournament in the quarter-finals against American Cliff Richey (6), coming back from 6/8, 5/7 to win the last three sets 6/4, 9/7, 7/5. The match started at 3.30 and lasted a minute under four hours. It was another tremendous performance by the 'Little Master' but Rosewall then suffered reaction and fell easily to his 1970 Final conqueror, Newcombe. Laver again went down in the quarter-finals, this time to American Tom Gorman.

This year saw the first use at Wimbledon of the tie-break. Many had thought that this device, brought in to shorten matches, would never come to Wimbledon. But with true British compromise it was used at eight all and not six all as in the rest of the world, the final set remaining an advantage one.

1972   In 1972, Billie Jean King (2) was intent on re-establishing her authority. Virginia Wade was also making a strong bid and had won the Australian title, beating Evonne Goolagong in the Final. In the French Championship Evonne again got to the Final, but there Billie Jean beat her.

So to Wimbledon. Evonne (1) got the top seed as reigning Champion. If the seeding ran true to form she was due to meet the new American sensation, Chrissie Evert (4), in the semi-finals. A year before, at only sixteen (even younger than Maureen Connolly when she first played Wightman Cup), Chrissie had been the main instrument in America winning that trophy and, with her relentless precision and attacking double-fisted backhand, had won forty-six consecutive singles before Billie Jean ended her precocious run in the US semi-finals. She had become the youngest player to reach that stage.

Evonne Goolagong, 1971
Champion, in the mood.

The tennis world awaited the Evert–Goolagong clash, for somehow these two rising stars had not as yet played each other. As the girls came out onto court to a tremendous welcome, seventeen-year-old Chrissie, her remarkable composure already a byword, appeared the senior to the twenty-year-old Champion. Both were beautifully dressed and looked delightful as they turned to make the traditional bow to the Royal Box. Evonne had already established her place in the crowd's affections. Chrissie, on the other hand, was immaculate not only in her dress, but also in the almost mechanical perfection of her length and accuracy. So many felt that she was cold and they responded to her as they did between the wars to Helen Wills. But the next year or two brought Chrissie almost as much affection and admiration as Evonne.

The match began with both playing tentatively, as though taking each other's measure, and the two opening service games were lost. Gradually Chrissie, gained slight ascendancy. It was a fascinating duel, with purity of stroke predominating. Chrissie's drives, particularly on the two-handed side, got ever nearer the lines. Her accuracy was a revelation. She took the first set after thirty-four enthralling minutes.

When Chrissie went to 3/0 in the second set it began to look as if Billie Jean's prediction would be fulfilled. She had said: 'I think Chrissie is the more mature. She is stronger mentally. She has basically only three or four shots and there is less to go wrong with her game.' But then it was as if pride had pricked Evonne with a spur. She struck an irresistible vein. Seven games in a row gave her the set 6/3 and 1/0 in the final set. Thrust and counter-thrust, with breathtaking shots by both girls, took Evonne to 5/4. With Chrissie serving, Evonne prepared the *coup de grâce*, with two superb shots, a backhand drop-volley for 0–15, and a chopped forehand cross-court passing shot for 0–30. She finished the game to love and with it the match.

It had been an hour and thirty-three minutes of sheer tennis delight, promising still more riches when these two candidates for all-time greatness met in the future. The crowd gave them a standing ovation.

This was 1972 Wimbledon's finest hour. Evonne was so popular and yet so unspoilt. Alf Chave, a Queenslander who came over yearly to be a brilliant summariser for BBC Radio, was staying with Vic Edwards during the fortnight. He told how Evonne, away from Wimbledon, was leading the ordinary life of a young girl. While weaving her way in glory through the Wimbledon draw, she was still doing her share of the washing-up and other chores, though she had been allowed one excursion to nearby Putney to buy herself a dress for the Wimbledon Ball.

Evonne was now through to the Final against Billie Jean, who on the way had vanquished Virginia Wade (7) and Rosie Casals (6). Billie Jean won the Final 6/3, 6/3, with a performance which recalled her dominance of earlier years. After knee operations, she herself said that she was back to full fitness

Smash and grab artists.
ABOVE LEFT & BELOW 1971. John Newcombe
takes Stan Smith.

ABOVE RIGHT 1972. In Newcombe's absence it's
Smith's turn.

and form: 'I could run and bend the way I did in 1966.' Once again she was queen.

Internecine quarrels between WCT and the ILTF had the effect of barring from this Wimbledon four of the leading players who had contracts with World Championship Tennis – Rod Laver, Ken Rosewall, Arthur Ashe and reigning Champion, John Newcombe. It was particularly sad that Big John was denied the chance of going for his hat-trick. He tried. He submitted a private entry but the management committee regretfully had to turn him down, since the ILTF had ruled that contract professionals must be barred.

In their absence, many took note of 19-year-old Wimbledon newcomer, left-handed Jimmy Connors, whose fierce hitting – especially with his two-handed backhand – disposed of Bob Hewitt (7) in the first round and brought him unseeded to the quarter-finals, having dropped only one set (to Panatta) on the way. Here he met his doubles partner to be, Ilie Nastase (2), who contained him 6/4, 6/4, 6/1 and in a glorious match of fine strokes then beat Manuel Orantes (3) 6/3, 6/4, 6/4 to reach the Final for the first time.

Nastase's opponent was Stan Smith (1), the previous year's Finalist and current American champion. In the quarters and semis respectively Smith had beaten Alex Metreveli (8) and Jan Kodes (5) – Finalists to be next year. The Final was postponed for twenty-four hours due to rain and was the first match ever played at Wimbledon on a Sunday. Stan Smith, blond, handsome and 6 feet 4 inches, with his straight-backed walk might well have stepped out of Sandhurst with the Sword of Honour. He was in fact a serving member of the US Army, had been in the American top ten since 1966 and was now the established No. 1. His was the big serve and volley game and, with his reach, he could command the net and was extremely difficult to lob.

Smith looked an officer but was in fact doing his draft service in the ranks. Nastase, though not of conventional military appearance, said with typical impish humour before the match, 'I am an officer.' He admitted that he was nervous after the day's postponement in a rain-bedevilled Wimbledon, but said with a familiar shrug, 'I will fight Godzilla' – a Rumanian horror film monster, whom he jokingly likened to Smith.

Nastase is a tennis genius and his deft but wayward style totally contrasted with the orthodox Smith. In a match which proved to be one of Wimbledon's most exciting finals, Nastase got the first edge and the first set 6/4. The twenty-four hours' delay had generated a lot of nervous tension which sparked off incredible service returns and brilliant rallies in the second set, which Smith took 6/3. It had been noticeable that 'Nasty', who had been behaving beauti-fully, was getting edgy – changing rackets often and showing other signs of tem-perament. This inevitably affected his own inspiration and Smith romped away with the third set to lead 2/1 and then 1/0 in the fourth. Nastase changed rackets yet again, found his touch and won the fourth set 6/4 to square the match.

All this had scarcely been Sunday-afternoon-on-the-vicarage-lawn tennis and the crowd delighted in the searing drives, the touch volleys, deceptive passing shots, the exquisite lobs and the thundering smashes. The final set provided a fitting climax. At 2/2 Smith was three times break-point down and held on only after seven deuces. At 4/4 Smith was 0–30. Nastase hit a forehand volley hard and true. Smith, with a mighty Godzilla leap of desperation, just reached the ball with the frame of his racket. It dropped dead – on the other side of the net. Had that shot failed Nastase must surely have won the title.

In the next game Nastase had to fend off two match-points. Again, at 5/6 down, he faced match-point and saved it with a forehand volley which defied even Smith's telescopic reach. A forehand volley gave Smith match-point again and he rammed it home for the title. The match had lasted two hours forty-four minutes and was classed by many as the best Men's Final since the Crawford–Vines epic in 1933.

Nastase had some comfort when he and Rosie Casals (2) won their second Mixed Doubles title, in straight sets against Kim Warwick and Evonne Goolagong (1). The Men's Doubles were also correctly forecast when Bob Hewitt and Frew McMillan (1) beat Stan Smith and Eric van Dillen (2) 6/2, 6/2, 9/7. Only the Women's Doubles strayed slightly from their seeding. Billie Jean King, partnered this time by Betty Stove (1), beat Judy Dalton and Frankie Durr (3) 6/2, 4/6, 6/3, giving Billie Jean her eighth doubles title. She was well on the way to the Wimbledon record of twelve doubles titles and nineteen titles in all, held by Elizabeth Ryan. Billie Jean now had fourteen.

13

CONNORS ASKS THE QUESTIONS 1973–6

1973 No sooner had one ugly political argument been settled than another was raised. As a result of Nikki Pilic being suspended by the ILTF for failing to play in a Davis Cup match, and his consequent barring from Wimbledon, the Association of Tennis Professionals called upon all its members to withdraw their entries. The arguments swung to and fro, always with the underlying feeling that nobody could do such a thing to Wimbledon. A formula would surely be found.

In the end, principle prevailed and seventy-nine players, including thirteen of the sixteen seeds, withdrew. There were three exceptions, two of them especially notable: Roger Taylor, with pressures from both sides, came down for Yorkshire and All England and overnight became still more a hero. With him as a strange pedestal-fellow was Ilie Nastase, a rebel and quixotic as one might expect.

The immediate effect was a surge of loyalty from the fans. Whenever Roger Taylor appeared he was cheered rapturously. Nastase (1) was given top place in the re-seeding with Kodes of Czechoslovakia (not a member of ATP) at 2, Taylor (3), Alex Metreveli of Russia (4) and Jimmy Connors (5). At No. 6 was a newcomer but with a reputation which had preceded him – straight from Valhalla it seemed – seventeen-year-old Bjorn Borg of Sweden. Squealing and screaming teenage girls followed his progress in droves. Never before has such a posse of policemen been needed to protect a player.

Nastase should have had a great chance for the title, but in the fourth round a newcomer, Alex 'Sandy' Mayer of the USA, beat him in four sets. Mayer went on to the semi-finals where he met Metreveli, whose all-round but unforceful game had contained the up-and-coming Jimmy Connors. Metreveli won the semi-final to become the first Russian to get to the Wimbledon Singles Final.

The other semi-final featured Roger Taylor as star billing. In a stirring five-set quarter-final he had dealt with that other precocious youngster, Borg. Taylor's semi-final opponent was Jan Kodes. Taylor, with his big serve game well in tune, had been showing his best form, and seemed to have a fine chance to take the title. He gave the semi-final all he had got, but it was Kodes who emerged the winner 8/9, 9/7, 5/7, 6/4, 7/5. Once there, the Czech's experience proved too much for a slightly overawed Metreveli and Kodes won 6/1, 9/8, 6/3. Connors got his first title and Nastase some consolation when they

1973. ATP withdraws its players. Alex Metreveli, the first Russian in the Men's Finals . . .

. . . but the first Czech, Jan Kodes, skis his chance . . .

. . . and just seventeen, Bjorn Borg makes his entrance to the squeals of the teenyboppers.

teamed up (1) to win the Doubles. But the biggest triumph belonged to Wimbledon – triumph of spirit over circumstance.

While Borg and Connors had been giving notice to their elders that a new order was imminent, in the Women's Championship Chris Evert (4) was again straining at the leash, putting out Margaret Court (1) 6/1, 1/6, 6/1 in the semi-finals. In the Final Chrissie came up against the indomitable Billie Jean King (2), who again had thwarted the challenge of Evonne Goolagong (3). Billie Jean clearly set out to repeat the lesson she had taught her young compatriot in the Forest Hills semi-final two years before. She took the first set in sixteen minutes, allowing her opponent just nine points. In the second set things started to look even worse for Chrissie. Billie Jean took the first two games for the loss of only one point.

Chrissie did not despair. She became Evert unremitting, and was rewarded. At 1/3 she took three games in a row and it was suddenly noticeable that Billie Jean had become uncertain. But yet again, when it was most needed, the Champion raised her game and at 5/5 broke service and held her own for the match and her fifth Singles title – a remarkable achievement. Billie Jean completed a clean sweep to gain her second triple crown.

1974   Billie Jean's (1) record-chasing was brought to a summary halt in the 1974 Women's Singles with quarter-final defeat by Olga Morozova (8), 7/5, 6/2. The popular and athletic Olga continued by beating Virginia Wade (5) 1/6, 7/5, 6/4 in the semi-finals, to become the first Russian woman to reach a Wimbledon Final. There she was to meet Chrissie Evert (2).

To get there Chrissie had only just survived a first-match marathon against Australian Lesley Hunt 8/6, 5/7, 11/9 – the forty-six games equalling the length of the King–Court final of 1970. In the Final her relentless accuracy was too much for Olga Morozova. The Russian fought valiantly in the opening game which went to five deuces but Chrissie won it and soon gained the set 6/0. In the second, Olga led 2/1, was pulled back to 2/4, recovered to 4/4 but Evert broke again and won the set and match 6/4 for her first Singles title.

In both the Men's and Women's Championships, the younger players were thrusting forward while the seasoned campaigners fought to hold off the challenge. In the thick of the battle there was still evergreen Ken Rosewall (9). In 1974 he beat successively Barry Phillips-Moore, Vijay Amritraj, Peter Kanderal of Switzerland, Roscoe Tanner, the left-handed service machine from Lookout Mountain, Tennessee (four sets), and John Newcombe (1), to come up against Stan Smith (4) in the semi-finals.

Big Stan turned on the power and at 8/6, 6/4, 5/4 was serving for the match. Rosewall staved off that crisis, survived a match-point at 5/6 and won the set 9/8. From then on the tide which had seemed to be engulfing Kenny turned completely. Smith's forehand weakened under Rosewall's consistent length. Rosewall took the fourth set 6/1 and the fifth 6/3, finishing with a love game.

So Ken got to his fourth Wimbledon Final, twenty years after the first. He faced an opponent playing in his first Final, Jimmy Connors (3), who at twenty-one was little more than half the age of thirty-nine-year-old Ken. Hitherto that year Connors had not looked a likely Finalist. His progress on an easy path was littered with dropped sets – one of them in the semi-final to Dick Stockton who, unseeded, had beaten Nastase (2) in the fourth round and then Metreveli (10). But once there Connors played devastating tennis. After Rosewall had won his opening service game, Connors blasted his way through ten consecutive games with strokes of unbelievable power and accuracy, hitting the ball early on the return of service and still controlling it down the line. He was at the net in an instant, commanding it with fierce stabbing volleys. After fifty-four minutes the scoreboard read 6/1, 6/1.

The Centre Court crowd was almost silent, as if present at an execution. In the third set Rosewall, ever the trier, slowed the rush, but Connors won it 6/4 to be respectfully, if rather silently acclaimed, as the most crushing winner since Hoad beat Cooper in 1957. All the emotion was reserved for the hapless Rosewall. Connors said afterwards, 'I just played unbelievable tennis today and it couldn't have been at a better time.' But not for Rosewall.

A year later the Men's Singles Final scoreboard was again showing 6/1, 6/1 with Connors (1) on court defending his title. But this time there was a difference. That score was against the Champion. His title was turning to Ashe's (6), as a rapt and cheering crowd was witnessing the most amazing upset of form and prediction ever seen in a Wimbledon Final.

In the bookmaker's tent, installed in the ground on the tea-lawns for the only time, the scene was that of a miniature stock exchange on a busy day as Arthur Ashe, the player who could not win, seemed to be doing just that. On the concourse between the two main courts and the outside ones the electric scoreboard flashed the scores to scarce-believing eyes.

Connors, who must have felt the almost solid impact of the crowd's concentration and applause on behalf of Ashe, gained many almost ashamed supporters when, having lost nine successive games, a voice (possibly with a bet at stake) implored, 'Come on, Connors.' Jimbo replied, 'I'm trying, for Chrissake!'

Ashe had approached the match with a most ingenious tactical plan. He had noted that in the semi-final against Roscoe Tanner, the biggest server in the Championships, Connors had fed on Tanner's pace to unleash an onslaught of service returns and passing shots. So, in the Final, Ashe deliberately slow-balled Connors, played wide of him, into his body, dinked short, sliced, top-spun, played down the line and across court to weave a web of soft intrigue. Connors's super-powerful game became disorientated.

Throughout this wondrous spell Ashe was in what he himself calls a 'serene high'. At every change of end he sat by the umpire's chair, deliberately facing away from his opponent, his eyes closed and inducing in himself a form of yoga or self-hypnotism. This shut out all distraction and enabled him to remain on that high plane for much longer than a player can normally achieve.

Jimmy Connors – 'the lion comes down to the fold'.

It could not last for ever and Connors, determined to end the humiliation, took and held the initiative for nearly a set and a half. He won the third 7/5 and got to 3/0 in the fourth. Knowing heads began to nod, and the odds to slide. Connors was back to form and a Connors in top gear could not be beaten. Wrong again. Ashe reimposed his skills, winning six of the next seven games to take his first Wimbledon like a conqueror of Everest. He was given the most tumultuous standing ovation seen or heard since the Drobny victory of 1954.

There were other men's singles matches in 1975, 126 of them, many extremely good. But then, and in retrospect, all paled beside the Final.

The quality of the women's line-up was as high as that of the Brough–du Pont era. Chrissie Evert (1), the Champion, found herself against unseeded Betty Stove of the Netherlands in the quarter-final. She made heavy weather of it initially, lost the first set but came back to take the next two, the final one to love. Billie Jean King (3) made certain that Olga Morozova (7) would not provide the upset of the previous year and won 6/3, 6/3. Virginia Wade (6) got to the quarter-finals for the sixth time, where she met Evonne Goolagong (now Mrs Roger Cawley) (4). Virginia gave the usual heart-stopping and often spectacular performance her fans had come to expect. She took an exciting first set 7/5 but lost the equally thrilling second and third sets 3/6, 7/9. The No. 2 seed was a newcomer to the higher ranks, Martina Navratilova, a husky left-hander from Czechoslovakia. She soldiered surely on to the quarter-finals where she found the experience of Margaret Court (5) too much.

What a semi-final line-up! The All-American Chris Evert v. Billie Jean King and the All-Australian Margaret Court v. Evonne Cawley. Billie Jean showed again what a tremendous competitor she is when she came back from a set down, 2/6, with a run of four games to level at one set all. Break-points were liberally sprinkled throughout the third set. First advantage was to Chrissie, who led 3/0 and at 15/40 on her own service Billie Jean's cause looked lost. She again raised her game, saved those two break-points, and a third, gave away no more chances and won six successive games for the match.

Evonne Cawley beat Margaret Court 6/4, 6/4. The score does not fairly reflect an exhilarating match. Evonne was golden. Her strokes flowed to give full rein to her natural genius. And for once her concentration never wavered. Margaret was physically herself but had to use every vestige of her power and athletic ability to try to stem Evonne's flow and to carry the attack to her opponent. Margaret managed a 4/2 lead, but then Evonne struck a winning sequence of four games to take the first set, after Margaret had saved four set-points. The second set was a tug-of-war, evenly balanced until Evonne came from behind with a run of three games for the set and the match.

After two such fine semi-finals, the Final was an anti-climax as far as thrills were concerned. But the tennis played by Billie Jean was masterful. She routed a bewildered Evonne Cawley with a display of serve and volley power of

The 1975 Final. Arthur Ashe in 'serene high' creates the upset of a century against 'certainty' Jimmy Connors.

which many a man would have been proud, her winning score 6/0, 6/1. The Billie Jean Wimbledon chart now read six Singles titles, putting her equal third with Suzanne Lenglen in the all-time list and behind Mrs Lambert Chambers (7) and Helen Wills Moody (8). Her overall tally of Singles and Doubles titles was now nineteen, level with the record of Elizabeth Ryan, who won all hers in Doubles.

Two results interested the connoisseur. In the Men's Doubles, won by Vitas Gerulaitis and Sandy Mayer, no seeds reached the semi-finals (Hewitt and McMillan (3) were the only pair to reach the quarters); and in the Women's Doubles Japan won its first title when Kazuko Sawamatsu, partnered by the American/Japanese Ann Kiyomura, a spontaneous and delightful pair, won an all-unseeded Final.

1976   The year 1976 gave Britain a heatwave and lightning fast courts at Wimbledon. Champion Billie Jean King, having announced her retirement from top-flight singles (she came for the Doubles), British hopes were high that the good form shown on the American circuit by Virginia Wade (3), and by new hope Sue Barker (7), could lead to a British Singles victory.

Virginia had promised much in the past. Her tempestuous talent had blown away senior seeds, but all too often that wind veered against her as she lost the tiller of her own temperament. On her day she had the most forceful game in women's tennis, a game spearheaded by her service. She had to attack. She had a good trained mind, but in play instinct prevailed, the instinct to attack. When attack failed and big shots were not going in, she found it hard to adapt to circumstances and play a waiting game until rhythm returned. But in recent years she had been an inspiring captain of the British Wightman Cup team. All this was true until 1977 and the miracle of Centenary year.

The fast courts of Wimbledon 1976 ideally suited Virginia's powerful game. She swept confidently through to the semi-finals, looking vulnerable only in the fourth round when she dropped a set to the challenge of the strong new-comer, Marise Kruger of South Africa. Alas again for British hopes. In the semi-finals she found Evonne Cawley (2) playing her best brand of winning tennis and, like Evonne against Billie Jean in the previous year's Final, Virginia was made to look a much lesser player. She was beaten 6/1, 6/2.

Sue Barker justified her seeding, reaching the quarter-finals, beating on the way old champion Maria Bueno, back for the first time since 1968. In the quarters Sue met Martina Navratilova (4), with whom she had had several battles on the American circuit. It was a fight, and one which ebbed and flowed. Like Virginia Wade, Sue Barker loves to play an attacking game and she always carried the attack to Martina. But, leading 5/3 in the final set and with Martina seemingly at her last gasp, instead of playing percentage shots Sue went for winners and hit too many losers. Martina was let off the hook and came back to win the set 7/5 and with it the match.

Martina went on to give Chrissie Evert (1) a good semi-final match which the

American won 6/4 in the final set. So the Final was between those two young rivals, Chrissie Evert and Evonne Cawley, and it was to produce an occasion to match the Court–King epic of 1970. The issue was in doubt throughout the two hours that the girls duelled on the sunny Centre Court. The conditions seemed ideally suited for Evonne with her faster shots, particularly on the backhand, and with her more forceful volleys.

But it was Chrissie who seized the advantage and kept it to take the first set 6/3. The rallies had been fierce, the shots scintillating. Back came Evonne to break Chrissie's service twice and win the second set 6/4. As in so many matches between Evonne and Chrissie, return of service was often better than service itself. In the long final set the advantage moved briefly one way, then quickly the other until 6/6 was reached. Two points then decided the issue. With Evonne serving, Chrissie got to advantage, and took it. On her own service she reached 40–30 and took that point, and the match. After two hours, her resolution just had the edge which enabled her to allow no mistake at the vital opportunity. Against most expectations Evert was Champion again.

More interest than usual was focused on both the Women's and the Mixed Doubles, which provided Billie Jean with the chance to win her twentieth Wimbledon title to set up an all-time record. She was seeded No. 1 in both, with Sandy Mayer in the Mixed and with Betty Stove in the Women's. Hope soon ended in the Mixed when she and Sandy were beaten in the second round by the combination of Bob Hewitt, that grand old doubles campaigner, and Greer Stevens. Only one seeded pair did better. Frew McMillan and Betty Stove (2) survived to the semi-finals with three unseeded pairs. There they were beaten by Tony Roche and Frankie Durr, who beat Dick Stockton and Rosie Casals in the Final. Frankie, with her extrovert French squeals and 'peculiar' backhand, finally, to the delight of everyone, achieved in her first Mixed Final what had eluded her in six Women's Doubles Finals.

So for Billie Jean it was to be all on the Women's. She and Betty Stove got through to their appointed Final place, to be met there by Chris Evert and Martina Navratilova. A 6/1 first set to Chrissie and Martina sent Billie Jean's hopes plunging, but she and Betty recovered to take the second 6/3. The decider was a fight to the last point, which Chrissie and Martina won. So Billie Jean was denied her record at a moment when she probably had greater crowd support than she had had throughout all her years of triumph.

When in 1974 Jimmy Connors ushered in a new era, he looked as if he might be invulnerable for years. Arthur Ashe momentarily stemmed the surge of youth, but in 1976 with many old heroes – Laver, Gonzales and Rosewall – finally bowing out, it became irresistible. Bjorn Borg (4) had already made an impact in 1973 as a seventeen-year-old. 1974 had marked the sudden rise of Guillermo Vilas (6) of Argentina, whose entry into the quarter-finals the following year went almost unnoticed against the epic Ashe–Connors Final.

Borg and Vilas had already had many tough battles around the world and

Chrissie Evert – a champion crystallised.

they came together in the 1976 quarter-finals. Here Borg, who had raised his game a class and had not dropped a set in the tournament, kept up his good form with a 6/3, 6/0, 6/2 victory. Jimmy Connors (2) had also been impressive in reaching the quarter-finals without dropping a set, beating on the way Stan Smith (16), the 1972 Champion. In the quarters Connors met up with Roscoe Tanner (7), a player of prodigious power, and at the outset it was felt that if Connors could get past him, he could recapture the title.

It was a clash of left-handers, with Connors double-fisted on the backhand. The fiery summer and the lightning-fast courts, especially the Centre Court, on which this match was played, favoured Tanner. His game depended so much on his service which, when firing well, was almost the ultimate tennis weapon. Tanner began in blistering form. He squandered his first service game by putting out a volley while Connors was lying on the ground, but from 0/2 he won seven out of eight games. His first service was so fast that it seemed to arc like a tracer bullet from a gun. This fire power is illustrated by his putting fifty per cent of those first serves into court (forty-five out of ninety-two). Nineteen of these were outright aces, and the rest were almost untakeable. He did not live by service alone, but it was the serve which crumbled Connors' confidence.

Tanner, who had beaten Connors in the Beckenham semi-final three weeks before, obviously sensed that this was his day, and one could feel his desire to eradicate the memory of the humbling he had received from Connors in the quarter-finals the previous year. He lashed the ball with all his power. His forehand fired continual winners, his volleys were sure and his smashes unanswerable. He took the second set even more easily and led 5/2 in the third. Serving at 0–40, Connors was in the situation of the victim in old Western films, tied to the rails and about to be run over by the train.

But hopeless though the position seemed to everyone else, Jimbo did not submit. The Champion spark, so near extinction, flickered still. He saved four match-points. On the next game he took Tanner's service, for the first time since the opening game of the match. He held his own to level 5/5. Tanner, serving first, then led 7/6 and suddenly Connors was down again 15/40. This time Tanner hammered home his advantage and the favourite was beaten.

This took him to the semi-final where Borg was to face his fire power. But neither velocity nor accuracy was the same. With his main weapon blunted, even metaphorically knocked out of his hand by some of Borg's service returns, Tanner seemed anxious to get to the net by chipping his approach shot. There, where he had dominated rallies against Connors, he became merely a signpost for the passing shots at which Borg was so adept. Borg's own service was fast and to a good length. It was so consistent that he did not lose it once in the whole match. Borg's performance was the more remarkable in the knowledge that he had pulled a stomach muscle early in the Championship and had needed pain-killing injections before each round that followed.

There were in fact only two service breaks in the entire match, in the first and third sets. The second set was decided on a tie-breaker when the score reached 8/8. So Borg became the first Swede to reach a Wimbledon Final.

His opponent was to be Ilie Nastase (3). The reigning Champion, Arthur Ashe (1), had been put out in the fourth round on Court 3 by up-and-coming Vitas Gerulaitis, beaten in turn by Raul Ramirez (8), who then fell to Nastase. Nasty for once had been doing his best to concentrate rather than communicate in a serious bid to win the elusive Wimbledon title. But in the semi-final he had returned to his volatile gesturing, especially in his running war with Press photographers. But his genius still flourished in a match which provided some of the best tennis of the tournament, and brought him a win in straight sets. So the Final promised a tennis feast.

For most of the crowd, it was not an occasion for hiding emotion. The blond good looks of Viking demi-god Borg carried even more teenage hearts than those of the dark, handsome Balkan, Nastase, stormy petrel of modern tennis. How much Nastase was affected by the memory of missing a title so near his grasp in 1972, or how much it was the sheer brilliance of Borg on the day, is hard to weigh in the scale. For brilliant Borg was. Nastase began by digging deep into the rich vein of his talent and was soon leading 3/0. In the fourth game, with Borg serving, Nastase had three break-points in five deuces. Had he won this game to lead 4/0 with his own service to follow, the door to the title could well have opened to him.

But Borg, who had again had pain-killing injections before the match, wanted to speed things on his own account. He became a man inspired. He saved that game and, twice in quick succession, had runs of three games to take the set 6/4. He was playing breathtaking tennis, going all out for pace on the fastest surface even the Centre Court had known for years. This sudden switch of ascendancy appeared to drain the spirit of Nastase, who seemed to sense that the prize was again slipping from him. Into the second set with the points brief and the scoreboard flickering fast, 3/2, 4/2, 5/2, 6/2. Two sets to love to Borg.

The third set continued at the same reckless pace, Borg capturing Nastase's service in the opening game and holding his own to lead 2/0. At last Nastase held service and, with service prevailing for a spell, it began to look like a match again. But Borg had that service-break in his pocket and at 4/5 Nastase faced the ultimate truth. He had to break. To his credit he did, after saving a match-point. The score went to 7/7. Borg broke Nastase's service again and held his own, this time to love.

He had become the first Swede to win a Wimbledon Singles crown. It sat well on him. Not only had he won, but he had done so in the grand manner, not losing a set, to become the fourth youngest holder of the Men's title. The Borg comet, first seen in fiery form in 1973, had now blazed through the Championship and would still be there to light up the Centre Court in Wimbledon's second century.

In harness – true teamwork.
LEFT AND OPPOSITE TOP Frew
McMillan (in cap) and Bob Hewitt,
winners in 1967, 1972 and 1978.

BELOW Stan Smith and Bob Lutz,
runners-up in 1974 and 1980 and US
champions in 1968, 1974 and 1978.
OPPOSITE BELOW Ilie Nastase and
Jimmy Connors, 1973 winners.

14

THE CENTENARY IS THE GREATEST

1977 So much had been thought, written and hoped for in advance of Wimbledon's Centenary Championships that many feared for a flop – perhaps an almighty one. Instead the Deity smiled on the occasion and in the outcome it was truly historic – a paean of sentiment and a pageant of play.

Save for a little spitting it did not rain once, but apart from that the weather was a poor ally. In the main it provided a drab backcloth for this glittering gathering of tennis skills and tennis greats. The skies were grey, though streaked at times by wayward shafts of sunshine; and cold breezes struck chill to crowds clothed for summer and traditional Wimbledon weather. This was probably the cause of a 'Wimbledon' throat that played havoc amongst fans, but fortunately not (as in 1934) amongst the players. Towards the end of the fortnight it did get warmer but never could it be called hot.

First on the Centre Court came the parade of champions, headed by Britain's Kitty McKane (Mrs Godfree) and France's Jean Borotra, both winners in 1924 and 1926. They were well matched to lead on (and arm-in-arm off) the past heroes and heroines of this stage, each of whom were presented with a commemorative medal by the Club's President, the Duke of Kent – each that is but Jimmy Connors, who chose instead to practise with Ilie Nastase. This apparently deliberate discourtesy caused a furore in the international media and throughout the tournament Connors was to feel the crowd's displeasure.

Being a cold, grey day the medal-giving was hurried through at an almost unseemly pace, so that some of the occasion's savour was never tasted, but there was enough to evoke floods of nostalgia and some tears. The Champions themselves were as moved as the crowds and Arthur Ashe admitted afterwards that he was glad to get off quickly, for he could not speak.

While the Centre Court had been savouring the past, first-round business on the other courts had as usual begun at 2 o'clock. Nostalgia on Centre was at times brought to heel when the sound of No. 1 court's applause broke closer and stronger as Britain's John Lloyd cast off the cringing memory of his recent Davis Cup performance in Bucharest, and began to apply his real skills against the blood and thunder of Roscoe Tanner's (4) big serve and volley. The court was dead and the turf juicy in its freshness, so that Tanner's service was by no means the lightning hammer that had sledged out Connors in the 1976

Centre Court 'old acquaintance' at Centenary Wimbledon.
Left to right: Peter Jackson (committee), Buzzer Hadingham (committee), Chris Evert, Jack Kramer, Arthur Ashe, Evonne Cawley, Stan Smith, Gp Capt. Freddie Judge (committee), Ann Jones, John Newcombe, Manuel Santana, Bimby Holt (vice-chairman), Karen Susman, Rod Laver.

John Lloyd's finest win at Wimbledon, over Roscoe Tanner (4), 9/7 in the final set in the first round.

quarter-finals. All the same Lloyd played an inspired game, using the deft supple-
ness of his service return more forcefully than usual and even producing some
blistering services of his own. He contained the new Australian Champion so
well that, although he lost the first set, an upset always looked likely. He gained a
real grip on the match and, his nerve holding well, he won the next three sets.
However, in the second round, having led Karl Meiler of Germany two sets to
love, he eventually lost to him 7/9 in the fifth. John still has to find the Toledo
tempering of unfailing steel, which American youth has in multi-lamination.
This was particularly exemplified by the eighteen-year-old American junior,
John McEnroe, whose resolute game was already forcing him through the field.

Borg (2) had leapt up the seniority ladder in the parade of champions, so
that he might be ready to open the defence of his title as soon as it was over. He
made short work of it, his harsh-hit top-spin drives subduing the subtler game
of Antonio Zugarelli, who fought with honour for a 9/7 third set. A second seed
to be blown away was Harold Solomon (16), somewhat overwhelmed by the
bludgeoning of 6 ft 5 inch Steve Docherty. So, despite his high ranking in the
game at large, little Solly found Wimbledon grass his undoing at the first hurdle
for the third time running.

A British favourite of many years, Roger Taylor, now a little over his Yorkshire hill, continued a losing first-round sequence when he just yielded a strong-
arm left-hander's battle to Australia's Ray Ruffels, who in turn, after holding
three match-points, went out to another of the up-and-now-it-seemed-come
American brigade, Billy Martin. Martin went on to beat two more left-handers,
both seeds, Vilas (3) and Cox (14), and reach the quarter-finals for the first
time. His match with Vilas, the new French champion, was played on No. 3
Court. The Argentinian may have suffered from crowd distraction, for not only
did he have an off day but seemed thoroughly depressed – as well he might to
lose in such spiritless fashion 2/6, 4/6, 2/6. In the first round he had looked
impressive when on the Centre Court he contained the 1974 Champion, Kodes,
9/8, 7/5, 6/4 in a delightful display of control and strokemanship. Admittedly
he had had little grass court play but against Martin he seemed to have no
Latin fire in his belly.

Nearly 34, Mark Cox (14) was having his best year and was seeded for the
first time on his high ATP Computer ranking. Before playing Martin he had not
dropped a set in three rounds. It was their first encounter and Mark must have
realised that the young American, twice winner of the Wimbledon junior title
and with nothing to lose, would be a tough opponent. Cox took the first set on
one break of serve, but dropped his own four times to lose the next two. The
fourth was all Cox, Martin winning only seven points. Breaking Martin's first
service game of the final set Cox led 4/1 and, holding his own to love, 5/2. It
seemed a convincing lead, but now Martin had a comfortable run of three
games to square at 5-all, and from then on looked and became the winner at
9/7. It was a curiously straightforward and undramatic match, there being

only twenty deuces throughout. A pity that in this Centenary year Mark could not quite go one better.

In the top half of the draw three seeds went out in the second round. Brian Gottfried (5), Paris finalist and whom many fancied as a strong challenger for the title, fell in four sets to the talent-come-true of South Africa's Byron Bertram. Byron's father, Max, had been an international player of note and, like Billy Martin, Bertram had won Junior Wimbledon two years running (1969/70). A tremendous but erratic hitter of the ball this was the first time his game had really come together at Wimbledon proper. Adriano Panatta (10), the 1976 Italian and French champion and spearhead of Italy's successful Davis Cup campaign that year, had the misfortune to meet Sandy Mayer (USA) for the first time at Wimbledon. Mayer is a very workmanlike and determined player, with good Wimbledon scalps to his name. Panatta saved the first set in a tie-break, after Mayer had led 5/1. Thereafter the Italian performed with the conviction of a man who thinks he cannot play on grass and only won six more games. He dropped his service eleven times in the course of the match. Tim Gullikson had an excellent win over Raul Ramirez (7) in five sets.

The Centre Court that day matched one of the Greats of the game, Rod Laver, with the No. 9 seed, Dick Stockton. Laver, who was making a Centenary comeback at the age of thirty-eight, had never lost to Stockton in five meetings, but the last of those had been in 1975, since when the Rocket had had little competitive play, whereas Stockton had developed his sound game and had only recently taken Connors to four sets in the WCT Dallas Finals. Laver started reasonably well, with many flashes reminiscent of his Champion days, but the first set fell to him more because Stockton was sluggish and unimpressive – indeed he appeared to be affected by the crowd's obvious desire for Laver to win. When Rod went to a 2/0 lead in the second set it seemed that their wishes would be met, but Stockton pulled back a service break, only to put three half-volleys into the net and one out and drop his own again. Laver led 4/2 but at 30-all he served a double-fault that eventually led to Stockton recovering the break. Games then went with service up to 7-all when Laver was suddenly 0/40. On the second break-point Stockton played a beautiful backhand cross-court lob that just landed in. The American then served out comfortably for the set.

Laver's ascendancy had gone and from then he was always struggling. Although still playing an unconvincing game Stockton, who was not helped by the nagging worry of a stubbornly troublesome back, now knew that he had only to stay in the match for victory to be assured. Laver still produced strokes of brilliant lawn-scape, especially some wondrous punched running forehands, but the old mastery and touch were no longer supremely sure and the finished canvas reflected the fitful gleams of a dying summer storm. In particular his service let him down at vital moments.

When Laver led 3/1 in the third set, two double-faults at 30-all squandered that advantage and a further service loss to love meant the set had gone. In the fourth set service prevailed to 5-all when Rod again double-faulted and lost his service to love. Though faltering with a double for 15/15 Stockton accepted victory gratefully at his first match-point. Laver had slaked some of the crowd's thirst for nostalgia without quenching it. As he left the court to a standing ovation he waved to the watchers, acknowledging it seemed that this really was for the last time.

Three seeds had failed to take root in the second round, and two others had stern struggles for existence. Borg needed five sets to subdue Mark Edmondson, the tough Australian Champion of 1976. Mark, with his brigand's moustache, always looks a battler but much of the struggle is against his own lack of con- viction in himself and his ability to turn advantage into victory. Leading two sets to love – and later 2/1, 4/4, 30/30 on Borg's service – Edmondson could not compound the interest on his capital. Borg only lost one more game. Edmondson said afterwards that he was unfit and ran out of steam – but was it more in the mind than the body?

Wherever Nastase (6) goes controversy is his shadow. Sometimes it is made for him, by the media or by quirking circumstance, but more often it is entirely Nastase-manufactured and stamped with his trademark. His own fitful nature refuses to give his genius fair play. With shrug and open-palmed expostulation he is for ever fretting about something – a linesman's call or silence, an umpire's over-ruling, the dancing cobra heads and whirrings of the cameramen, or just the murmurs and reactions of the crowd. And it seems an unlikely coincidence that these posturings almost always occur when his opponent is doing well. In fact, to coin a word, he is the master of the temptrum – the timely tantrum. On No. 2 Court he was playing Andy Pattison, sandy-haired Pretorian-born Rhodesian, now representing the USA. A solid player with a powerful all-round game, Pattison took the first two sets 9/7, 6/3 and only lost the third 5/7. In the fourth he had a break and led 4/3 when 'Nasty' started a temptrum to end all temptrums. His ill manners riled his opponent, the umpire and the crowd. He sent for the referee just before the umpire did. He held this bear garden of a stage for nearly a quarter of an hour and at the end, instead of a deserved disqualification, he met with surrender, abject on the part of authority, furious on the part of Pattison, who had predictably lost all his concentration and with it the match. Nastase had got away with it again. In the next round, 'banished' to Court 14 where his ardent followers jammed up the sidewalks to a dangerous degree of overspill (even onto the court), Nastase defused the situation by his impeccable behaviour. But then Elliott Teltscher, his American Junior oppo- nent, was probably distracted enough. He was certainly no worry to the No. 6 seed.

Besides Vilas, another seed to fall on the first Friday was Bob Lutz (15). He was beaten by Kim Warwick, who had always threatened to go places but whose lack of inner conviction had kept the threat empty. In Lutz Warwick faced a man who, despite fine doubles talent and deftness of touch, was capable of the same qualms as the Australian. In a five-set see-saw Kim just got the verdict.

From Kim to Tim, the right-handed of the American Gullikson twins, who had taken out Ramirez. Gullikson had been riding high on a crest which started to spume in the French Championships, where he beat Ray Moore and then took Nastase to five sets, and then foamed to the final at Beckenham and to the rained-off final and a shared title at Nottingham, before finally dumping him at Wimbledon – but only 7/9 in the fifth set of his fourth-round match with Dent (13).

While Mark Cox justified his No. 14 seeding and so nearly reached the last eight, another British hope, Buster Mottram, fell in the third round to Poland's Wojtek Fibak (12). In four meetings Mottram had never won, but Wimbledon grass gave his serve–volley game some advantage over the more precise and flexible but less powerful game of the talented Pole. Buster had the Centre Court crowd sensing a good win that would blot out the memory of previous Wimbledon failures when he took the first set 6/3 and led 5/4, 0/40, on Fibak's service in the second. But he could not clinch it, nor later when at 8/8 he led 5/1 in the tie-break. From then on, although Mottram took the fourth set, Fibak always looked the more likely of two diffident winners.

So the fourth round found only nine of the sixteen seeds surviving, and six of them were in the bottom half of the draw. Connors (1) was handicapped by a bad right thumb, which was said to have sustained a hairline fracture on the Tuesday of Queen's (his Wimbledon first-round match had been postponed a day to give him more recovery time). It did not seem to affect his stroke production or cause him pain but he was finding it difficult to get into real form. He struggled in a long second-round four-setter with Marty Riessen and now was given a fight and a real fright by Stan Smith (11), who had himself had a three-hour match with doughty New Zealander, Onny Parun, in the previous round.

Smith this year had fought hard to regain his halcyon Champion's form of 1972. Advised by an expert in calisthenics, between points he was constantly doing little exercises which did indeed seem to loosen the straight jacket of his guardsman's back. And he had altered the aspect ratio of his stance when receiving service. He was more upright and certainly more effective. He was a man who believed again that he could win Wimbledon and his refound conviction nearly carried him through against Connors. He led him 2 sets to 1 and pulled all the battling best out of Jimbo in a match lasting more than three and a half hours.

For a place in the semi-final Connors now had to reckon with Byron Bertram, who after beating the seeded Gottfried had had convincing straight-set wins over Australians Paul Kronk and Kim Warwick. Although, like Connors, twenty-four years old, Bertram had been a much slower developer, whose early potential seemed unlikely to be fulfilled. But he had now got some bite between his teeth and, with only reputation to win, gave Jimbo almost more than he wanted – even on the progressively toughening assault course that a Wimbledon medal demands. Bertram deservedly won the third set and could look back on Centenary Wimbledon with the satisfaction of one who has climbed to a higher rung of the ladder.

In the second quarter the astonishing John McEnroe went steadily marching on, more guts perhaps than soul, as he disposed in turn of El Shafei, Dowdeswell, Meiler and Mayer, dropping only three sets in the process. Many might have thought that enough – especially since it brought him opposite Phil Dent (13), who had already doused the urgent fire of Tim Gullikson. But not McEnroe, who had taken Dent to five sets in the recent French Championships and, nothing daunted when beaten, had captured the Junior title as well as winning the Senior Mixed Doubles.

So battle was joined on No. 1 Court. The big Australian was having a good year, having reached the semi-finals of both the Italian and French Championships, as well as the quarter-finals of the Australian, and at twenty-seven his experience and weight of shot looked to be too much for the young aspirant. But McEnroe is no respecter of reputation. He won the first set 6/4 and had a set point at 7/6 in the second-set tie-break. Here a double-fault, which he bitterly disputed, cost him concentration and the set.

McEnroe now charged the net on every possible – but often improbable – occasion and his errors were legion. Dent won the set and seemed in command of the match, but McEnroe fought his way back inch by pressure inch till suddenly the barometer of the game was 'set fair' for him. At two sets-all Dent, who had double-faulted thirteen times, lost his service for 3/4 – the final point won by McEnroe's flashing cross-court backhand, hit on the run and leaving Dent helpless at the net. At 3/5 Dent saved four match-points with fierce winners but McEnroe served out the next game to 30. The youngster had done it again and had stamped his passport to the tennis Hall of Fame with the clear visa of being both the only qualifier and the youngest player to reach the Men's Singles semi-finals at Wimbledon, having played more matches (9) than anyone before.

In the third quarter Vitas Gerulaitis (8) had played his own brand of Rolls Royce (he owns two) tennis to cruise through three rounds. Let it not be thought that Vitas is sedate. He is not but his game is as urgently smooth as the accelerator of his favourite car. In the fourth round he lost a set to Stockton (9) but he always had the measure of his compatriot, seeded one below him but ranked 7 in the States, two above him. Stockton's back had been plaguing him and he was well below his early season form. Gerulaitis then exerted his senior citizen's status to quell the young bull, Billy Martin, in four sets and so reach the semi-finals for the first time.

The bottom quarter saw Borg, after his escape from Edmondson, making straight-sets progress over Pilic and Fibak to reach the quarter-finals and Nastase. Nastase in the previous round had dropped one set in a beautiful match with Tom Okker. Fleetness of foot, artistry of touch and sheer genius combined in a scintillating display by both. It was as if both players knew that Nastase must win but were determined that it should be a good show – and it was.

So Borg and Nastase met in a replay of their last year's final. Then Nasty had started brilliantly, only to be sent reeling by the stream of winners which flowed from Borg's racket and his spirit had been easily subdued. This time his countenance at the start showed a stern 'niceness' of purpose, but it was soon belied. He served first and lost the game to love. There had been a corrected call and already he was showing signs of irritation and bad court behaviour. Borg was brilliant. He was like a master who knows that the only way to cope with a clever but awkward pupil is to be ahead of him from the start. No matter what Nastase tried, Borg was more than equal to it and took only seventeen minutes to win the set to love, allowing the Rumanian just seven points.

In the second set Borg's super-control lapsed a little and he became almost human. The rallies were good, with Nastase making many a superb shot and bringing off coups that only his genius could contrive. But, although there was little in it, the really important points were being won by Borg. Nastase had break-points against him in his first two service games, but survived them. He then broke Borg's service and led 4/1 on his own. Borg countered with a run of three games and they played level up to 6-all, when Nastase played a poor game to drop service and Borg, saving two break-back points, served out for the set.

From the start of the match there had been ruffled wavelets on the sea of Nastase's temperament and now suddenly it was blowing a gale and his good ship tennis was heading straight for the rocks. At 1/0 to Nastase and Borg serving, the Swede won a point that Nasty thought was lucky. Nastase then hit a ball with tremendous force straight at Borg. When Borg queried why, Nastase swore at him and was immediately reprimanded by the umpire. On the very next point there was a correction to a service call that went in Borg's favour. Nastase made an exaggerated scene and started a running campaign against the umpire – a campaign that became not only insulting but almost obscene. The umpire gave him a warning for swearing and stalling. After the normal time-wasting and repeated shows of resentment by the Rumanian the third set and match went to Borg, who kept his composure remarkably well, at 6/3.

Afterwards Nastase abused the umpire and claimed that he had been totally biased and looking for trouble. Possibly the umpire's authority was fully cocked and primed from the start, but little wonder in the light of the disputes and temptrums that Nastase had perpetrated earlier in the Championships. So once again this genius of the courts had wrecked his Wimbledon chances – this time quite evidently on the shoals of his temperament. It was clear that at thirty-one the door of opportunity was almost closed to him.

The semi-finals on the second Thursday before a capacity crowd were to go down in Wimbledon annals, the first because of left-handed John McEnroe, the boy who was making history, the second because it was the finest match for sustained brilliance anybody could remember seeing, and almost certainly the finest ever played in the hundred years of Wimbledon. It was as well they took place in that order – or there could have been a terrible anti-climax.

Connors, as he had been throughout the Championships, was struggling to find real form. McEnroe, wearing a head-band very like Borg's – but presumably so far for comfort only – with his dark appearance seemed like young Hiawatha,

> 'and his heart was hot within him,
> Like a living coal his heart was.'

But his great Wimbledon adventure (it could have come straight out of a pre-war *Boy's Own Paper*) had reached the point of no return. Connors knew it, the crowd knew it and one sensed that the boy knew it deep down in his gut feel but, such is the determination of this champion-to-be, his conscious self never admitted it for one moment.

It was McEnroe's first time ever on the Centre Court (and he was the youngest semi-finalist). What a burden to take out into the world's most important tennis arena against a player like Connors. Yet he adjusted so well to the wide open spaces of the court, which have baffled many fine players at their first appearance, that he looked a familiar in accustomed surroundings – a shade of things to come. The first few games were evenly, if rather ineptly, played. Then Connors managed to put together a dribble of good service returns and, helped by two double-faults by McEnroe, broke the boy's service for the first time. The dribble became a minor spate and soon Connors had won five games in a row for the set at 6/3 and 1/0 in the second. Games then went easily with serve till Connors, leading 3/2, broke McEnroe again at his fifth break-point. This game, for which McEnroe fought fiercely, weighed heavily in the scale of the outcome. It turned the lock of the second set and a two-set deficit was asking a lot – even of McEnroe's skill and courage.

But he still showed both in forcing a ragged Connors to a fourth set. The third set was a see-saw affair, governed by seven service losses and McEnroe, leading 5/4, took it with three superb backhand passing shots, one across court and two down the line. His backhand is reminiscent of Laver, played with upright stance, the shoulder rising into the stroke. It is a sparkling shot but as yet inconsistent. In the fourth set Connors led 2/0 but McEnroe broke back for 2/3 and the crowd's backing was urgent for him. But Connors regained his stride and, breaking service again for 4/3, took the set and the match 6/4.

Vitas Gerulaitis has yet to beat Borg, but in the semifinal, the finest match at Wimbledon that anyone could remember, it was touch and go.

The new young hero, 17-year-old qualifier John McEnroe. 'And his heart was hot within him.'

So ended McEnroe's first Wimbledon Crusade. He was the No. 1 seed for the Boy's Singles but his Open exploits had denied him the chance of that title. There seemed little doubt that, even if he were not to succeed in his second or third crusade, it could not be long before the inner keep fell to him.

If the Connors–McEnroe match had been disappointing in its uneven quality, what followed was literally 'out of this world' – in the realms of a tennis paradise – and all at the courtside were transported there. It was a match that was difficult to describe in retrospect because its very brilliance had a mesmeric effect, so that the watcher felt suspended in an unbelieving animation of sheer delight at the magic being continually wrought before his eyes.

These two young gods of the game look curiously alike. Both have long fair hair, Borg's held in place by his well-known headband, Gerulaitis's styled and fashioned to frame his face and give it the swept-back look of an eager hound. Both are tall and long-legged, their build similar but for Borg's broader shoulders. Both Adonis-like of aspect, easy to hero-worship. Both are fair to look at – and both play fairly. They like to get on with it. They know each other's game as if it were their own, for all their pre-Wimbledon practice was against each other.

From the first stroke the ball shuttled at lightning speed between their rackets, weaving wonderful and intricate patterns of shimmering brilliance. Perfect counter followed perfect stroke at mach speeds. Their footwork, positioning and poise were breathtaking. Their anticipation was so good that it seemed as if every coup de main was countered by its own radar reflection.

And it went on and on. A superlative top-speed display that was supernatural. Excellence was pulled out to its thinnest elasticity and yet it held. There was no let-up, no breathing spell, no time to stand and stare at their own Olympian arrogance – and lose it. They were playing so well, their concentration was so intense, they were so evidently enjoying it that fatigue never lit upon them. They were as fast and accurate at the end as they had been all the way through.

The crowd sat enthralled, scarce daring to breathe in case the spell were broken. They did not care who won but they did not want either to lose. They were just utterly content to be part of the most marvellous display of lawn tennis *un*imaginable. It was the aurora borealis of a hundred years of Wimbledon. Two shining knights had jousted to the limits of their powers and in doing so had become blood brothers. When finally, after three hours and three minutes of sustained magic, Gerulaitis *missed* a smash he was suddenly match-point down. Realisation hit him and he *fluffed* a forehand volley. The greatest match of a century was over.

In the aftermath of that match scores do not matter. The scales were so evenly balanced that only one or two points in a set were really significant. Gerulaitis lost his opening service game and that profit was enough to give Borg the first set. Similarly Borg yielded his third service game of the second and Gerulaitis was soon home. A double-fault gave away Gerulaitis's first service game of the third set but he broke back easily. The fourth game had eight deuces and five break-points to Borg before Gerulaitis squared at 2/2, but at 3/4 he dropped service again and Borg had the set 6/3. In the fourth Borg returned the compliment with a double-fault at break-point in his second service game. That was enough. Two sets all.

In the final set at 2/2 Borg looked dispirited and immediately dropped his service to love. It seemed for the moment as if the crack had come. But, like Rosewall, the Swede is never so dangerous as when he looks down. Gerulaitis had his chance when he served at 40/30. He did not follow to the net and Borg survived, breaking back for 3/3. Games then went with service until Borg led 7/6 and Gerulaitis came to that air-smash. The rest were better silence.

And so to the seeded Final – Connors v. Borg. They are total opponents – both double-fisted on their backhand but Connors left-handed, Borg right-handed. Connors the brash 1974 Champion, Borg the quiet and popular title-holder. Connors, the winner of WCT in Dallas (the previous two WCT Champions, Ashe and Borg, had won Wimbledon in the same years) and conqueror of Borg in the 1975 semi-final and the 1976 final of the US Championships. Indeed, Borg had only won two out of their nine encounters but, significantly, he had won their first and their last – *and they had never met on Wimbledon grass*.

Everyone knew that Jimmy Connors would produce better form for the Final than he had managed in previous rounds. He had to if he was to live with the speed and skill of the Swede. There was only one question-mark above Borg's head. Had he burned himself out in his historic semi-final with Gerulaitis? He soon showed that he had not, though he admitted after the Final that he had never felt so tired on a tennis court.

The match started with Connors in better control of his shots than at any time in the tournament. Despite this, it was Borg who could have broken first when he had three game-points on Connors' second service game. This crisis averted, Jimmy, profiting by a double-fault and some poor, short driving by Borg, broke the Swede for 5/3 and served out to 15 for the first set. So far it had been mainly a baseline clay court-type duel as the players felt each other out.

Borg was looking depressed and aware that his length had deserted him. He puts so much top-spin on the ball, particularly on the forehand, that he is able to hit it tremendously hard and yet normally ensure good length. The head of the racket comes up so steeply across the ball that it seems incredible that he does not mishit and send it skeetering miles out of court. His control is phenomenal and it gives him the ability to delay his stroke until his opponent is committed.

But he had temporarily lost that control. Connors was gaining confidence and had begun the familiar cocky march up and down the baseline. He started coming in more and was soon going for his favourite lunging coups at the net. At 1/1, Borg was quickly down 15/40 and altogether, in a game of five deuces, he had to save four break-points. Had Connors broken then, with a set already to his credit, he could well have taken charge of the match. As it was, Borg suddenly seemed to find again the tactics he had started the match with but had soon mislaid, the by now classic approach to beating Connors, first fully formulated by Arthur Ashe in 1975. He began varying his shots more, in length, speed, height and manner of hitting. In this he could not match the wide spectrum ranged by Ashe in that famous match but his ability, so to speak, to open or close the throttle of his top-spin had much the same effect. At 2-all Borg fell to 0/30 when Connors played a hurricane cross-court forehand that passed him at spatial speed, but that was the nadir of Bjorn's fortunes. He fought well to hold that game, which started a winning run of eight and altogether ten out of eleven games, giving him the second and third sets 6/2, 6/1.

Connors had been in a slump and, fighter that he is, he worked his way back into the match while Borg reacted and slackened his grip. Connors broke first for 4/2 but at once dropped his own when Borg 'softly, softly' caught his monkey. At 4/4 Borg, with two break-points, had a marvellous chance to clinch the match but instead at 5/6 committed only his third double-fault to be 0/40. Connors nailed him with a perfect lob and the match was square. Suddenly the scene had changed and it seemed as if Borg's great efforts in beating Gerulaitis, followed by two and a half hours of tilting with Connors, had run his mental and physical batteries completely down. The Swede looked bowed and spent.

Like a boxer, whose head is ringing from a well-timed punch, Borg drew on unknown depths of courage and stamina and started a charge. He captured Connors' service to 15 and at 40/30 on his own played the shot of the Centenary. It was a forehand passing shot down the line, hit on the low rising ball (almost a half-volley), and it flashed down the line with the accuracy of an arcing tracer bullet. Because he hit it so near the ground and with the head of the racket nearly vertical, it was quite different to his usual awkward-looking top-spin. It was an unforgettable stroke, as if played from the edge of a table-tennis table.

Borg's run continued to 4/0 and on Connors' next service, the longest game of the final set, Borg had two break-points. His position seemed impregnable, but gritty Connors, forced like a losing duellist to the brink of an abyss, fought his way back inch by fierce inch until in turn he had his opponent going backwards and had reached four games all. Now the impetus was with the Challenger and the Champion looked sore pressed. But, as so often happens after a player has made a major effort to wipe out a large deficit, there is overdraft interest to be paid in the form of slight relaxation – the feeling of safe harbour in sight. Connors reached 15/0 and then double-faulted for only the second time in the match. Burning the last drops of his inspiration and stamina, Borg played a good forehand stop-volley and forced two errors from Connors to lead 5/4. Serving for the title, he hit a good smash, forced Connors to net,

Bjorn Borg wins the centenary title after two five-setters – a fantastic match of the highest quality with Gerulaitis, and a death-struggle with Jimmy Connors (*below*).

served a cracker of a near ace and at match-point played a fine passing shot which Connors, desperately diving to cover, could only ricochet into the stands.

Where the Borg–Gerulaitis match had been the most finely poised perfection throughout its length, the Borg–Connors final had seen the scales rising and falling convulsively as the desperate gamblers lost their stakes and then threw more chips into play to convert into winnings. The one had been resplendent, the other was one of the best finals ever, scene upon scene full of high tension, the players two of the most dramatic performers the Wimbledon stage has known.

The Men's Doubles had more than its quota of upsets and heroic perform-ances. The Champions and No. 1 seeds, Gottfried and Ramirez, reacted to their Singles defeats and went out in the first round to the scratch pair of Delaney and Menon. The No. 8 pair, Charlie Pasarell and Eric van Dillen, were also tame first-round casualties in three sets to the Australians, Syd Ball and Kim Warwick. The Lutine bell must have tolled when Britain's Davis Cup heroes of 1976, the Lloyds, went down in the second round to the No. 2 seeds, Hewitt and McMillan, winning only nine games. But the old maestri met their match in the new, Ross Case and Geoff Masters, the 1976 Finalists but only seeded 7. Their quarter-final was a blazing scrap that more than held the Centre Court gallery – even after the excitement of the Women's semi-finals.

Hewitt, broody general of four Wimbledon titles (two with Stolle for Aus-tralia, two with McMillan for South Africa), had cast his strong influence over the World doubles scene for more than fifteen years and his partnership with Frew McMillan, whose widely-angled, punched two-handed volleys are potent tactical weapons, was always more feared than any. Having won the Australian title in 1974, Case and Masters really thrust themselves into world reckoning in 1976 when, after being runners-up for the Australian title, they took Gottfried and Ramirez to 7/5 in the fifth set of the Wimbledon Final. Since then their understanding had deepened, so that both pairs had that instinctive intuition and inspiration that calls the tune in the close rat-a-tat-tat of modern doubles – rather like expert high-speed morse senders and receivers who can read each other's signatures.

With deference to the eventual runners-up, Alexander and Dent, this match should have been the Final. It was desperately close all the way, the old Champions forcing their way back from two sets down and saving ten match-points before the gloaming called a wicked halt at 6/6 in the final set. Next day, transferred to No. 1 Court, it was a tame ending. Hewitt dropped his service with a bad volley and Case and Masters emerged from a long tunnel 6/2, 9/8, 5/7, 7/9, 8/6.

Case and Masters then stamped hard on the unseeded scratch pair of Cox and Drysdale, who could muster only seven games. This was the more surprising since the latter had also survived a five-set quarter-final when they beat the

No. 6 seeds, Riessen and Tanner. But the Anglo–South African combination was not firing well, especially the elegant Springbok who was at his most lackadaisical.

In the top half Delaney and Menon, the first-round giant-killers, had succumbed in straight sets to Amaya and Hagey, who in turn went down to another pair of mixed nationality in Australian 'Nails' Carmichael and American Brian Teacher. These two then won comfortably against Fibak and Stockton (5) to reach the semi-finals opposite another unseeded pair, Alexander and Dent, big men in a forceful partnership that was carrying all before them, including Lutz and Smith (3) in the third round.

Even when lacking top-flight singles players, Australia is seldom at a loss to provide good doubles teams, as the semi-finals showed. The all-Australians, Alexander and Dent, just beat the mixed pair of Carmichael and Teacher and so qualified to meet Case and Masters in the twelfth all-Australian Final since the war. This also went all the way, the seeded pair having match-points in the fourth set and getting home 6/3 in the fifth. This was the twentieth all-Australian title in the thirty-two championships since the war.

Though Margaret Court, Evonne Goolagong (recovering from having her baby) and Dianne Fromholtz (laid low by an allergy) were missing and few looked beyond Evert as the winner, the challenge for the Women's title brought into conflict most of the established names and some exciting new prospects. The first one and a half rounds (the first has 32 byes) provided interest enough. The Champion, Chris Evert (1), was in merciless form against newcomer Ruta Gerulaitis, sister of Vitas, as she issued a clear declaration that she intended to keep her status. In the next round Britain's Winnie Wooldridge found her in the same formidable mood. When Chrissie is playing like this her opponents are entitled to look on the games they win as campaign medals.

Anne Smith, third-ranking American Junior and new Junior Champion of France, made an impressive Wimbledon début when she beat the hard-hitting Swede, Mimi Wikstedt, and then took the first set 8/6 against Billie Jean King (5). Marise Kruger, 18-year-old South African, proved that it was no bubble reputation she was blowing when she nearly beat Virginia Wade in 1976, putting paid in the third round to the No. 10 seed, Mima Jausovec of Yugoslavia, and taking the first set off Mrs King in the fourth. Helga Masthoff, the elegant ex-Champion of Germany, needed all her experience to contain Uruguay's 16-year-old Fiorella Bonicelli, whose name seemed rather to echo the sweet notes of Italy's Dante Alighieri.

If the Men's event had seen an unexpected foray into the semi-finals by an American junior, John McEnroe, the Women's included the arrival of American starlet Tracy Austin, who at fourteen and a half became the youngest competitor at Wimbledon since two Austrian sisters, Mita and Willy Klima, aged thirteen and fourteen, were easily beaten in the 1907 first round. The media had heralded her arrival with such a fanfare that she might well have been crushed by the weight of realisation. That she was not was a sign that she too had Toledo temperament to go with her remarkably mature strokes and tactical game.

She had a bye in the first round and in the second, on Court 7, disposed comfortably of Elly Vessies-Appel of the Netherlands. With her two-handed backhand her game looked very similar to that of the Champion, whom she now met. There was something bizarre about this Centre Court confrontation, for Chrissie could well have felt that she was playing against her younger self. There was the same meticulous length and application, the same pattern play until an opponent was worked out of position, and the same kind of coup de grâce – quietly and efficiently executed. The only difference was that Tracy possibly hit the ball harder. The sense of unreality was heightened by Tracy's dress, which had been very cleverly designed, with a big bow at the back, to have a pinafore effect and to make her look astonishingly like Tenniel's Alice, who was contemporary with the earliest graftings of the game. But there the likeness ceased, for this girl had a brace on her teeth and the tennis bit between them.

Chrissie Evert beat her 6/1, 6/1 but the score sins against the game, which was played on level terms except in one regard. The young girl's still coltish legs could not carry her as fast as her already mature tennis brain urged. She was thwarted by her own stage of physical development. This was especially evident whenever Chrissie drop-shotted her, for it made her look pathetically helpless and the Champion almost sadistic. Chrissie Evert used this telling weapon as sparingly as possible and only when her authority seemed momentarily in doubt. Despite this handicap the youngster sustained long rallies and brought off many fine coups. She fought hard, brought near the best out of the Champion and gave exceptional promise for the future. It was an astonishing début – not less because this historic match was the first meeting between two players whose names will surely shine for all time in the annals of the game. Indeed, Chrissie may have reflected ruefully what hard labour a match against Tracy Austin would be in even one year's time.

In 1976 Maria Bueno, that very gifted Champion, had made a fine and welcome return to the Wimbledon scene after an eight-year absence caused mainly by recurring illness and injury. She had gone out in three sets in the fourth round to the youth and free-hitting game of Sue Barker. It was good to see her back again in Centenary year giving, like Laver, many glimpses of her former imperious majesty. This time, having survived a close call with Janet Newberry, she was beaten in the third round by her old foe, Billie Jean King, in a match that revived many memories; and, as they left the Centre Court to a big ovation, it seemed, as with Laver, that for Maria it was for the last time.

As far as the quarter-finals the Women's seeding worked out impeccably. In the bottom half there was nary a scare, but the top half saw a few anxious moments. Chrissie Evert, who had only allowed Greer Stevens one game in

Ross Case and Geoff Masters home and dry.

The youngest yet: Austrian Mita Klima, who played in 1907, aged thirteen.

Tracy Austin, the youngest at New Wimbledon, in play against Chris Evert.

each of two previous encounters, found herself 5/1 down in the first set to a charging young South African lioness, who actually had two set-points; but little Miss Icicle, as the Champion used to be called, kept her cool and won 8/6, 6/4.

However, the South African under-21 brigade had shown no little mettle for, besides this gallant fight by Greer, Marise Kruger we have already seen took the first set from Billie Jean King, and neat little Linky Boshoff disposed of two Australians in straight sets before giving the same treatment to Frankie Durr (11). Now Linky took on Rosie Casals (6), whom she led 2/1 on previous meetings. But Rosie's success had been in the 1975 Wimbledon, whose grass suits her serve–volley game more than the good-length driving of Linky's baseline armoury. Rosie won again this time, but only after a good fight – 8/6, 6/3.

Virginia Wade (3) had beaten in straight sets successively Jo Durie, Betsy Nagelsen and Yvonne Vermaak – another of the young South Africans who could look back on a successful Wimbledon sally, in which she lost to the eventual Champion before winning the Plate. Now Virginia found she had to work hard to beat Bjorn Borg's fiancée, Rumania's Mariana Simionescu, 9/7, 6/3. But there was a new look about the British No. 1, both in her game and in her appearance. Her tennis seemed more purposeful and her short bushy hairstyle gave her a different outward personality. She had looked good – but then she so often did – in the first week.

The easiest quarter-finals were then played by the British hopes, Wade and Barker. Although only 9/10 down to Rosie Casals in a career count of their meetings, Virginia had lost to her in their three encounters of the current year. But when her big game is going right, as this Wimbledon it was, grass suits its power even more than it suits Rosie's. Having led 3/0 Wade was pulled back to 4-all and 0/40. The old Virginia might have 'blown', but the new coolly fought her way out by skilful use of lob and passing shot against the net pressure of Casals. She still had to fight off break-points before taking Rosie's service to love for the set at 7/5. In the second set at 2/0 she slipped to 2-all but then cruised ever more powerfully into her second semi-final. Rosie Casals, who on her advent at Wimbledon in 1966 had looked a potential winner, had been in four semi-finals between 1967 and 1972. But little Rosie had never quite been able to make it – perhaps mainly because of her size. In a game that depends almost entirely on serve and volley, reach is at a greater premium.

Sue Barker (4) and Kerry Reid (8) had somewhat similar games and records – the difference being mainly age and experience – nearly nine years. Sue, the French and German Champion in the depleted year of 1976 and three sets runner-up to Chrissie Evert in the 1977 Virginia Slims Final, had developed steadily in the last year, the main improvement being in her backhand, which could now be confidently hit through. It was not the devastating winner that her forehand could be, but it gave no comfort to an opponent fondly thinking that she was playing to the weaker side. Kerry's forehand had been widely known for years – as well as her all-round driving ability. Both girls preferred the back-court to the net, but neither looked helpless there. Neither had a great service but Reid's was as yet the better.

Had she needed it Sue had the mental backing of a 4/1 record against the Australian, current holder of her own open title; but, after a jerky start that found the server the loser for five games, Barker's forehand began to hit the lines and the rest of her game was running comfortably. It was pleasant to watch these two delightful girls exchanging their drives in long rallies till the kill or the soft death came. Sue finished with a deserved win 6/3, 6/4.

The top match by far provided an unforgettable exhibition by Chris Evert, who was playing the old Queen of the Courts, Billie Jean King. Billie Jean, after yet another knee operation at the end of 1976, had not spared herself to get back to physical shape. She had literally put herself on the rack of phy-siotherapy, and there was no question of her bodily fitness. But at thirty-three, and with little competitive play behind her, could she be match-fit to meet a champion like Evert and give her eleven years? Evert led 9/7 in previous meetings but at Wimbledon there is always the x-factor of the World's premier title being at stake and in 1975, her last Champion year, Billie Jean had won a memorable victory over Chrissie.

The simple score of 6/1, 6/2 to Evert perjures the game, which was a classic and much, much more finely poised. Evert had never played better. Her generalship was supreme, her tactical game uncanny and her use of the passing shot and lob – especially the lob – was devastating. But how bravely King fought with every skill at her command. Perhaps her interceptions at the net were not quite as incisive as they used to be nor her volleying quite as categorical; but she was trying to stem a tide of inspiration that was running strongly for Chrissie.

At 0/4 down, Evert serving, King played a desperately brave game and was oh so unlucky. Evert put a forehand lob out, 0/15; King netted a backhand, 15/15. Then followed a superb rally that drew gasp after gasp from the crowd and ended with King playing a marvellous backhand cross-court smash from behind her shoulder; it landed plumb on the sideline, 15/30. King *just* failed to clear the net with a cross-court forehand passing shot, 30/30. King again *just* failed to clear the net with a peach of a forehand drop-shot across court, 40/30. King then *just* failed with a backhand return of serve down the line.

So much, like that game, was touch and go. But the margins for Billie Jean were being forced finer and finer by the sheer excellence of Chrissie's play, and inevitably the old Champion found it more and more difficult to withstand the pressure. She was having to try too hard and the demands of super-accuracy, to combat the brilliance of Evert, were too great. It was a much closer-run thing than perhaps most appreciated – one of the great matches of these superlative Centenary Championships. Chrissie Evert had played the game of her life and Billie Jean had forced her to it.

So far the correct seeds had won through to the semi-finals. Not so in the match between Betty Stove (7) and Martina Navratilova (2). Before the Championships started many thought that Martina, the brilliant young left-hander from Czechoslovakia, who had moved to America, was the only player with a real chance of beating Chrissie Evert. She had lost her tennis way for a while and had put on a lot of weight, but in the past year had made a determined and largely successful effort to get back to peak form and fitness. Both she and Betty Stove, the big-hitting, well-built Dutch girl, had comfortable passages to the quarter-finals. Betty's game was as fitful and erratic as usual, big winners booming in and unaccountable losers zooming out – or into the net. Martina was playing badly or she must have won. The first set went to a tie-break, in which Martina led 6–2, but the four set-points eluded her and Betty had a run of six to win the set. The second and third sets followed similar courses of ineptitude, lightened by moments of brilliance, and in the end Betty Stove took the match 9/8, 3/6, 6/1; but she cannot so much be said to have won it as Martina to have lost it. At least Betty Stove, hitherto much better known for her doubles results, was the first Dutch player to reach a Wimbledon Singles semi-final.

The semi-finals were uneven in quality. The first between the Champion and Virginia Wade was another historic match, Chrissie Evert not quite at her best but Virginia giving the most amazingly controlled performance of her career. Evert had an overwhelming lead of 22/5 but two of Wade's wins had been in the last eight months. After Chrissie's marvellous display in her quarter-final many thought that she might suffer a reaction. She did and was certainly not at her best, but nor can she have reckoned with a totally new Virginia Wade, one who could not only play the big game but was playing it to such a consistent, controlled length and was actually *rallying* with her. Chrissie must have been dumbfounded, for nobody by choice rallies with her. It is the slowest way to tennis suicide. You may prolong the rallies but you will almost certainly lose them.

Not so. Virginia's length was the better and soon Chrissie was making the mistakes. After a marathon third game (Evert had six break-points) to hold her service, Wade led 4/0, dropped her service for 4/1, took Evert's for 5/2, dropped her own again but once more captured the Champion's (the last point being a double-fault) for the set at 6/2. It had been a curious set, Virginia holding her own service twice, all the other six games going against service. The balance shifted in the second set, a slight relaxation by Virginia combining with intensified effort by Chrissie. In the opening game at 30/40 Wade saved the break-point with a smash to the forehand but could not deny the next at 'advantage Miss Evert'. She fought hard to break back and had an advantage, whereat Evert got a net-cord and Wade, disturbed in her stroke, put a forehand out down the line to lose that chance. The rallies were now longer and the standard even higher, since Chrissie was beginning to match Virginia's impeccable length

Virginia Wade in full cry for her title.

with her own. Significantly she was managing in her normal way to win the really important points. A dropped service game by each left Chrissie still ahead and she ran out the set at 6/4.

Had the Champion turned the corner? Before 1977 she probably would have done, but Virginia had in the early part of the year appealed in despair to Jerry Teeguarden (father of Pam), the coach who had done so much for Margaret Court – especially in helping her to find the right mental approach. Teeguarden had wrought a marvellous miracle and it was a new Virginia that we were watching. Composed, refusing to be pressured back to her old confused fears.

The opening game of the final set was vital. Recovering from 0/30, Wade double-faulted to give Evert advantage and break-point. The next service was twice a let. Many a player would then have served another double. Virginia served an ace, clean down the centre. That crisis overcome, she swept majestically through the set in two three-game sequences, Chrissie winning one service to be 1/3. There were no more break-points to fight off, there was never a qualm – the final score 6/2, 4/6, 6/1. It was Virginia Wade's most famous Wimbledon victory and now who would gainsay her real chance at last – at her sixteenth attempt – to grasp the glittering crown? Only perhaps Sue Barker, who had already beaten her two or three times.

But in the second semi-final, to which honour both Barker and Stove were new, things did not go according to plan. It was almost a repeat performance of their 1975 third-round match on No. 2 court, when an abusive wind had torn the players' patience – particularly Sue's – to shreds and their match had been a neurotically tattered canvas. There was no wind this day – except perhaps the capricious and impish breezes that seem to criss-cross the Centre Court – but poor Sue could not get going and Betty was not much better. Stove is difficult to play against, for there is little pattern to her performance. At one moment she is hitting great shots of superior weight, the next making footling mistakes. Sue's forehand could not feed on the slices Betty offered her.

The first set went to the Dutch girl 6/4 and she led 2/1 in the second. Sue predictably fought back with the desperation of the damned and won six games in a row to make it set-all and 1/0 in the final set, having captured Betty's service. Now, surely, she could sail on to victory. But no. In turn Stove fought back to lead 5/2. Desperation pumped adrenalin again and Barker at 3/5 fought and fought to break back. All honour to her, at her fourth break-point she did, having saved a match-point into the bargain. In the next game she was 30/40, match-point down, but Betty Stove netted her forehand volley. A short reprieve, for Sue condemned herself by double-faulting to give Betty her third match-point. This was converted and a Dutch player reached a Wimbledon Singles Final for the first time.

The 1977 Ladies' Final had all the prospects of being a fitting first climax to Centenary Wimbledon. The Queen was coming to mark her Jubilee. The favourite for the title was a British girl, whom the public had for so long supported, so long believed in, but who, until this year, had never seemed to be able to believe sufficiently in herself, in front of that public at the home of Lawn Tennis. On that Friday, 1 July, Virginia Wade was 31 years and 356 days old, Betty Stove was 32 years and 7 days old. Only separated by sixteen days they were the oldest pair to contest a Singles Final since 1913 and, whoever won, she would be the oldest first-time woman winner since 1912. There was, too, coincidence enough for a believer to wallow in. Both finalists came from nations with great seafaring traditions, nations which had once held sway over vast empires, and were now ruled by beloved Queens. To cap it all, Virginia has the same birthday as Arthur Ashe. When he won for the first time in 1975 against the odds he was the same age as Virginia if she won this day.

There were three main reasons why it was not a good match. First, like Chrissie Evert who had reacted slightly after her great win over Billie Jean King, Virginia suffered reaction from her amazing performance against Chrissie. Then, as we have already seen, Betty Stove's type of game makes it very difficult for good rallies to evolve. Finally, the pressure of the *occasion* – both were first-time Finalists – was so great that even Virginia's new-found belief and resolution faltered briefly. She said afterwards that she had been day-dreaming of the scenes when she would win, have her trophy presented by the Queen, hold it aloft and be out on the Centre Court again in the first women's match next year. As she played these dreams kept straying back and her greatest difficulty was to shut her mind to them. Inner conviction, like Arthur Ashe in 1975, told her that it was her year and that nobody was strong enough to deny her, but that knowledge still had to be brought to fruition.

Inept and inconsistent play by both caused crisis after crisis as the balance of the first set swayed. There were good shots to be seen – they mostly came from Betty Stove. There were plenty of bad ones and they, too, came in the main from Betty's racket. Her power, generated by a stalwart Dutch frame and magical timing, was prodigious. It did so much for her and undid her so much. But it was enough to give her the edge in a 6/4 first set over the incoming tide of Virginia's old temperament.

Virginia, her dream now in acute danger, began the second set more positively, making fewer mistakes and serving better. Having won her first service to 15, she clinched Betty's at her second break-point, forcing a forehand volley error with her own forehand cross-court, and then held her own serve to 15 again. The crowd, which had become rather silent, relaxed and became noisier in her support. But now the Dutch girl had a run of three games and, at one set up and 3-all, things began to look ominous for British hopes. Wade responded to the crisis and won the next three games for the loss of only two points.

Virginia continued her winning sequence to 4/0 in the final set and she and the crowd were gathering confidence all the way. They were getting more and more vociferous and even applauding Stovian double-faults. It was very nearly 5/0 but at 0/40 down Betty Stove found desperate inspiration to play again like the winner she had once looked and save the game from the fire. It was only a temporary setback for Virginia Wade, whose dream was now so near reality. She won her service to love and soon had Betty Stove 15/40. One match-point was saved but on the second Virginia's forehand return of service was much too good. Britain had a Queen at Wimbledon again.

In the second that victory became fact all the Centre Court spectators rose as if jerked by the same pull on a puppet string. Hands went up in unison and beat together in crackling thunder, like migrating birds tuned to their leader's instinct, taking off hurriedly from dense treetops. The spontaneous combustion of this ovation was stupendous. Certainly not since the war had there been scenes at Wimbledon like it – not even when Drobny beat Rosewall or Ashe beat Connors. The crowd went wild. Before the match they had sung the National Anthem. Now, as the Queen stepped out onto the court for the presentation, they broke wholeheartedly into 'For she's a jolly good fellow', ending with a great cheer and embracing equally, one felt, Her Majesty and Virginia Wade. It seemed appropriate for both so well deserved it, the one for her unswerving loyalty and sense of duty so magnificently maintained for a quarter of a century, the other for her unswerving determination to achieve the highest goal and prove all the critics – including probably herself – *wrong*.

Amid all the jubilation Prince Philip did not forbear to rescue Betty Stove from a modest and self-imposed effacement. What a delightful girl the President of the Women's Tennis Association is and how sportingly she took defeat and the not unpleasant jingoism of the crowd. Indeed, much as Betty Stove wanted and strove to win, in her subconscious mind she may have felt that on the day her fate was inevitable and that in truth it were better that way, or *she* might stand convicted of lèse-Majesté!

On the final Saturday, after Borg's great triumph, the crowd paid the interest they owed Betty Stove in their desire for her to win at least one of her other two Finals, but it was not to be. In the Women's Doubles Betty and Martina Navratilova were the No. 1 seeds. They had adventures on their way to the Final, just winning a long three-set match against the veteran but still shrewd tactician, Ann Jones, partnered by Winnie Wooldridge; and dropping the opening set in their semi-final against Frankie Durr and Virginia Wade (4). Through to the Final against them were Mrs R. L. Cawley (Helen Gourlay, not Evonne Goolagong) and Joanne Russell, who had reached there by dint of a straight-sets third-round win over the No. 2 seeds, Rosie Casals and Chrissie Evert; then beating Jackie Fayter and Regina Marsikova, second-round conquerors of the 1961 and 1962 champions, Billie Jean King and Karen Susman (8); and in the semi-final downing that excellent British pair, Leslie Charles and Sue Mappin (7). Helen Cawley and Joanne Russell proved that theirs was no fluke partnership when they outplayed Navratilova and Stove to the tune of 6/3, 6/3 and so became the fifth unseeded pair to win the event.

The same claim could be made by Bob Hewitt and Greer Stevens, who put

Virginia's dream comes true against Betty Stove.

Rule Virginia, Virginia Rules OK.
Queen Elizabeth II watches Virginia in the by now traditional press photograph, with Club Chairman Air Chief Marshal Sir Brian Burnett, Club President the Duke of Kent, LTA President Sir Carl Aarvold and Club Secretary Major David Mills.

out two seeded pairs on their way to the Mixed Doubles Final, Marty Riessen and Frankie Durr (3) in the third round and Phil Dent and Billie Jean King (2) in the semis. In the top half the No. 1 seeds, Frew McMillan and Betty Stove, had to fight to reach the Final and never more than in their semi-final against Dennis Ralston and Martina Navratilova (4), who took them to 5/7, 6/4, 12/10. Perhaps that Friday fight coming hard on the heels of the emotion of the Women's Final, followed by Saturday's Women's Doubles Final, proved too much for even the gallant Betty Stove. It could well have made the difference in a three-set Final that went to Hewitt and Stevens 3/6, 7/5, 6/4.

So Betty Stove, who got so near to the triple crown, came away without a title – as did Billie Jean King, who was therefore still joint record holder with Elizabeth Ryan at nineteen Wimbledon titles each. The odds against Billie Jean making it twenty were lengthening but the lure was still bright.

It was a year of records. The total attendance fell only 2000 short but the record for a day was broken on Wednesday 22 June with 37,389. John McEnroe made a glorious entry onto the Wimbledon stage by fighting his way through a record nine matches (four in the Qualifying Competition) to become the only qualifier and the youngest man ever to reach the semi-finals. At just over fourteen and a half Tracy Austin became the youngest competitor ever to appear at New Wimbledon. For the first time the top seeds were beaten in every event. Wimbledon had its first pair of European Champions since 1934.

At just twenty-one Borg was the youngest man to win the title two years running since Wilfred Baddeley in 1891/2. (In 1891 there were only twenty-two entries in the All Comers and in 1892 Baddeley, as Champion, only had to play the Challenge Round.) Betty Stove was the first Dutch player to reach a singles Final. Virginia Wade was the second-oldest woman first-time winner. She and Betty fought out the first over-thirty Final since 1913.

The Centenary Championships were undoubtedly the greatest. More world-wide attention was focussed on them than on any other. The Borg/Gerulaitis semi-final was the finest match for sustained quality ever played at Wimbledon. The Evert/King and Evert/Wade matches were two of the best Women's singles ever seen. The Borg/Connors Final, with all its up and down of quality, was a superbly fought duel, one of the best Finals in memory. Throughout the Championships, from the nostalgia and history of Day 1 to the last rites of Day 12, the organisation and pageantry were superb. From July 1877 to July 1977 Wimbledon had marched a very long way. It has always been the colour-bearer of the game that Britain gave the world, and these Championships underlined why Wimbledon has always been and ever more firmly remains the premier title.

In Jubilee and Centenary year what a fitting dish to set before a Queen.

15

BORG, BORG AND MORE BORG

1978   If Centenary Wimbledon had been a great tennis milestone, Wimbledon 1978, far from being a let down (despite appalling weather), opened in dramatic and almost historic fashion. Borg (1), the Champion, going for his third title running, so nearly fell in the first Centre Court match to gentle giant Victor Amaya, 6 ft 7 inch left-hander from America. In their only previous encounter, Borg had dropped a set to him in the US Championships, but nobody expected him to be in real trouble when opening his title defence. Although liberally sprinkled with double faults, Amaya's big serve and hard-hit volleys and ground strokes gave him the edge in a first set that went to 8-all. In the tie-break, Borg squandered two set-points at 6/4, the second with a double, but Amaya got home on his second at 9/7.

At 1/1 in the second set Borg won five games and, it seemed, was running into his normal ruthless form. But in the third Amaya gave him tit for tat. And now 1/2 down in sets, the Champion looked really vulnerable, often casting almost abjectly bewildered glances towards his Svengali, Bergelin, who sat as impassively as possible in the competitors' friends' box. Worse was to come, for Borg served two doubles to drop his service to love at the start of the fourth set. When the American led 3/1 and had a point to break the Champion's serve for the second time, Borg looked completely beaten. But at this critical moment he still had steel enough to put his second serve deep to Amaya's forehand and the return hit the tape. Champion's luck, maybe, but Borg now lifted his head and, though nowhere near his best, gradually assumed ascendancy. Amaya was never given another chance, Borg winning 8/9 (7–9), 6/1, 1/6, 6/3, 6/3,

The courts had lacked sunshine to harden them and the low bounce of the soft Centre Court had been a prime cause of Borg's poor form. This was even more evident on the outside courts and probably accounted for three seeds falling in the first round. Ashe (15) just went down in a long five-setter to the big-hitting Steve Docherty; McEnroe (11), youthful hero of last year, found the wait till fourth match on Court 7 on Tuesday, combined with the poor bounce and an unusually aggressive Eric van Dillen, just too much; and Stockton (10), who the previous year had halted Laver's progress, was beaten in straight sets by John Marks of Australia. The final irony was that all three winners failed at the next hurdle.

Of fourteen British starters, ten crashed in the first round and the remainder in the second. Of these last Mottram (12) found his usual Wimbledon hoodoo, this time in the shape of South African double-hander Frew McMillan, who won in straight sets – only to lose in three himself against Masters, who then fell to Borg.

Despite a rain-bedevilled first week (there was no play at all on Thursday), the crowds kept coming, a spirit – distilled no doubt by Centenary fervour – which seemed proof against anything. Wednesday's 38,291 was an all-time record for one day and so was the first week's total of 198,197. By Friday night the schedule was ninety matches awry and the Committee was forced to start play two hours early for the next five days.

The 34-year-old Flying Dutchman, Tom Okker, was never more quicksilver than this year. He had a tremendous run to reach the semi-finals for the first time, scalping Parun, Noah, Vilas (4), Leonard and finally Nastase (9), before bowing his head with dignity to the Lord High Executioner, Borg. Against Vilas, particularly, he was scintillating and made the Argentinian look clumsy and lacklustre. Vilas' mentor, Ion Tiriac, had no courtside answers to the appealing glances directed at him.

In the bottom half, after the early exit of McEnroe and Stockton, results had gone with the form book. Gottfried (5) had made his persevering way to a quarter-final against the wing-footed Gerulaitis (3), whose greater flexibility and seniority in US ranking were too much for him. A rapidly sharpening Connors (2) surged through the bottom quarter, sinking Warwick, Gorman (both of whom took a set off him), Alexander (14) and Ramirez (7) (neither of whom were allowed one) in his wake.

Gerulaitis, who with Borg had provided such a marvellous spectacle in their Centenary semi-final, was very anxious to go one better but was now up against the jinx of an opponent who, like Borg, had the psychological advantage of a string of wins against him. Against Connors he fought very hard for the first set. Having dropped his opening service game, he recovered the break at second bite and ran level to 6/6; then Connors put on the pressure and broke him again at his sixth break-point. All honour to him, Gerulaitis at once broke back, only to drop his own service again. Connors, with his sights firmly on a return joust with Borg, gave no second chance and took the set 9/7. He now had Gerulaitis haltered and took the next two sets with fair ease.

And so to the Final rematch, for which Connors had waited impatiently since their great Centenary battle of a year ago. This time his preparation had seemed sharper and his development through the tournament appeared right. However, Borg, after his horrific fright on the opening day at the hand of Amaya, had also slipped into higher and higher gear. On the day a match full of quality, which lasted for an hour and three-quarters, looked sadly one-sided from Connors' point of view, for Borg beat him 6/2, 6/2, 6/3. He was inexorable with the accuracy of his top-spin forehand. Despite the tightness of the strings (70–80 lbs pressure) he holds the ball so long on the racket that he can literally 'feel' it to a precise landing. His action reminds one of an expert cowboy, lassoing from the hip with his snaking lariat and always getting his steer.

Jimbo had an early success, when he took Bjorn's service to lead 2/0, but then the Champion ran into super form, reeling off nine out of the next ten games, to lead 6/2, 3/1 and have the match by the throat. The final game of this run was perhaps Connors' last chance. Borg was serving at 0/40. One mistake by Connors and good serving by Borg saved those break-points. Connors had one more, but Borg killed with a beautiful high backhand volley across court. When Borg led 4/2, it was clear that Connors, although always trying, was losing his grip. In the third set, he had only one break-point, and again Borg finished with a triumphant run, this time four games.

Despite the score, the crowd had been enthralled by some marvellous patterns of play and superb rallies. Perhaps the real difference was that Borg was now showing himself a much more complete grass-court player. If in trouble, he could control his length with his amazing top-spin and all sorts of angle. Whereas Connors, always gambling with a fine margin of error on his ground strokes, had no other answer when his accuracy deserted him. As Connors made his last mistake, Borg sank to his knees, clasped his hands in front of him, and seemed to give thanks for equalling the achievement of Fred Perry on winning the title three times running. After his opponent, Perry was the first to congratulate him.

The women's Championships provided few surprises, the top four seeds all reaching the semi-finals, though Chris Evert (1) twice needed a final set to get there. Her quarter-final opponent was the gallant Billie Jean King (5). She broke first to lead 3/2 but then Chrissie, with her immaculate ground strokes, took four games to finish the set. The second set swayed to and fro, five of the nine games going against service, before Billie Jean squared at 6/3, set-all. She now looked as if she might well take the match; but again Chrissie had a run of four games to win the final set more easily than she might have expected, 6/2.

She now met Virginia Wade (4), the reigning Champion. Chrissie was nearly ten years her junior and had a big overall lead in their encounters; but in her glorious zenith in the Centenary year, Virginia had played an inspired semi-final against her, and it began to look as if she might repeat history. She broke first to lead 3/1, but like Billie Jean in the previous round she was immediately broken back. Games then went without incident to the server up to 6/6 when at 30/40 the door was opened for Evert and she did not miss with her two-handed cross-court passing shot. In the next game, serving for the set, one set-point was enough. That long 8/6 set which took sixty-five minutes had clearly drained Virginia. When Chrissie swept into a 4/1 lead, the Champion gave a dying kick to take Evert's service, but immediately lost her own and Chrissie went out for the match 6/2.

In the bottom half, Martina Navratilova (2) was seeded to meet Evonne Cawley (3) in the semi-finals. Martina dropped a set to Kathy Jordan of

Bjorn to be King. Borg – grandmaster of top-spin and super-champion.

America but Evonne sauntered through to meet her. She seemed to be limping slightly half-way through the first set, but this did not prevent her from playing the most glorious tennis against the somewhat lacklustre Czech. She took the first set 6/2. Navratilova then lifted her game and masterfully forced the net position, risking all against Cawley's ground strokes. Her challenge took her to 4/0 and, though she dropped one service game, she won the set 6/4. The final set was littered with break-points, but it was the Czech who won most of them and got home to reach her first Final.

Born just after Maureen Connolly won the last of her three titles, Chrissie Evert was nearly two years the senior of Martina Navratilova and led her 20/5 in previous meetings; she was also far more experienced and in her fourth Final, having won the title twice. As expected it was a very edgy match, especially the first set where the quality of play was poor, though the emotions on and around the court were tense. Then Chris Evert, at a see-sawing 2/2, had one of her familiar four-game runs to take the set. The second opened with three service breaks and the players were giving the impression of puppets on poorly manipulated strings. However, suddenly Navratilova found something of her service, though she had to fight off three break-points on it when leading 3/2. She levelled the match at 6/4, then took Evert's service at the start of the final set and held hers for 2/0 before another string of four games saw Chrissie forge ahead to 4/2. This was her purple patch and she ended it with a love game on Navratilova's service, after a very long rally, with a two-handed cross-court shot that left the Czech standing. Now Martina's temperament, hitherto, one had felt, suspect on the very big occasions, held firm. She broke back and held service. She was now back in the match with a vengeance. She surged to the net in an overwhelming attack and won twelve out of the last thirteen points to take the set 7/5 and her first Wimbledon title. Having done it, it seemed she would take a lot of stopping in the future.

In the Men's Doubles the experienced partnership of Bob Hewitt and Frew McMillan (1) prospered again. They lost only one set, to Gerulaitis and Sandy Mayer (5) in the quarter-finals. The beaten finalists were two names to be conjured with in the future, unseeded Peter Fleming and John McEnroe, who had put out those established pairs Lutz and Smith (3) and Fibak and Okker (2). In the Women's Doubles, Billie Jean King, seeking her elusive twentieth Wimbledon title, seemed to be playing a strong hand, partnered by Martina Navratilova. They were the No. 1 seeds but curiously fell in the quarter-finals to Sue Barker and Mona Guerrant (6), who themselves were beaten by Kerry Reid and Wendy Turnbull (4), the eventual winners.

In Centenary year, Betty Stove had been in three finals and won no titles. This time, in the enforced absence of the holders through Greer Stevens' knee injury, she took the Mixed Doubles with Frew McMillan (1). In the Final they beat Ray Ruffels and Billie Jean King (2), and it began to look as if Billie Jean would never get that twentieth title.

Like Borg the previous year, Ladies Champion Martina Navratilova (1) was given a real fright in her opening Centre Court match. Her opponent, Tanya Harford, a 20-year-old from South Africa with nothing to lose, played an inspired first set. Her serve–volley game was so aggressive and so well controlled that it outplayed even the Champion. Possibly Martina was a little nervous, since her mother, whom she had not seen for four years, was in the competitors' friends' box at the special invitation of the All England Club. True or not, nothing could take away from the marvellous play of Tanya, and she very deservedly took the first set 6/4. Perhaps this brilliance was partly derived from Tanya having had to play through the qualifying competition; she certainly revelled in the Centre Court atmosphere. But after the first set, she lost her 'serene high' of concentration and Martina was able to dictate the match comfortably, winning 4/6, 6/2, 6/1.

Though the sun shone unusually brightly on the women's first round, fortune did not smile on Sue Barker (12), the only seed to fall at the first hurdle. Again it was Court Two, the seed cemetery. Perhaps she had memories of her woeful match there in blustery conditions with Betty Stove in 1975. Her opponent this time was Argentina's Ivanna Madruga, at eighteen now very much improved and with sets off Chris Evert (now married to the British Davis Cup player John Lloyd) in the Italian and French Championships to her credit but, at thirty-three places below Sue in the women's table, not expected to win and with nothing to lose. It was a nervy see-saw game in which sixteen of the thirty-three games went against the server. The court was slow which did not help the British girl, especially her potent, hard-hit forehand. Moreover, she served thirteen double-faults, twice at game-point against her in the final set. Madruga was the bolder, Barker was uncertain. Attack just carried the day 6/3, 4/6, 8/6.

Billie Jean King (7), who had withdrawn from the Eastbourne tournament with a pulled muscle, played very convincingly to beat Yvonne Vermaak 6/4, 6/1. In doing so, she created a record, playing her 91st singles at Wimbledon, more than any other player before her. She sailed through the next three rounds majestically, in the fourth beating the talented young Czech Hana Mandlikova 6/4, 6/3. Hana was perhaps reacting from a great win over her senior country-woman, Regina Marsikova (13). Regina probably reacted herself from a terrific match with Britain's Anne Hobbs, who really deserved to reach the third round, for she fought a very brave fight against Marsikova. In the final set she twice had the Czech No. 1 at 0/40 – but could not clinch the break. At 5/5 she did and served for the match. But cramp was now the greater enemy for Anne and Regina just struggled through 6/3, 5/7, 9/7. So the only British second-round survivors were Virginia Wade (5) and Debbie Jevans, who sadly had to meet in the fourth round where Virginia exerted her authority, winning 6/1, 6/2.

The women's quarter-final line-up was therefore as the seeding predicted. Navratilova to play Dianne Fromholtz (6), who had survived two nervy tie-breakers against Betty Stove (15), Tracy Austin (4) to play Billie Jean King, and in the bottom half, Virginia Wade to play Evonne Cawley (3) and Wendy Turnbull (8) against Chrissie Evert-Lloyd (2).

Dianne Fromholtz when going well is a lovely player to watch, and she started this left-hander's battle in excellent form. She can only play an attacking game and to begin with – as in Tanya Harford's first set against the Champion – she was the better player. She won the first nine points and broke service twice to take the first set with ease, 6/2. Her momentum gave her another break of service in the opening game of the second set. As with all Champions, this unexpected challenge brought the best out in Navratilova. So far she had only won three points from Dianne's service but now she broke it to love and took it again next time. The scales were moving up fast in her favour and eventually she had a run of seven games to win the match. Australia did no better in the other quarter-final on No. 1 Court, when Chris Lloyd comfortably contained Wendy Turnbull, who no doubt was suffering a complex after her drubbing at Chrissie's hands in the French final, 6/2, 6/0.

The opening Centre Court match between Virginia Wade and Evonne Cawley probably hinged on the very first game, when Virginia lost her service to 15. After that, games went fairly comfortably with service until Virginia, at 3/5, had two set-points against her. These she saved, the second with a rather lucky backhand volley across court, and the game went to eight deuces before Wade won it. With Evonne serving 5/4, Virginia had break-point at 30/40 but she put up a very weak lob, and at her next set-point Evonne got home. Evonne Cawley was now playing that beautiful brand of tennis of which only she is capable, and the second set was very quickly hers, 6/0.

Next followed the first meeting between the six-times Champion, Billie Jean King, and the new double-fisted challenger, Tracy Austin, nineteen years her junior. King is such a magnificent Champion and match-player, and wields such obvious authority in her game, that many of her opponents are intimidated and this encounter was unquestionably a tremendous test for young Tracy. She came through it with flying colours. The match lived up to anticipation. Tracy took the early advantage to lead 4/1. Billie Jean responded in kind, but at 4/5 found herself 0/40. She saved these three set-points but, after three deuces, on the fourth failed to get to a good forehand cross-court return of serve from Tracy, which passed her easily. The second set was full of breaks of service. King led 3/1, was pulled back to 3/3, led again 5/4, trailed 5/6 and forced the tie-break. Here, her depth of experience got her home, 7/5.

Set-all and Billie Jean took first blood in the final set, breaking Austin to lead 2/0. Tracy Austin won the next six games for set and match. That sounds easy, but it never was, for Billie Jean was ever a bonnie fighter. It was probably youthful stamina just having the edge on the old Champion's fading powers. It was a classic contest. The serve–volleyer against the accurate groundstroke player. It might well have gone either way. But the result was certainly a new feather in Tracy's cap.

A la Françoise – Frankie Durr gets down to it.

Greer Stevens makes light of it.

Dianne Fromholtz makes sleight of it.

264 WIMBLEDON

Tracy Austin, who two years previously had been the youngest player ever at New Wimbledon, was now the youngest semi-finalist since Christine Truman. She was up against the Champion, Martina Navratilova, who after starting the tournament rather shakily seemed now well into her stride. However, there may have been a niggling memory in her mind of Tracy ending her streak of thirty-seven wins in the Virginia Slims tournament of the previous year.

Austin struck first. In a long opening game, she broke service at her second advantage when Martina netted a backhand volley. Navratilova then won three games for the loss of two points but again was broken after another long game and only at the fifth break-point. This game was the start of a run of four won by Tracy Austin – to give her a 5/3 lead in a set in which so far five games out of eight had gone against service, three of them against the Champion's powerful delivery. Austin's passing shots, which had so often pierced the guard or eluded the reach of the incoming server in her match against Billie Jean King, had been sharpened by that encounter and were now doing the same against Navratilova.

At this point the Champion wore a very careworn look, the look of one stretched to the full, on a road that she knew was long and full of hazards. She held service and then Tracy faltered. At 15/30 Martina drove very deep and many thought her shot out but, on appeal, the umpire supported the linesman. This gave Martina 15/40 on Tracy's serve and the younger girl could not cope with a fierce top-spin forehand across her backhand. That disputed point was surely immensely significant, for although she still fought and rallied hard, Tracy won only one more game and that only after Martina had had a run of nine games to lead 7/5, 5/0. Navratilova finished the match 7/5, 6/1. To be fair to the Champion, whatever the significance of that doubtful point, she imposed her will on the junior player, playing a more complete game and very often, by playing short, forcing Tracy into the net, where she does not particularly like to be.

The first semi-final, especially the first set, had been of an extremely high class. But the second between Evonne Cawley and Chrissie Lloyd fell well below their high standard. Lloyd won 6/3, 6/2, but it was unhappy tennis, noticeably on the part of Cawley, who could not bring her normal brilliance to bear at all.

In prospect, the Final should have been a wonderful piece of women's tennis. Although Chrissie Lloyd led Martina Navratilova by a considerable margin in their overall meetings, they had each won twice on grass, all four matches going to three sets. In 1978, Martina had won the Eastbourne final and repeated that in the Wimbledon Final. This year, just before Wimbledon, these two had played the best women's tennis anyone could remember for a long time in the Eastbourne final and Chrissie had got home only 13/11 in the final set, after having had a match-point against her. If last year's precedent were fateful, she should win Wimbledon this time.

The sun shone and the Centre Court crowd was agog for the drama and brilliance they expected. It was never quite that good. Both players were tense, performing in this, the greatest of all Championships, before their greatest of loved ones, Martina's mother and Chrissie's new husband. Martina survived the early edginess the better, sensed it in her opponent and felt her own confidence waxing. She was ahead throughout the first set, which she took 6/4, and the pattern of the second set was almost identical – as indeed the score was. It was never the humdinging thriller it should have been, as evidenced by only one game going to deuce – when Navratilova was serving, leading 4/2 in the first set. At deuce she netted a forehand volley that gave Lloyd her one real opportunity of getting into the fight and developing her tactical methodical rhythm. Martina saved it with a good service which bounced badly and gave Chrissie no chance. It was a pity that the promised climax had not been fulfilled, but on the day Martina Navratilova deserved to retain her title.

In most experts' minds, there could only be one of three men to win Wimbledon 1979: Bjorn Borg (1), the Champion, going for a record fourth win running since the Challenge Round was abolished, John McEnroe (2), the new Grand Prix Masters and WCT Champion (the thrusting if somewhat uncouth pretender to Borg's throne), and Jimmy Connors (3), the 1974 Champion, who had often said that he would pursue Borg to the ends of the earth. The draw favoured McEnroe, for Borg and Connors were drawn to meet in the top-half semi-final, which meant that McEnroe would only have to beat one of them.

In the run-up to Wimbledon McEnroe's reputation for 'temperament' as to umpire, linesmen and crowd had been amply upheld. So much so that, after some disgraceful scenes in his match with Sandy Mayer at Queen's, at matchpoint he demanded silence so vehemently that Mayer capped him with 'rigor mortis is required'. On the other hand, in his final against Pecci the crowd had become so drilled to his requirements that they seemed more like deaf mutes presided over by McEnroe, who behaved with impeccable decorum.

A postponed start and a later 63-minute break for rain did not help the chances of the seeds on opening day. On his familiar Centre Court territory, Borg found himself with a handful in Tom Gorman, who at thirty-three should have left his best days behind him. However, hoping no doubt to profit from Borg's vulnerability in an early round, he attacked him from the start, playing better than he had for years – certainly since he beat the great Rod Laver in 1971. At 4/3 to Gorman with service the rain came down and, when they resumed over an hour later, Borg immediately fell to 0/40. Even he could not save this game against a rampaging Gorman, who then served out the set. Indeed, Gorman's concentration was so high for this period that he forgot to change ends at 0/1 down in the second set. Gorman maintained the pace and at 4/4 had Borg 15/40; but the Swede, as ever, reacted well, saved the break and immediately Gorman faltered, letting Borg square at set-all. In the third set, Gorman again broke to lead 5/4 but Borg always has extra resources to

Potentially one of the Greats –
Martina Navratilova.

John McEnroe and Peter
Fleming, masters of the
doubles game.

draw on and Gorman's own nerves helped with two double faults. So Borg won three games in a row for the set and had no trouble in the fourth.

Three other seeds fared worse. Arthur Ashe (7) could get into no stride on No. 2 Court – that unfertile ground for so many seeds – and was beaten in straight sets by Chris Kachel, an Australian with no great previous performance to his name. Even more surprising was the demise of Gerulaitis (4), again on Court 2. He was beaten by the American Belgian, Pat Dupre, in five sets – an inhibited Gerulaitis this, at no time showing confidence in his high-ranking capabilities. The last first-round seed to fall was blown away on Tuesday. Corrado Barazzutti (14) fell to the strong grass-court game of Andrew Pattison, again in five sets. This was no real surprise, as the Italian is much more a clay-court player.

Only three out of ten British starters survived the first round. The Lloyd brothers, David and John, went down to Onny Parun and Ove Bengtsson respectively – the latter in very spiritless fashion. Evergreen Yorkshire favourite Roger Taylor went to Vilas (6) in straight sets and John Feaver was beaten in five by Kirmayr. Of the survivors, Jonathan Smith put up a good five-set fight against Panatta and Buster Mottram raised Centre Court spirits by taking a first-set tie-break against McEnroe, who eventually won 6/7, 6/2, 7/6, 6/2. Mark Cox, almost thirty-six, had a real Indian summer. He beat in succession Meiler, Taroczy and Moretton before losing to an impressive Connors.

The second-round rainy skies and soft turf were too much for three more seeds – Orantes (13), that delightful touch player; Vilas (6), beaten by Tim Wilkison, at nineteen fast improving and already NSW Champion; and Higueras (12), all of whom much prefer clay courts. In each case their conquerors bowed out in the next round. And so it went on in the third round. John Alexander (11) found Gene Mayer in strong mood and did not get a set. Brian Gottfried (9), whose methodical game was in low gear, went out to Brian Teacher ranked eleven below him in the United States; and Victor Pecci (8), the giant from Paraguay, who had recently beaten both Vilas and Connors to reach the French Final and taken a set off McEnroe in the Queen's final, was beaten by Aussie Brad Drewett, in very sharp form winning two critical long tie-breakers.

The sensation of the fourth round on the first Saturday was the encounter between Tim Gullikson (15) and John McEnroe, who had beaten his left-handed twin Tom Gullikson, the day before. The venue was the same – the dreaded Court 2. It has been the graveyard of so many hopes, for the crowd are very close to the players and there is plenty of noise from the concourse and the snack bars under the players' restaurant. Perhaps not least daunting when things are going wrong is the knowledge that so many peers are watching critically from the restaurant roof.

John McEnroe, who was not a hundred per cent fit, was in trouble from the start. By the third game he was complaining of crowd movement, by the fifth – when he lost his own service – it was the noise that was upsetting him, and by the end of the seventh he was anointing his knee and left shoulder joint with linament. That one fifth-game breakthrough gave Gullikson the set, 6/4. With Gullikson serving 0/1, 30/40 in the second set, McEnroe argued long on a service decision. On this game may have hung the match. There were five deuces and McEnroe had five break-points, but each time Gullikson served and saved well. It was again in the fifth game that he broke McEnroe, who was now looking more and more disconsolate: towards the end of the set, which Gullikson won 6/2, McEnroe twice changed his racket and was seen to take a tablet.

Gullikson was playing very well but McEnroe was letting him, making many unnecessary mistakes and lacking any of his normal confidence. A run of nine games took Gullikson to two sets to love and 4/0. As the match wore on and an upset for 'Superbrat' became likely, more and more people crowded in for the kill and the physical pressure and atmosphere were tangible. Indeed, the crowd sitting in their seats for Court 6 were totally ignoring their own game and stood up to watch Court 2. They had to be ordered to sit down. Players and Press were no better, for every impossible vantage point was somehow contrived. One almost felt sorry for McEnroe, who looked like a small boy who had lost his mother and had none of his natural aggressive fight. Sitting at the chair on odd games, he would shake his head and look bemused. He did try to get back into the match: but Tim still had a break in hand. Leading 5/4 and serving for the match he saved two break-points and got home on his second match-point. It was his first win over McEnroe and a very famous victory.

Havoc among the seeds meant that only four reached the quarter-finals. No. 1 Court was the venue for the two top-half matches, in which the senior men were engaged. Tom Okker, although not having to play a seed, had done well again but had to bow out to Borg one round earlier this year, and with a smaller score, for the Swede was in masterful form, winning 6/2, 6/1, 6/3. The whole execution lasted only sixty-seven minutes and Okker's post-match remark said it all: 'I'm not tired – I didn't have enough time on court to get tired.' Borg contented himself with: 'I feel I'm playing very well' – perhaps the understatement of the tournament.

Connors followed against Bill Scanlon, who also had wended his way to the quarter-finals against unseeded players, dropping a set each to Pattison and Drewett. Unusually in Americans, Scanlon paid no lip service to his own national No. 1 (he himself being ranked 37). In the first set he had break-points (a total of seven) in all but one of Connors' service games, but still lost the set on the one break-point on his own service that Connors successfully converted, when he forced Scanlon to net his smash from a high two-handed lob across court. Nothing daunted, Scanlon started winning his break-points and raced to 4/0 in the second set. Connors fought back with four of the next five games, including three breaks of serve, but dropped his own for the fourth time for Scanlon to win the set and square the match 6/4. In the third set, Scanlon led at 5/2 but with only one break: Connors was able to pull that back and in the eventual tie-break he was all over his opponent, winning it 7/1. So, as so often, through sheer resolution not to be beaten, Connors surmounted the crisis and was in command throughout the fourth set.

In the first Centre Court match, Roscoe Tanner (5), though dropping the third set in a tie-break to Tim Gullikson, never really gave McEnroe's conqueror any hope. Not only was Tanner's service working well but so were his ground strokes, which had certainly sharpened in accuracy and pace from the previous year. The last quarter-final between Pat Dupre and Adriano Panatta, both unseeded, was a long-drawn-out, fluctuating affair, as the Italian's matches so often are. He has great talent and can be inspired, especially before a home crowd, but his performance is often wayward and long runs of success are counterbalanced by inept failure. Indeed, it seemed almost a home crowd, for there were Italians aplenty in the open standing room and they did not fear to let their hero know they were there. Panatta led two sets to one but Dupre, who had fought his way up to half a class higher this year, never gave up and eventually triumphed after nearly three and a half hours.

Nobody would have expected that both semi-finals would be over in three sets, but they were. Borg played almost as if from Valhalla, so merciless and accurate was the genius with which he crushed Connors 6/2, 6/3, 6/2 in only an hour and three-quarters. After Connors led 2/1 with service, Borg reeled off five games for the first set. In the third set Connors broke Borg's service for the only time and led 2/0 on his own. At this slight hint of rebellion, the Emperor raised his game again and Connors was only allowed eleven more points. The annihilation was as complete as in their 1978 Final.

After the sheer magnificence of Borg, the Tanner–Dupre semi-final was an anti-climax. It depended upon good service and the ability to contain it. Dupre only had two break-points on Tanner's and could not win either; whereas Tanner won two out of the three he had on Dupre's service. Those gave him the first and third sets on his service plate, the middle set going to a tie-break which Tanner won 7/3.

So to the Final – Borg in it for the fourth time, Tanner unexpectedly there for the first. But anyone who had watched his progress through the tournament had realised that this was a Tanner who no longer depended on his scintillating service, but had developed his ground strokes into thunderous weapons. Could he achieve what Connors had failed to do, use his swinging left-hand service to beat Borg's two-handed backhand – especially as the Swede loves to stand well back and receive the ball on its way down from the top of its bounce? Could Tanner's flame-gun of a service melt the ice-Borg?

Tanner came very near, playing perhaps the finest tennis of his career against the Champion, who was also near his peak. Service dominated the first set, in which there were only three deuces and one break-point against Tanner, which he contained with a flashing ace to the backhand. In the tie-break, his great service just gave him the advantage 7/4 to lead one set to love. At 1-all in the second set, Borg had one of his super streaks to finish off the set in nineteen minutes, 6/1. It was suspected that Borg had developed a hamstring injury in his opening round and had needed injections for it. Serving at 0/1 in the third set and 0/30, he seemed unwilling to stretch up for a smash and one wondered whether this injury was going to affect him too much. He lost the game and, although he fought very hard at 2/4 to regain the break, he could not do so and the set was Tanner's at 6/3. One hour forty minutes gone, and the buzz that ran round the court seemed to say: 'Is the impossible about to happen? Is Borg at last going to lose at Wimbledon?' At 2/1 to Borg, Tanner played three very bad points to drop his service and that was enough to let the Champion eventually take the set 6/3 – with all to play for in the final set.

The first three games were very hard fought. Tanner, with the advantage of serving first, made two mistakes to be 0/30 and netted a backhand volley for 15/40. A blinding ace down the middle saved one break-point, but Borg took the second with a terrific two-handed backhand top-spin shot of high trajectory, which fell just in. At the umpire's chair Tanner changed his shirt for the third time and, seemingly refreshed, attacked Borg's service in turn. The Swede served an uncharacteristic double-fault for 15/30, Tanner hit a tremendous forehand return of serve for 15/40, Borg saved with a good service, 30/40, and Tanner going for another terrific return of serve then missed his backhand for deuce. Tanner had advantage but again missed his backhand return of serve. Borg then held on to lead 2/0. Tanner in turn had to fight to hold his service game, defying three break-points to do so. His next and only chances to break back came when Borg at 4/3 was 15/40 on his service. Tanner put a down-the-line forehand pass well out and then netted a backhand volley. He was not given another chance, Borg taking his fourth title running 6/7 (3–7), 6/1, 3/6, 6/3, 6/4 in two hours, forty-nine minutes. As usual he sank to his knees, but this time held his hands in an attitude of prayer. Well he might, for he had written another page in the history of Wimbledon.

McEnroe's failure in the Singles was partly compensated when he and Fleming (1) confirmed their mastery of the doubles game by beating former champions in their last three rounds – Case and Masters (13), Hewitt and McMillan (4) and, in the Final, Gottfried and Ramirez (2) 4/6, 6/4, 6/2, 6/2. In the Mixed Bob Hewitt and Greer Stevens (2), happily back on the scene with Greer apparently unhandicapped by a metal support to her knee, repeated their Final success of centenary year against McMillan and Betty Stove (1), the holders, in two close-fought sets, 7/5, 7/6 – the first occasion on which the tie-break settled a Final.

The dramatic dénouement of Wimbledon 1979 was both sad and glad – sad because that great doubles Champion, Elizabeth Ryan, who jointly held with Billie Jean King the record of nineteen Wimbledon titles, died on the second Friday of the Championships; glad because she did so without knowing that next day Billie Jean, partnered by Martina Navratilova (1), won the Women's

Doubles for the tenth time, beating Betty Stove and Wendy Turnbull (2) in a rather nervy Final 5/7, 6/3, 6/2. She now held the outright record with twenty titles. It was a crowning moment for the redoubtable Mrs King – and a thoroughly deserved one.

1980   Rain bedevilled the opening day of Wimbledon 80 and continued to do so throughout the first week, so that perforce the first Thursday saw play starting at twelve o'clock and this went on right through to the end of a marathon Championships. Despite this, two important innovations – four new courts on the north side, carved out of what used to be Barker's cricket field and the present car-parking space, and the introduction of the 'magic eye' on the Centre and No. 1 Courts to make service line decisions – were an immediate success. The new outside courts gave the complex a more rounded whole, more freedom of movement for the crowd and a new meaning to the old title 'Centre Court', a relic of Worple Road days. After one or two players had early looked askance at the eye – particularly Nastase who seized on it as a marvellous prop for some humorous antics – they soon realised that, if not infallible, it was the nearest thing to it. It certainly cut out many an argument with linesmen and umpires. The seating on the notorious No. 2 Court was also increased down to court level, giving an extra 370 seats (2020 in all).

New records were in prospect with the performance of the Champion, Bjorn Borg. If he reached the quarter-finals he would have won thirty-two singles matches running and so have beaten the achievement of the great Rod Laver. If he went on to win the title for the fifth year running, he would have extended his own superlative record at New Wimbledon and would equal the performance of Laurie Doherty, who won the title from 1902 to 1906, exceeded only by Willie Renshaw 1881–6 and 1889 (seven in all), though of course in those days the Champion only played one match – the Challenge Round. Even before the start a new record was set by Andrea Jaeger (14), who was given the deserved honour of being, at fifteen years and eighteen days, the youngest seed ever.

Although all seeded players got through the first round of the Women's Championship, four minor ones fell at the second fence: Sylvia Hanika of Germany (16) 9/7 in the third to the big American youngster, Pam Shriver; Virginia Ruzici (12) 6/4 in the third to Joanne Russell; Sue Barker (13) 6/2 in the third to Betty Ann Dent; and Regina Marsikova (15) 6/1 in the third to Sue Saliba of Australia. Nine British girls started in the singles, six appeared in the second round but only one, Virginia Wade (7), reached the third. Such is the sad reflection of our standard against the world's – and especially the USA's – today.

By the quarter-final stage, there had been another seeding upset in both halves of the draw. In the bottom, Greer Stevens (11) had easily beaten an off-form Dianne Fromholtz (8). In the top half, Andrea Jaeger (14) had beaten Virginia Wade, 6/2, 7/6. Her steadiness and precocious competitiveness were too much for the Centenary Champion. Andrea then took a real spanking from

King's record twentieth title. Martina smiles but Billie Jean is constrained for once.

Another fine doubles pair, Wendy Turnbull and Betty Stove.

Roscoe Tanner, the Chattanooga choo-choo and 1979 runner-up, letting off steam.

Chrissie Lloyd (3), who put her firmly in her place, 6/1, 6/1, and so reached her appointed semi-final. But Andrea had made a star's entrance on the Wimbledon stage, and already a second record was hers – that of youngest quarter-finalist ever in the Women's Singles.

At thirty-six and her twentieth Wimbledon, Billie Jean King (5) was still a formidable obstacle for any would-be Champion to overcome. She had only just beaten 18-year-old Pam Shriver in a fascinating duel, 5/7, 7/6, 10/8, and now in the top quarter-final she met Martina Navratilova (1). The Champion ('the lightest I've been for seven years'), in going for her third successive title, had had no match-play for three weeks before competing at Eastbourne, where she had been beaten by Betty Stove. Moreover, she had dropped a set to Tanya Harford, who had given her a first-round fright in 1979. Her confidence a bit shaken, this was just the situation for Billie Jean to bring off a famous victory.

And well she might have done. The conditions did not favour Martina, for although both players are serve–volleyers, the soft court took more of the bite out of Martina's severe service. For the first set the light was stygian, with rain threatening at any moment. The bespectacled Billie Jean should have been the more affected but, out of sorts with herself, it was Martina who shrugged repeatedly at the skies and gave every sign of discontent with the ambience. The first set, without loss of serve on either side, went to a tie-break. Billie Jean led 5/2 when the first rain pelted down. Now she was clearly in trouble. Martina seized her chance and took six of the next seven points to win the set. That was the end of play for that day. When they resumed on Wednesday, it was in sunshine for most of the time. Billie Jean revelled in it, winning the first five games and taking the set 6/1 to be all square. Her play had been virtually faultless – quite remarkable and reminiscent of her hey-days.

The final set was as dramatic as any that Billie Jean had fought in her long militant career. She at first fell from her high grace of the second set, winning only one of the first eight points, but she immediately broke back, and held serve for 2/2. At 3/3 she had Navratilova at 0/40 but could not clinch it, so it went on with service up to 5/5. Here she had an advantage on Martina's service and broke her when the Champion netted a backhand volley. Alas for Billie Jean! Serving for the match, she 'choked' and lost a love game with four *volley* mistakes! When Navratilova led 7/6, King saved three match-points; when the Champion led 8/7, King saved another three. That might sound matter-of-fact but anyone knowing Billie Jean would expect, nay bet, on her doing so. They would know, too, what blood and guts, what sweat and toil in the gymnasium and what iron resolution combined in her Champion's nature and capacity to respond to crises in this way.

It was beginning to be like that fantastic duel in 1970 when Margaret Court beat Billie Jean King in the longest women's Final ever, 11/9, 14/12. That was ten years earlier and Billie Jean was still a supreme fighter. But luck was against her, for when Martina led 9/8, Billie Jean's spectacles broke and she had to change them. It transpired that this had never happened to her before in her whole playing career. By an odd quirk of prescience, she had talked about the possibility with Rosie Casals in the dressing-room just before the match. Whether affected or not, she still put up a remarkable fight, saving two more match-points before Martina found a forehand passing shot down the line, which literally just nicked it. The cheers rang round the court, mainly for the fantastic effort by the old Champion, whom the crowd had now very much taken to their heart.

Evonne Cawley (4), sunny-natured and playing her old carefree game, had no difficulties with her fellow Australian, Wendy Turnbull (6), for run and fight, as 'Rabbit' always does, she was outplayed. In the last quarter-final it was a similar story. Tracy Austin (2), favourite in many prophets' eyes to take her first title, was in her best accurate form against Greer Stevens. The South African has a free hard-hitting game and had so far come through without losing a set; but in this mood Tracy Austin's pinpoint rallying forced too many errors from her, and the American won 6/3, 6/3.

So it was, from the Seeding Committee's point of view, the perfect semi-final line-up – the Champion, Martina Navratilova, against the ex-Champion, Chrissie Lloyd, in the top half, and in the bottom, Evonne Cawley, Champion nine years before, against Tracy Austin.

The rain's vagaries had caused the programme to become so lopsided that on the second Wednesday, traditional Ladies' semi-final day, King and Navratilova had only finished their great quarter-final match as the first Centre Court offering. The third match, though, was the semi-final between Evonne Cawley and Tracy Austin. Evonne had had plenty of practice in playing Tracy's kind of game in her previous Wimbledon duels with Chrissie Lloyd. Tracy, the reigning American Champion, was now just as clever and scheming in her rally ploys, and as honed in the hard school of American tennis as ever the youthful Chrissie Evert had been; and she was tenacious in her fight for the title, to which – even at only seventeen – she now felt she could lay a just claim. The inherent defect in Evonne Goolagong's (as she then was) play, when she first came to Wimbledon and conquered all hearts there, was her sometimes sudden departure mentally – or so it seemed – from the tennis scene which she had hitherto been flawlessly gracing. The media had immediately seized on this trait of hers and, since she was in part Aborigine, liked to say that she was going 'walkabout'. These moments had been unpredictable, and opponents who were struggling in her toils when she was playing on a high plane could only pray that a 'walkabout' would overtake her. Sometimes it did and so there was often a stay of execution.

The new Evonne, happy in the compass of a husband and daughter, seemed no longer to stray from the business in hand. One break-point was enough to give her a 3/0 lead. But Tracy broke back and, at 2/3, 30/40, had what many felt was a very unlucky decision against her, when a backhand from Evonne, which looked longish, was called in. 4/2 to Cawley and, after another service-break each, Evonne went out 6/3. Tracy now showed her tempered steel and meticulously set about destroying her opponent. She fought off break-points against herself and successfully seized three in her favour, to take a bloodless set 6/0. It was not as one-sided as the score seemed. The rallies were still brilliant, weaving their cat's cradle patterns around the court, but more often ending in point to Austin.

The first two sets had been played mainly from the baseline, the normal happy hunting ground for either player. But, seeing she was now being out-played there, Evonne sounded the charge to herself and surged into the net with startling success, taking four games in a row, to have what looked to be a winning lead. Tracy jutted her jaw and fought back to only one break of serve down. With Evonne serving for the match at 5/4, Tracy had one chance to draw level, but at 30/40 she was beaten by a good service down the centre. Evonne then made advantage and match-point and Tracy netted a backhand.

In any match between Martina Navratilova and Chrissie Lloyd, the balance swayed continually and grippingly as mastery faltered imperceptibly on one side or the other. The standard was usually superb and the battle long, the exception being the 1979 Final, which had disappointed anticipation. Not so this time: 3/1 Navratilova, 4/3 Lloyd, but now a run of three gave Martina the set 6/4. It had been a see-saw with only four break-points and one deuce played. One thing had been noticeable, Chris Lloyd was coming to the net more than usual and often succeeding. As in the 1979 Final, though, she was making too many mistakes in her general play; although Martina was also nervous, her big serve began to take effect and was perhaps the deciding factor in the opening set.

In the second, Martina again broke to lead 3/1 and it looked as if it might be a repetition of their previous year's encounter: but Chrissie fought back valiantly to lead 4/3, saving three break-points in her first service game of this recovery. At 4/5, Martina's service let her down with two double-faults, the second giving set-point at 30/40. She saved that with a good backhand volley across court, but lost the next set-point on Chrissie's advantage. This, though, was a very questionable decision, for a return of Chris Lloyd's seemed to land three or four inches over the baseline, but was not called out.

The final set started edgily, both players dropping two service games each fairly easily, but Chrissie Lloyd now seemed to gain the crest of an ascendancy on which she planed comfortably to 5/2 and which just sustained her in a hard-fought battle for the match at 6/2, but only at her fourth match-point in a game of six deuces.

So the Champion was deposed, and two former Champions now met in renewed rivalry for the chance of another title. On their lifetime record Lloyd led 22–12 and at Wimbledon 2–1 but Evonne Cawley, in superb touch, made such a serene start that it almost seemed she was giving an unnecessary rehearsal

After nine years Evonne makes her point again, only the second mother ever to win.

for a carping producer, rather than the performance itself. She won the set 6/1, five games going against service, and she won it on merit, for Chrissie Lloyd was also playing well, although unusually she had played her semi-final only the day before. It was just that Evonne was better.

This 'serene high' took Evonne to 2/0 in the second set, when she seemed to have the match in her pocket. However, a gloomy sky had darkened perceptibly throughout the set and now rain stopped play for an hour. On the restart, Evonne held service for 3/0, but then Chrissie made one of her familiar four-game charges to get back in the match. Evonne stole back the service-break and, holding her own after an eventful game containing three break-points, now led 5/4. Chrissie served to 5/5 and, when Evonne dismally lost hers, it seemed that Lloyd might be able to make it set-all. But she in turn failed badly, so that at 6/6 the tie-break was called. At 3/3, with Lloyd serving, there was a very, very long rally, which just went to Evonne and probably settled the final issue. A run of three points took her to 6/3, match-point, when she put a backhand return of serve out. At 4/6, still with match-point against her, Chrissie netted a backhand volley and Evonne had succeeded where only Bill Tilden had before her – a great Champion again, nine years after her last title – and only the second mother to win (the other being the redoubtable Dorothea Lambert Chambers).

The Centre Court crowd had been thrilled and enthralled, half wishing the golden Australian girl to have her glorious comeback, half wanting Chrissie Lloyd – now married to an Englishman – to bring home something for the country's colours. This was the first Singles Final decided by tie-break.

Because of the programme pile-up, this was the only Final played on the Friday, and the Mixed Doubles was the first item on an early Saturday agenda. In a competition littered with walk-overs, unseeded John and Tracy Austin seized their opportunity to make Wimbledon history and become the first brother and sister champions. The inveterate Billie Jean King, hoping for her 21st title in the Women's Doubles which she held with Martina Navratilova (1), was denied in the semi-finals by her junior compatriots Kathy Jordan and Ann Smith (4), who went on to win the Final.

Australian doubles, which had been in a slight doldrum, came good again with that onomatopoeic pair Peter McNamara and Paul McNamee (7), the national champions, whose effervescent doubles technique was a refreshing draught for the spectators. Like Fleming and McEnroe the previous year, they finished their home run by disposing of former champions in their last three rounds – Gottfried and Ramirez (3), Fleming and McEnroe themselves (1) and, in the Final, Lutz and Smith (4) 7/6, 6/3, 6/7, 6/4 – in a match which, because of the rain and the long Men's Singles Final, was relegated to the comparative backwater of No. 1 Court.

In the Men's Championship Borg (1), luckily for his chances, had an easy draw, with all his main opponents – particularly the left-handers to whom he was more vulnerable (he had not lost to a right-hander since 1977) – in the bottom half, where McEnroe (2) was seeded to meet Connors (3) in the semi-finals (the reverse of the previous year when Borg and Connors met there). An Amaya or an Amritraj might so easily have upset Borg in an early match this year, for the weather – as was almost becoming the rule – was atrocious. Rain had been prevalent for a long time before the Championships, so that the preparation which Borg meticulously likes to give himself on grass had been halved – only some sixteen hours of practice.

Oddly it was a left-hander, El Shafei, against whom the Champion opened on the Centre Court. But the Egyptian – probably a little over-Borged in the situation – knew there was no hope of repeating his feat of 1974, when he was one of only three players ever to beat Borg at Wimbledon (the others being Roger Taylor (1973) and Arthur Ashe (1975)). Borg had then been eighteen and his great potential had not fully developed, whereas El Shafei had been a much fitter and faster player. But the rain-interrupted match evidenced one new aspect of the Champion's play. He went to the net much more than usual and this he continued to do throughout the tournament. When asked why on the first day, he replied that he had done so 'because of the soft court and low bounce'. But as the fortnight wore on, it became clear that he had improved his volleying and that net play was now a more integral part of his game. In the third round he dropped a set to Frawley of Australia, in the quarters needed two vantage sets against Gene Mayer (6), and in the semis yielded one to Gottfried, but never looked in danger on his way to the Final. His second round opponent, Glickstein, made history in a small way. He was the first Israeli to get through a round at Wimbledon and, in doing so, he won a distinguished scalp, Raul Ramirez.

Unlike the previous year, there was no great early carnage amongst the fourteen seeds who started (Harold Solomon (11) and Yannick Noah (12) had withdrawn). Only Amaya (14) went in the first round – and he in five sets to the equally big serving of his doubles partner, Hank Pfister. After him Stan Smith (15) was the next to go – in the third round. This was not surprising, for he was no longer the force of some years before and was beaten in straight sets by Brian Gottfried.

Gottfried had been a very convincing winner at Surbiton, dropping not a set; and he proceeded in the same vein at Wimbledon, clearly out to prove that his unseeded status for the first time for years was all wrong. He reached the semi-final for the first time – and without loss, the only man to do so. In his quarter-final he beat Fibak (13), who in the fourth round had just got home (over two days) against Gerulaitis (4) 8/6 in the final set. Taking a set from Borg meant that Gottfried was playing very well indeed and could look back on Wimbledon 1980 with real satisfaction.

Four other seeds went out in the third round. The brilliant young Czech, Ivan Lendl (10), was beaten in four sets by Colin Dibley (who then lost to

Gene Mayer); and Victor Pecci (8) succumbed to another big server in Phil
Dent, whom Gottfried then only allowed five games. In the bottom half Pat
Dupre (9), semi-final hero of 1979, was beaten by Nick Saviano, in a big-serving
marathon match, 11/9 in the fifth; and Clerc (16) succumbed to that solid
campaigner Onny Parun – a qualifier this year, as was an impressive newcomer,
Kevin Curren of South Africa, who beat Brian Teacher in the third round
and forced John McEnroe to two tie-breaks in the fourth.

Of ten British starters only Cox (who beat Moretton for the second year
running), Jarrett and Mottram reached the second round. Cox was beaten in
four sets by Ramesh Krishnan, just nineteen, whose father Ramanathan Krishnan was a semi-finalist in 1960 (the year Cox started his Wimbledon career)
and 1961. Jarrett lost to Gene Mayer in straight sets but Mottram had a titanic
match with Nick Saviano (USA), who just survived 6/7, 7/6, 6/3, 4/6, 13/11 – 69
games – one of the longest matches since the advent of the tie-break.

The quarter-finals in the bottom half lined up as scheduled, Tanner (5)
against Connors, Fleming (7) versus McEnroe. In the left-handers' battle the
seventh game in the third set, at one set all and 3/3, was a big one. Connors,
serving, having saved two break-points, half fell in saving a third and seemed
to hurt his left knee temporarily. Despite this, he fought off another break-point
and eventually won the game after six deuces. However, Tanner broke him
next time and served out the set 6/4. Connors started the fourth set well, holding
twice and taking Tanner's serve at his third advantage. Another service-break
gave him 5/1 and Connors, although he dropped his own service, took the set
6/2 by capturing Tanner's for the third time. The final set went with service up
to 3/2 to Connors. Then, in a hard-fought game, he broke Tanner, held his
own and broke Tanner again to take the match 6/2. It was a contest full of
spasmodic play, in which the two were seldom performing well at the same
time. It still pleased a pinprick-packed crowd, who especially appreciated the
thunderbolts which gave Tanner seventeen aces.

The other quarter-final in the bottom half was a forthright win for John
McEnroe against his doubles partner. Peter Fleming, a very big man, depends
on his very big service and some booming ground strokes to see him through.
In other words, he is a very straightforward player who, unusually for today,
does not even bother to bounce the ball two or three times in his service
preparation. Perhaps McEnroe was a jinx for him, but certainly he was off his
game, and was beaten convincingly in straight sets.

In his semi-final, Connors, bent intently to receive service – like a frescoed
Assyrian lion, proved a much sterner foe and it was not long before McEnroe's
temperament, slightly less evident so far at this Wimbledon, began to show its
Hyder side. Serving at 4/2 and 40/15, he thought he had aced Connors. The
linesman gave a fault. In his own emphatic way, McEnroe made no bones
about querying the decision, and asked for the referee (quite wrongly because
he can only decide a question of law or stoppage, not of fact), almost as a pre-

condition of talking to the umpire. The umpire agreed with McEnroe and over-ruled the linesman, calling for a let. McEnroe argued violently that, if right, it was an ace and the point belonged to him. He became so unnecessarily vehe-ment that he was given an official warning, the first ever at Wimbledon. The referee, on arrival, supported this action.

By now the crowd, always ready on reputation to view McEnroe with suspicion, was totally prejudiced against him and right behind Connors, who himself had often felt their disapproval in the past. It was not surprising that with two such pugnacious opponents the match turned into a slugging contest in which for a while deuces abounded. McEnroe took the first set with one break of service 6/3, Connors the second in similar fashion, though when serving for 5/2, in a game of ten deuces, he had to fight off no fewer than eight break-points. After a fall in the second game of the second set, Connors was again showing signs of left knee trouble and this may have slowed him up a bit, for in the third set the games and rallies became shorter and McEnroe was winning his services easily. Again one break was sufficient and 'Superbrat' led two sets to one. Connors struck back in the fourth to lead 2/0, dropped his own service but again won McEnroe's for 4/2. Just as it seemed he would be taking the match to the final set, McEnroe raised his game and only allowed his opponent two points in each of the next four games. It was a three hours five minutes encounter that was belligerent, pugnacious, unpleasant, ragged, rugged and rascally.

So McEnroe was through to his first Final. He had promised as much ever since his first appearance three years before. Would he now dethrone Borg, who had shown himself to be coming up strongly to the winning post when he played superb tennis to beat a much improved Gottfried in the other semi-final? For all who saw it, the Men's Final was a high point in any afficionado's career. There was always tension, there was superb drama, there was scintillating attack and equally brilliant riposte. It was a clash of two giants of the game, which after each rally sent shivers of anticipation rippling contagiously through the crowd in thrilled expectation of the next one.

As the players came on court, it was quickly clear that the crowd were totally behind Borg. They booed – and almost hissed – McEnroe, such was their dislike after his behaviour against Connors. That attitude did not last long, for 'Superbrat' was transformed. His scowl cast off, McEnroe managed to hold himself in check and yet play good tennis. Unbelievably, he swept through the first set in twenty minutes, Borg looking a shadow of the Champion we knew – perhaps even his steel nerve influenced by the dread realisation that this must be the supreme test and the zenith of his game, if he were to grasp the Grail of a fifth successive title.

The start of the second set was more normal, though things still looked precarious for Borg when, at 2/2 with service, he had to survive a break-point and four deuces before emerging from the crisis. Indeed it was perhaps this crisis that began to tune his game. At 4/4 adversity was again staring him in the face – with three break-points to overcome – but again he was equal to the challenge. Leading 6/5, at 15/40 he had his first break-points against McEnroe. He missed a forehand return of service on the first, but got home on the second. Somehow, against all McEnroe's belief and the early run of play, Borg had squared the match.

As many had expected, it was McEnroe's swinging service, particularly to the Borg two-handed (restricted-reach) backhand that had forged the way for his brilliant start. Now he seemed to lose some of the confidence of his early charge. At 0/1 and 30/40 in the third set he was lucky when Borg's fierce two-handed cross-court return of serve, struck acutely, just went out. McEnroe then changed his racket and immediately netted a forehand volley. At this second break-point, Borg ran round his backhand and hit his forehand return of serve for a clean winner.

When Borg led 3/0 on service, McEnroe looked really punch-drunk and nearly out, but still won his service and his next one, both to 30. With Borg leading 4/2, McEnroe made his big effort. He had the Champion at 0/40, but Borg saved well in a game that went to seven deuces. Both players had clearly felt that this was a mid-match crisis of high degree. A service gain on either side then left the set in Borg's grasp 6/3. The Champion led 2/1 after nearly two hours' play. It had been enthralling stuff but clearly the crowd felt that the writing was now on the wall.

How wrong McEnroe proved them, for there followed one of the best and most exciting sets of tennis ever seen, with a climactic tie-break that drew its suspense out so far that the nerves of all watching were at scream pitch. There were no break-points up to 4/4. McEnroe then survived one at 30/40, but at Borg's advantage he was beaten by the Champion's two-handed return of service. Surely now it was a formality, and when Borg reached 40/15 no one would have taken a bet on McEnroe at any odds.

He saved both those match-points with scintillating shots, the first a backhand down the line, the second a forehand dink. Now a netted Borg forehand gave him his chance, which he gratefully took with another backhand pass down the line. At the ultimate crisis he had shown his mettle with a sequence of four superlative points. Two love service games followed and then came that unforgettable tie-break – almost impossible to describe in retrospect. Suffice that each player in turn played unbelievable strokes, called on unknown depths of resilience, and raised their games to a height probably never seen before. In the thirty-four points played over twenty-two and a half minutes, Borg had five match-points, and McEnroe seven set-points, on the last of which he got home. McEnroe had somehow miracled his way through seven match-points, and that title that had seemed safe again in Borg's hold was now as elusive as ever.

If that tie-break was the Everest in a Himalayan match, the final set was incredibly sustained. Borg could so easily have reacted badly and lost his

John McEnroe – super-
service, supercharge,
'superbrat'.

opening service. Instead he seemed to grow in stature, his wide but hunched shoulders even broadening till he looked like the ace ice-hockey player he could surely have been. It was his Champion's quality that sustained him, for he was 0/30 down and then won four points. McEnroe was in worse distress, 0/40 with a double-fault compensated by three fine services, two of them aces. Then another double-fault gave a fourth break-point to Borg, but he could not clinch it. At 3/4, McEnroe was again 0/40. Borg netted a backhand return of serve, McEnroe played two good volleys and another crisis was over. It was hardly surprising that tiredness was now creeping in, for they had been playing for three and a half hours. For five games each won his service easily. With McEnroe trailing 6/7, he suddenly teetered on the tight-rope, and at 15/40 down faced his eighth match-point. Borg played a two-hander across court and McEnroe could not meet it. After fifty-five games and nearly four hours, it was all over bar the tumult and the shouting.

What tumult! The overwhelming ovation was for both players, but especially for McEnroe, who had not only jousted with heart and soul and gut, but had fought the good fight in a most sporting spirit, and was at last loved by one and all. 'For sure that was my best match at Wimbledon,' said Borg at his Press interview, and for sure it was McEnroe's too. Most who saw it felt it was the best Final they had ever witnessed and probably the best there had ever been.

Tennis in the eighties had already some clear outlines. Among the men Borg was the Emperor, his kingdom firmly based on his French and Wimbledon thrones; but his New World territories were mainly under the sway of McEnroe – with the banished Connors always fuming rebellion. If McEnroe was undoubtedly the most likely usurper, of whom Borg must be constantly aware, there were emerging from the wings a polished Pretender, Ivan Lendl of Czechoslovakia, and some gifted youngsters, notably Frenchman Thierry Tulasne, the new Wimbledon junior champion, and Dutchman Eric Wilborts.

Among the women there was no one pre-eminent. If Navratilova had the clearest potential, she lacked consistent authority; while from America there was issuing a succession of young players from the same fiercely competitive mould, players like Lloyd, Austin, Jaeger and Bettina Bunge – each likely to deny the others any long-lasting mastery. Aside from these only one threatened future supremacy – another Czech, the highly gifted but too often disappointing Hana Mandlikova – and perhaps America's Kathy Horvath, regarded as of exceptional promise. Never to be forgotten – and still able to threaten the best – was the fabulous Billie Jean King, alas now on the sidelines, having succumbed to the siren command of television. Sic transit gloria Reginae.

As for Wimbledon, that charismatic and gracious lady had never looked or performed better. Despite the turmoils and power struggles of the game's last decade and the larger looming presence of an omnisport surface, her grass was just as green, the Centre Court still the players' greatest stage and the titles she sparingly bestowed on eager aspirants always the most coveted in the world.

Paul McNamee and Peter McNamara, the effervescent Aussie Champions, 1980.

Tracy Austin in 1980. Is the inevitable of 1977 still so inevitable?

Youth to the fore.
Andrea Jaeger.

Ivan Lendl.

Hana Mandlikova.

Bettina Bunge.

APPENDICES

MEN'S SINGLES – FINALS

	Champion	Runner-up	Score
1877	F S.W. Gore	W. C. Marshall	6/1, 6/2, 6/4
1878	P W F P.F. Hadow	S.W. Gore	7/5, 6/1, 9/7
*1879	F J.T. Hartley	V. 'St Leger' Goold	6/2, 6/4, 6/2
1880	O^7 J.T. Hartley *31.188*	H.F. Lawford	6/3, 6/2, 2/6, 6/3
1881	Y^5 W. Renshaw *20.191*	J.T. Hartley	= SF 6/0, 6/1, 6/1 (20 games)
1882	W. Renshaw	E. Renshaw	6/1, 2/6, 4/6, 6/2, 6/2
1883	W. Renshaw	E. Renshaw	2/6, 6/3, 6/3, 4/6, 6/3
1884	W. Renshaw	H.F. Lawford	6/0, 6/4, 9/7
1885	W. Renshaw	H.F. Lawford	7/5, 6/2, 4/6, 7/5
1886	W. Renshaw	H.F. Lawford	6/0, 5/7, 6/3, 6/4
*1887	O^4 H. F. Lawford *36.53*	E. Renshaw	1/6, 6/3, 3/6, 6/4, 6/4
1888	E. Renshaw	H.F. Lawford	6/3, 7/5, 6/0
1889	W. Renshaw	E. Renshaw	6/4, 6/1, 3/6, 6/0
1890	W.J. Hamilton	W. Renshaw	6/8, 6/2, 3/6, 6/1, 6/1
*1891	Y^1 W. Baddeley *19.174*	J. Pim	6/4, 1/6, 7/5, 6/0

	Champion	Runner-up	Score
1892	W. Baddeley	J. Pim	4/6, 6/3, 6/3, 6/2
1893	J. Pim	W. Baddeley	3/6, 6/1, 6/3, 6/2
1894	J. Pim	W. Baddeley	10/8, 6/2, 8/6
*1895	W. Baddeley	W.V. Eaves	4/6, 2/6, 8/6, 6/2, 6/3
1896	H.S. Mahony	W. Baddeley	6/2, 6/8, 5/7, 8/6, 6/3
1897	R.F. Doherty	H.S. Mahony	6/4, 6/4, 6/3
1898	R.F. Doherty	H.L. Doherty	6/3, 6/3, 2/6, 5/7, 6/1
1899	R.F. Doherty	A.W. Gore	1/6, 4/6, 6/2, 6/3, 6/3
1900	R.F. Doherty	S.H. Smith	6/8, 6/3, 6/1, 6/2
1901	A.W. Gore	R.F. Doherty	4/6, 7/5, 6/4, 6/4
1902	H.L. Doherty	A.W. Gore	6/4, 6/3, 3/6, 6/0
1903	H.L. Doherty	F.L. Riseley	7/5, 6/3, 6/0
1904	H.L. Doherty	F.L. Riseley	6/1, 7/5, 8/6
1905	H.L. Doherty	HN.E. Brookes	8/6, 6/2, 6/4
1906	H.L. Doherty	F.L. Riseley	6/4, 4/6, 6/2, 6/3
*1907	ZN HN.E. Brookes (A'lia)	A.W. Gore	6/4, 6/2, 6/2
*1908	A.W. Gore	H. Roper Barrett	6/3, 6/2, 4/6, 3/6, 6/4
1909	O¹ A.W. Gore 41.182	M.J.G. Ritchie	6/8, 1/6, 6/2, 6/2, 6/2
1910	N A.F. Wilding (NZ)	A.W. Gore	6/4, 7/5, 4/6, 6/2
1911	A.F. Wilding	H. Roper Barrett	6/4, 4/6, 2/6, 6/3 retired
1912	A.F Wilding	OR¹ A.W. Gore 44.188	6/4, 6/4, 4/6, 6/4
1913	A.F. Wilding	M.E. McLoughlin	8/6, 6/3, 10/8
1914	HO³ N.E. Brookes 36.235	A.F. Wilding	6/4, 6/4, 7/5
1915–18	No competition		
1919	FG.L. Patterson	HN.E. Brookes	6/3, 7/5, 6/2
1920	NFW.T. Tilden (USA)	G.L. Patterson	2/6, 6/3, 6/2, 6/4
1921	W.T. Tilden	B.I.C. Norton	4/6, 2/6, 6/1, 6/0, 7/5
*1922	G.L. Patterson	R. Lycett	6/3, 6/4, 6/2
1923	W.M. Johnston	F.T. Hunter	6/0, 6/3, 6/1
C 1924	NJ. Borotra (Fr)	YR¹ R. Lacoste 19.3	6/1, 3/6, 6/1, 3/6, 6/4
C 1925	Y³ R. Lacoste 20.2	J. Borotra	6/3, 6/3, 4/6, 8/6
1926	J. Borotra	H.O. Kinsey	8/6, 6/1, 6/3
C 1927	H. Cochet (4)	J. Borotra (3)	4/6, 4/6, 6/3, 6/4, 7/5
1928	R. Lacoste (2)	H. Cochet (1)	6/1, 4/6, 6/4, 6/2
1929	H. Cochet (1)	J. Borotra (2)	6/4, 6/3, 6/4
1930	O² W.T. Tilden (2) 37.145	U W.L. Allison	6/3, 9/7, 6/4
C*1931	Y² S.B. Wood (7) 19.243	F.X. Shields (3)	w.o.
C 1932	Y⁶ FH.E. Vines (2) 20.278	H.W. Austin (6)	6/4, 6/2, 6/0
C 1933	J.H. Crawford (2)	H.E. Vines (1)	4/6, 11/9, 6/2, 2/6, 6/4
C 1934	F.J. Perry (2)	J.H. Crawford (1)	6/3, 6/0, 7/5
1935	F.J. Perry (1)	G. von Cramm (2)	6/2, 6/4, 6/4
1936	F.J. Perry (1)	G. von Cramm (2)	SF 6/1, 6/1, 6/0 (20 games)

	Champion	Runner-up	Score
C*1937	T J.D. Budge (1)	G. von Cramm (2)	6/3, 6/4, 6/2
1938	G T W J.D. Budge (1)	H.W. Austin (2)	6/1, 6/0, 6/3
C*1939	Y7 T F P R.L. Riggs (2) 21.132	E.T. Cooke (6)	2/6, 8/6, 3/6, 6/3, 6/2
1940–45	No competition		
C*1946	O9 Y. Petra (5) 30.119	A G.E. Brown (3)	6/2, 6/4, 7/9, 5/7, 6/4
C 1947	J.A. Kramer (1)	T. Brown (3)	6/1, 6/3, 6/2
C*1948	R. Falkenburg (7)	A J.E. Bromwich (2)	7/5, 0/6, 6/2, 3/6, 7/5
C 1949	P F F.R. Schroeder (1)	H J. Drobny (6)	3/6, 6/0, 6/3, 4/6, 6/4
C*1950	J.E. Patty (5)	F.A. Sedgman (1)	6/1, 8/10, 6/2, 6/3
C 1951	F R. Savitt (6)	K. McGregor (7)	6/4, 6/4, 6/4
C 1952	T F.A. Sedgman (1)	J. Drobny (2)	4/6, 6/2, 6/3, 6/2
C*1953	E.V. Seixas (2)	U K. Nielsen	9/7, 6/3, 6/4
C 1954	N H O5 J. Drobny (11) (Eg) 32.263	Y R2 K.R. Rosewall (3) 19.242	LF 13/11, 4/6, 6/2, 9/7 (58 games)
C 1955	W M.A. Trabert (1)	U K. Nielsen	6/3, 7/5, 6/1
C*1956	Y8 L.A. Hoad (1) 21.225	K.R. Rosewall (2)	6/2, 4/6, 7/5, 6/4
1957	L.A. Hoad (1)	Y R4 A.J. Cooper (2) 20.293	6/2, 6/1, 6/2
C*1958	Y9 A.J. Cooper (1) 21.291	H N.A. Fraser (4)	3/6, 6/3, 6/4, 13/11
C*1959	A. Olmedo (1)	U H R.G. Laver	6/4, 6/3, 6/4
C*1960	H N.A. Fraser (1)	H R.G. Laver (3)	6/4, 3/6, 9/7, 7/5
C 1961	H R.G. Laver (2)	Y R3 C.R. McKinley (8) 20.187	6/3, 6/1, 6/4
1962	G H R.G. Laver (1)	U M.F. Mulligan	6/2, 6/2, 6/1
C*1963	W C.R. McKinley (4)	U F.S. Stolle	9/7, 6/1, 6/4
C 1964	R.S. Emerson (1)	F.S. Stolle (6)	6/4, 12/10, 4/6, 6/3
1965	R.S. Emerson (1)	F.S. Stolle (2)	6/2, 6/4, 6/4
C 1966	N M. Santana (4) (Sp)	R.D. Ralston (6)	6/4, 11/9, 6/4
C 1967	J.D. Newcombe (1)	U W.P. Bungert	6/3, 6/1, 6/1
1968	H R.G. Laver (1)	H A.D. Roche (15)	6/3, 6/4, 6/2
1969	G O8 H R.G. Laver (1) 30.330	J.D. Newcombe (6)	6/4, 5/7, 6/4, 6/4
1970	J.D. Newcombe (2)	K.R. Rosewall (5)	5/7, 6/3, 6/2, 3/6, 6/1
1971	J.D. Newcombe (2)	S.R. Smith (4)	6/3, 5/7, 2/6, 6/4, 6/4
C*1972	S.R. Smith (1)	I. Nastase (2)	4/6, 6/3, 6/3, 4/6, 7/5
C*1973	N J. Kodes (2) (Cz)	A. Metreveli (4)	6/1, 9/8 (7-5), 6/3
1974	H Y10 J.S. Connors (3) 21.307	O R2 K.R. Rosewall (9) 39.246	6/1, 6/1, 6/4
C 1975	O6 A.R. Ashe (6) 31.360	H J.S. Connors (1)	6/1, 6/1, 5/7, 6/4
C 1976	Y4 W N B. Borg (4) (Swe) 20.27	I. Nastase (3)	6/4, 6/2, 9/7
1977	B. Borg (2)	H J.S. Connors (1)	3/6, 6/2, 6/1, 5/7, 6/4
1978	B. Borg (1)	H J.S. Connors (2)	6/2, 6/2, 6/3
1979	B. Borg (1)	H R. Tanner (5)	6/7 (3-7), 6/1, 3/6, 6/3, 6/4
1980	B. Borg (1)	H J.P. McEnroe (2)	1/6, 7/5, 6/3, 6/7 (16-18), 8/6

MEN'S DOUBLES – FINALS

	Champions	Runners-up		Score
1879	L.R. Erskine/ H.F. Lawford	F. Durant/ G.E. Tabor		4/6, 6/4, 6/5, 6/2, 3/6, 3/6, 5/6, 10/8
1880	W. Renshaw/ E. Renshaw	O.E. Woodhouse/ C.J. Cole		6/1, 6/4, 6/0, 6/8, 6/3
1881	W. Renshaw E. Renshaw	W.J. Down/ H. Vaughan	Played at Oxford	6/0, 6/0, 6/4
1882	J.T. Hartley/ R.T. Richardson	J.G. Horn/ C.B. Russell		6/2, 6/1, 6/0
1883	C.W. Grinstead/ C.E. Welldon	C.B. Russell/ R.T. Milford		3/6, 6/1, 6/3, 6/4
1884	W. Renshaw/ E. Renshaw	E.W. Lewis/ E.L. Williams		6/3, 3/6, 6/1, 1/6, 6/4
1885	W. Renshaw/ E. Renshaw	C.E. Farrar/ A.J. Stanley		6/3, 6/3, 10/8
1886	W. Renshaw/ E. Renshaw	C.E. Farrar/ A.J. Stanley		6/3, 6/3, 4/6, 7/5
1887	H.W.W. Wilberforce/ The Hon P.B. Lyon	J.H. Crispe/ E. Barratt Smith		7/5, 6/3, 6/2
1888	W. Renshaw/ E. Renshaw	H.W.W. Wilberforce/ The Hon P.B. Lyon		2/6, 1/6, 6/3, 6/4, 6/3
1889	W. Renshaw/ E. Renshaw	E.W. Lewis/ G.W. Hillyard		6/4, 6/4, 3/6, 0/6, 6/1
1890	J. Pim/ F.O. Stoker	E.W. Lewis/ G.W. Hillyard		6/0, 7/5, 6/4
1891	W. Baddeley/ H. Baddeley	J. Pim/ F.O. Stoker		6/1, 6/3, 1/6, 6/2
1892	E.W. Lewis/ H.S. Barlow	W. Baddeley/ H. Baddeley		4/6, 6/2, 8/6, 6/4
1893	J. Pim/ F.O. Stoker	E.W. Lewis/ H.S. Barlow		4/6, 6/3, 6/1, 2/6, 6/0
1894	W. Baddeley/ H. Baddeley	H.S. Barlow/ C.H. Martin		5/7, 7/5, 4/6, 6/3, 8/6
1895	W. Baddeley/ H. Baddeley	E.W. Lewis/ W.V. Eaves		8/6, 5/7, 6/4, 6/3
1896	W. Baddeley/ H. Baddeley	R.F. Doherty/ H.A. Nisbet		1/6, 3/6, 6/4, 6/2, 6/1
1897	R.F. Doherty/ H.L. Doherty	W. Baddeley/ H. Baddeley		6/4, 4/6, 8/6, 6/4
1898	R.F. Doherty/ H.L. Doherty	H.A. Nisbet/ C. Hobart		6/4, 6/4, 6/2
1899	R.F. Doherty/ H.L. Doherty	H.A. Nisbet/ C. Hobart		7/5, 6/0, 6/2
1900	R.F. Doherty/ H.L. Doherty	H. Roper Barrett/ H.A. Nisbet		9/7, 7/5, 4/6, 3/6, 6/3
1901	R.F. Doherty/ H.L. Doherty	D.F. Davis/ H. Ward		4/6, 6/2, 6/3, 9/7
1902	S.H. Smith/ F.L. Riseley	R.F. Doherty/ H.L. Doherty		4/6, 8/6, 6/3, 4/6, 11/9
1903	R.F. Doherty/ H.L. Doherty	S.H. Smith/ F.L. Riseley		6/4, 6/4, 6/4
1904	R.F. Doherty/ H.L. Doherty	S.H. Smith/ F.L. Riseley		6/1, 6/2, 6/4
1905	R.F. Doherty/ H.L. Doherty	S.H. Smith/ F.L. Riseley		6/2, 6/4, 6/8, 6/3
1906	S.H. Smith/ F.L. Riseley	R.F. Doherty/ H.L. Doherty		6/8, 6/4, 5/7, 6/3, 6/3
1907	N.E. Brookes/ A.F. Wilding	B.C. Wright/ K. Behr		6/4, 6/4, 6/2

	Champions	Runners-up	Score
1908	A.F. Wilding/ M.J.G. Ritchie	A.W Gore/ H. Roper Barrett	6/1, 6/2, 1/6, 1/6, 9/7
1909	A.W. Gore/ H. Roper Barrett	S.N. Doust/ H.A. Parker	6/2, 6/1, 6/4
1910	A.F. Wilding/ M.J.G. Ritchie	A.W. Gore/ H. Roper Barrett	6/1, 6/1, 6/2
1911	A.H. Gobert/ M. Decugis	M.J.G. Ritchie/ A.F Wilding	9/7, 5/7, 6/3, 2/6, 6/2
1912	H. Roper Barrett/ C.P. Dixon	A.H. Gobert/ M. Decugis	3/6, 6/3, 6/4, 7/5
1913	H. Roper Barrett/ C.P. Dixon	F.W. Rahe/ H. Kleinschroth	6/2, 6/4, 4/6, 6/2
1914	N.E. Brookes/ A.F. Wilding	H. Roper Barrett/ C.P. Dixon	6/1, 6/1, 5/7, 8/6
1915–18	No competition		
1919	R.V. Thomas/ P. O'Hara Wood	R. Lycett/ R.W. Heath	6/4, 6/2, 4/6, 6/2
1920	R.N. Williams/ C.S. Garland	A.R.F. Kingscote/ J.C. Parke	4/6, 6/4, 7/5, 6/2
1921	R. Lycett/ M. Woosnam	F.G. Lowe/ A.H. Lowe	6/3, 6/0, 7/5
1922	J.O. Anderson/ R. Lycett	G.L. Patterson/ P. O'Hara Wood	3/6, 7/9, 6/4, 6/3, 11/9
1923	R. Lycett/ A. Godfree	Count de Gomar/ E. Flaquer	6/3, 6/4, 3/6, 6/3
1924	V. Richards/ F.T. Hunter	R.N. Williams/ W.M. Washburn	6/3, 3/6, 8/10, 8/6, 6/3
1925	R. Lacoste/ J. Borotra	H. Hennessey/ R. Casey	6/4, 11/9, 4/6, 1/6, 6/3
1926	H. Cochet/ J. Brugnon	V. Richards/ H.O. Kinsey	7/5, 4/6, 6/3, 6/2
1927	F.T. Hunter/ W.T. Tilden	J. Brugnon/ H. Cochet	1/6, 4/6, 8/6, 6/3, 6/4
1928	H. Cochet/ J. Brugnon (2)	G.L. Patterson/ J.B. Hawkes (4)	13/11, 6/4, 6/4
1929	U W.L. Allison/ J. van Ryn	J.C. Gregory/ I.G. Collins (4)	6/4, 5/7, 6/3, 10/12, 6/4
1930	W.L. Allison/ J. van Ryn (2)	J.H. Doeg/ G.M. Lott (1)	6/3, 6/3, 6/2
1931	G.M. Lott/ J. van Ryn (1)	H. Cochet/ J. Brugnon (2)	6/2, 10/8, 9/11, 3/6, 6/3
1932	J. Borotra/ J. Brugnon (4)	G.P. Hughes/ F.J. Perry (3)	6/0, 4/6, 3/6, 7/5, 7/5
1933	J. Borotra/ J. Brugnon (1)	U R. Nunoi/ J. Sato	4/6, 6/3, 6/3, 7/5
1934	G.M. Lott/ L.R. Stoefen (2)	J. Borotra/ J. Brugnon (1)	6/2, 6/3, 6/4
1935	J.H. Crawford/ A.K. Quist (2)	W.L. Allison/ J. van Ryn (1)	6/3, 5/7, 6/2, 5/7, 7/5
1936	G.P. Hughes/ C.R.D. Tuckey (2)	U C.E. Hare/ F.H.D. Wilde	6/4, 3/6, 7/9, 6/1, 6/4
1937	J.D. Budge/ C.G. Mako (2)	G.P. Hughes/ C.R.D. Tuckey (1)	6/0, 6/4, 6/8, 6/1
1938	J.D. Budge/ C.G. Mako (1)	H. Henkel/ G. von Metaxa (4)	6/4, 3/6, 6/3, 8/6
1939	E.T. Cooke/ R.L. Riggs (2)	C.E. Hare/ F.H.D. Wilde (4)	6/3, 3/6, 6/3, 9/7
1940–45	No competition		
1946	T. Brown/ J.A. Kramer (2)	G.E. Brown/ D. Pails (1)	6/4, 6/4, 6/2

	Champions	Runners-up	Score
1947	R. Falkenburg/ J.A. Kramer (1)	UA.J. Mottram/ O.W. Sidwell	8/6, 6/3, 6/3
1948	J.E. Bromwich/ F.A. Sedgman (3)	T. Brown/ G. Mulloy (2)	5/7, 7/5, 7/5, 9/7
1949	R.P. Gonzales/ F.A. Parker (3)	G. Mulloy/ F.R. Schroeder (1)	6/4, 6/4, 6/2
1950	J.E. Bromwich/ A.K. Quist (2)	G.E. Brown/ O.W. Sidwell (4)	7/5, 3/6, 6/3, 3/6, 6/2
1951	GK. McGregor/ GF.A. Sedgman (1)	J. Drobny/ E.W. Sturgess (4)	3/6, 6/2, 6/3, 3/6, 6/3
1952	K. McGregor/ F.A. Sedgman (1)	E.V. Seixas/ E.W. Sturgess (4)	6/3, 7/5, 6/4
1953	L.A. Hoad/ K.R. Rosewall (1)	R.N. Hartwig/ M.G. Rose (3)	6/4, 7/5, 4/6, 7/5
1954	R.N. Hartwig/ M.G. Rose (1)	E.V. Seixas/ M.A. Trabert (2)	6/4, 6/4, 3/6, 6/4
1955	R.N. Hartwig/ L.A. Hoad (2)	N.A. Fraser/ K.R. Rosewall (3)	7/5, 6/4, 6/3
1956	L.A. Hoad/ K.R. Rosewall (1)	UN. Pietrangeli/ O. Sirola	7/5, 6/2, 6/1
1957	UG. Mulloy/ J.E. Patty	N.A. Fraser/ L.A. Hoad (1)	8/10, 6/4, 6/4, 6/4
1958	US. Davidson/ U. Schmidt	A.J.Cooper/ N.A. Fraser (1)	6/4, 6/4, 8/6
1959	R.S. Emerson/ N.A. Fraser (1)	R.G. Laver/ R. Mark (4)	8/6, 6/3, 14/16, 9/7
1960	UR.H. Osuna/ R.D. Ralston	UM.G. Davies/ R.K. Wilson	7/5, 6/3, 10/8
1961	R.S. Emerson/ N.A. Fraser (1)	UR.A.J. Hewitt/ F.S. Stolle	6/4, 6/8, 6/4, 6/8, 8/6
1962	R.A.J. Hewitt/ F.S. Stolle (2)	UB. Jovanovic/ N. Pilic	6/2, 5/7, 6/2, 6/4
1963	UR.H. Osuna/ A. Palafox	UJ.C. Barclay/ P. Darmon	4/6, 6/2, 6/2, 6/2
1964	R.A.J. Hewitt/ F.S. Stolle (3)	R.S. Emerson/ K.N. Fletcher (4)	7/5, 11/9, 6/4
1965	J.D. Newcombe/ A.D. Roche (2)	K.N. Fletcher/ R.A.J. Hewitt (4)	7/5, 6/3, 6/4
1966	UK.N. Fletcher/ J.D. Newcombe	W.W. Bowrey/ O.K. Davidson (4)	6/3, 6/4, 3/6, 6/3
1967	R.A.J. Hewitt/ F.D. McMillan (2)	R.S. Emerson/ K.N. Fletcher (4)	6/2, 6/3, 6/4
1968	J.D. Newcombe/ A.D. Roche (4)	K.R. Rosewall/ F.S. Stolle (2)	3/6, 8/6, 5/7, 14/12, 6/3
1969	J.D. Newcombe/ A.D. Roche (1)	T.S. Okker/ M.C. Riessen (6)	7/5, 11/9, 6/3
1970	J.D. Newcombe/ A.D. Roche (1)	K.R. Rosewall/ F.S. Stolle (6)	10/8, 6/3, 6/1
1971	UR.S. Emerson/ R.G. Laver	UA.R. Ashe/ R.D. Ralston	4/6, 9/7, 6/8, 6/4, 6/4
1972	R.A.J. Hewitt/ F.D. McMillan (1)	S.R. Smith/ E.J. van Dillen (2)	6/2, 6/2, 9/7
1973	J.S. Connors/ I. Nastase (1)	J.R. Cooper/ N.A. Fraser (2)	3/6, 6/3, 6/4, 8/9, 6/1
1974	J.D. Newcombe/ A.D. Roche (4)	R.C. Lutz/ S.R. Smith (3)	8/6, 6/4, 6/4
1975	UV. Gerulaitis/ A. Mayer	UC. Dowdeswell/ A.J. Stone	7/5, 8/6, 6/4
1976	B.E. Gottfried/ R. Ramirez (1)	UR.L. Case/ G. Masters	3/6, 6/3, 8/6, 2/6, 7/5

	Champions	Runners-up	Score
1977	R.L. Case/ G. Masters (7)	UJ.G. Alexander/ P.C. Dent	6/3, 6/4, 3/6, 8/9, 6/4
1978	R.A.J. Hewitt F.D. McMillan (1)	UP. Fleming/ J.P. McEnroe	6/1, 6/4, 6/2
1979	P. Fleming/ J.P. McEnroe (1)	B.E. Gottfried/ R. Ramirez (7)	4/6, 6/4, 6/2, 6/2
1980	P. McNamara/ P. McNamee (7)	R.C. Lutz/ S.R. Smith (4)	7/6, 6/3, 6/7, 6/4

WOMEN'S SINGLES—FINALS

	Champion	Runner-up	Score
1884	Y[7]F Miss M. Watson *19.284*	Miss L. Watson	6/8, 6/3, 6/3
1885	W Miss M. Watson	Miss B. Bingley	6/1, 7/5
1886	W Miss B. Bingley	Miss M. Watson	6/3, 6/3
1887	Y[1] P W F Miss L. Dod *15.285*	Miss B. Bingley	6/2, 6/0
1888	Miss L. Dod	Mrs G.W. Hillyard	6/3, 6/3
*1889	Mrs G.W. Hillyard	Miss L. Rice	4/6, 8/6, 6/4
*1890	W Miss L. Rice	Miss M. Jacks	6/4, 6/1
*1891	W Miss L. Dod	Mrs G.W. Hillyard	6/2, 6/1
1892	Miss L. Dod	Mrs G.W. Hillyard	6/1, 6/1
1893	Miss L. Dod	Mrs G.W. Hillyard	6/8, 6/1, 6/4
*1894	W Mrs G.W. Hillyard	Miss L. Austin	6/1, 6/1
*1895	Miss C. Cooper	Miss H. Jackson	7/5, 8/6
1896	Miss C. Cooper	Mrs W.H. Pickering	6/2, 6/3
1897	Mrs G.W. Hillyard	Miss C. Cooper	5/7, 7/5, 6/2
*1898	Miss C. Cooper	Miss L. Martin	6/4, 6/4
1899	Mrs G.W. Hillyard	Miss C. Cooper	6/2, 6/3
1900	O[2] Mrs G.W. Hillyard *36.242*	Miss C. Cooper	4/6, 6/4, 6/4
1901	W Mrs A. Sterry	Mrs G.W. Hillyard	6/2, 6/2
1902	Miss M.E. Robb	Mrs A. Sterry	7/5, 6/1
*1903	Miss D.K. Douglass	Miss E.W. Thomson	4/6, 6/4, 6/2
1904	Miss D.K. Douglass	OR[2] Mrs A. Sterry *41.290*	6/0, 6/3
1905	Y[3] Z N W F Miss M.G. Sutton (USA) *18.286*	Miss D.K. Douglass	6/3, 6/4
1906	W Miss D.K. Douglass	Miss M.G. Sutton	6/3, 9/7
1907	W Miss M.G. Sutton	Mrs Lambert Chambers	6/1, 6/4
*1908	O[1] W Mrs A. Sterry *37.282*	Miss A.M. Morton	6/4, 6/4
*1909	Miss D.P. Boothby	Miss A.M. Morton	6/4, 4/6, 8/6
1910	W Mrs Lambert Chambers	Miss D.P. Boothby	6/2, 6/2
1911	Mrs Lambert Chambers	Miss D.P. Boothby	SF 6/0, 6/0 (*12 games*)
*1912	O[4] Mrs D.R. Larcombe *33.27*	Mrs A. Sterry	6/3, 6/1
*1913	W Mrs Lambert Chambers	Mrs R.J. McNair	6/0, 6/4
1914	O[3] Mrs Lambert Chambers *35.304*	Mrs D.R. Larcombe	7/5, 6/4
1915–18	No competition		
1919	Y[9] P N F Miss S. Lenglen (Fr) *20.42*	Mrs Lambert Chambers	10/8, 4/6, 9/7
1920	T Miss S. Lenglen	OR[1] Mrs Lambert Chambers *41.302*	6/3, 6/0
1921	Miss S. Lenglen	Miss E. Ryan	6/2, 6/0
1922	T W Miss S. Lenglen	Mrs M. Mallory	6/2, 6/0
1923	W Miss S. Lenglen	Miss K. McKane	6/2, 6/2
C 1924	Miss K. McKane	YR[2] Miss H. Wills *18.271*	4/6, 6/4, 6/4
1925	T W Miss S. Lenglen	Miss J. Fry	6/2, 6/0
1926	Mrs L.A. Godfree	Miss L. de Alvarez	6/2, 4/6, 6/3
C 1927	Y[12] Miss H. Wills (1) *21.269*	Miss L. de Alvarez (4)	6/2, 6/4
1928	W Miss H. Wills (1)	Miss L. de Alvarez (2)	6/3, 6/3
1929	W Miss H. Wills (1)	Miss H.H. Jacobs (5)	6/1, 6/2
1930	W Mrs F.S. Moody (1)	OR[3] Miss E. Ryan (8) *38.149*	6/2, 6/2
*1931	N Miss C. Aussem (1) (Ger)	Miss H. Krahwinkel (4)	6/2, 7/5
*1932	W Mrs F.S. Moody (1)	Miss H.H. Jacobs (5)	6/3, 6/1
1933	Mrs F.S. Moody (1)	Miss D.E. Round (2)	6/4, 6/8, 6/3
C *1934	Miss D.E. Round (2)	Miss H.H. Jacobs (1)	6/2, 5/7, 6/3
1935	Mrs F.S. Moody (4)	Miss H.H. Jacobs (3)	6/3, 3/6, 7/5
C *1936	Miss H.H. Jacobs (2)	Mrs S. Sperling (5)	6/2, 4/6, 7/5
1937	Miss D.E. Round (7)	Miss J. Jedrzejowska (4)	6/2, 2/6, 7/5

	Champion	Runner-up	Score
*1938	O^5 *W* Mrs F.S. Moody (1) *32.269*	*U* Miss H.H. Jacobs	6/4, 6/0
C*1939	*T W* Miss A. Marble (1)	*H* Miss K.E. Stammers (6)	6/2, 6/0
1940–45	No competition		
C*1946	*P W F* Miss P.M. Betz (1)	Miss A.L. Brough (3)	6/2, 6/4
C*1947	*W* Miss M.E. Osborne (1)	Miss D.J. Hart (3)	6/2, 6/4
C 1948	*T* Miss A.L. Brough (2)	Miss D.J. Hart (4)	6/3, 8/6
1949	Miss A.L. Brough (1)	Mrs W. du Pont (2)	10/8, 1/6, 10/8
1950	*T* Miss A.L. Brough (1)	Mrs W. du Pont (2)	6/1, 3/6, 6/1
C1951	*T W* Miss D.J. Hart (3)	Miss S.J. Fry (4)	6/1 6/0
1952	*P Y²F* Miss M. Connolly (2) *17.291*	Miss A.L. Brough (4)	7/5, 6/3
1953	*G W* Miss M. Connolly (1)	Miss D.J. Hart (2)	8/6, 7/5
1954	*W* Miss M. Connolly (1)	Miss A.L. Brough (4)	6/2, 7/5
*1955	O^6 *W* Miss A.L. Brough (2) *32.113*	*A* Miss J.G. Fleitz (3)	7/5, 8/6
C1956	Miss S.J. Fry (5)	Miss A. Buxton (6)	6/3, 6/1
C*1957	*W* Miss A. Gibson (1)	Miss D.R. Hard (5)	6/3, 6/2
1958	O^9 Miss A. Gibson (1) *30.314*	*U* Miss A. Mortimer	8/6, 6/2
C*1959	*N Y⁶* Miss M.E. Bueno (6) *(Braz) 19.266*	Miss D.R. Hard (4)	6/4, 6/3
1960	Miss M.E. Bueno (1)	Miss S. Reynolds (8)	8/6, 6/0
C*1961	Miss A. Mortimer (7)	Miss C.C. Truman (6)	4/6, 6/4, 7/5
C1962	*Y⁵ W* Mrs J.R. Susman (8) *19.208*	*U* Mrs V. Sukova	6/4, 6/4
C*1963	*N Y¹⁰* Miss M. Smith (1) *(A'lia) 20.357*	*U* Miss B.J. Moffitt	6/3, 6/4
1964	Miss M.E. Bueno (2)	Miss M. Smith (1)	6/4, 7/9, 6/3
1965	*W* Miss M. Smith (2)	Miss M.E. Bueno (1)	6/4, 7/5
C1966	Mrs L.W. King (4)	Miss M.E. Bueno (2)	6/3, 3/6, 6/1
1967	*T W* Mrs L.W. King (1)	*H* Mrs P.F. Jones (3)	6/3, 6/4
1968	Mrs L.W. King (1)	Miss J.A.M. Tegart (7)	9/7, 7/5
C1969	HO^{10} Mrs P.F. Jones (4) *30.260*	Mrs L.W. King (2)	3/6, 6/3, 6/2
1970	*G* Mrs B.M. Court (1)	Mrs L.W. King (2)	*LF* 14/12, 11/9 (46 game
C1971	*Y⁸* Miss E.F. Goolagong (3) *19.337*	Mrs B.M. Court (1)	6/4, 6/1
1972	Mrs L.W. King (2)	Miss E.F. Goolagong (1)	6/3, 6/3
1973	*T* Mrs L.W. King (2)	*YR¹* Miss C.M. Evert (4) *18.198*	6/0, 7/5
C1974	*Y⁴* Miss C.M. Evert (2) *19.196*	Mrs O. Morozova (8)	6/0, 6/4
1975	O^8 Mrs L.W. King (3) *31.244*	Mrs R. Cawley (4)	6/0, 6/1
1976	Miss C.M. Evert (1)	Mrs R. Cawley (2)	6/3, 4/6, 8/6
1977	O^7 Miss S.V. Wade (3) *31.356*	Miss B.F. Stove (7)	4/6, 6/3, 6/1
1978	*H N* Miss M. Navratilova (2) *(Cz)*	Miss C.M. Evert (1)	2/6, 6/4, 7/5
1979	*H* Miss M. Navratilova (1)	Mrs J.R. Lloyd (2)	6/4, 6/4
1980	Mrs R. Cawley (4)	Mrs J.R. Lloyd (3)	6/1, 7/6 (7-4)

WOMEN'S DOUBLES–FINALS

	Champions	Runners-up	Score
1913	Mrs R.J. McNair/ Miss D.P. Boothby	Mrs A. Sterry/ Mrs Lambert Chambers	6/4, 2/4 (retd)
1914	Miss E. Ryan/ Miss A.M. Morton	Mrs D.R. Larcombe/ Mrs F.J. Hannam	6/1, 6/3
1915–18	No competition		
1919	Miss S. Lenglen/ Miss E. Ryan	Mrs Lambert Chambers/ Mrs D.R. Larcombe	4/6, 7/5, 6/3
1920	Miss S. Lenglen/ Miss E. Ryan	Mrs Lambert Chambers/ Mrs D.R. Larcombe	6/4, 6/0
1921	Miss S. Lenglen/ Miss E. Ryan	Mrs A.E. Beamish/ Mrs I.E. Peacock	6/1, 6/2
1922	Miss S. Lenglen/ Miss E. Ryan	Mrs A.D. Stocks/ Miss K. McKane	6/0, 6/4
1923	Miss S. Lenglen/ Miss E. Ryan	Miss J. Austin/ Miss E.L. Colyer	6/3, 6/1
1924	Mrs G.W. Wightman/ Miss H. Wills	Mrs B.C. Covell/ Miss K. McKane	6/4, 6/4
1925	Miss S. Lenglen/ Miss E. Ryan	Mrs A.V. Bridge/ Mrs C.G. McIlquham	6/2, 6/2

	Champions	Runners-up	Score
1926	Miss E. Ryan/ Miss M.K. Browne	Mrs L.A. Godfree/ Miss E.L. Colyer	6/1, 6/1
1927	Miss H. Wills/ Miss E. Ryan	Miss E.L. Heine/ Mrs I.E. Peacock	6/3, 6/2
1928	Mrs Holcroft-Watson/ Miss P. Saunders (3)	Miss E.H. Harvey/ Miss E.B. Bennett (2)	6/2, 6/3
1929	Mrs Holcroft-Watson/ Mrs L.R.C. Michell (2)	Mrs B.C. Covell/ Mrs D.C. Shepherd-Barron (3)	6/4, 8/6
1930	Mrs F.S. Moody/ Miss E. Ryan (1)	Miss E. Cross/ Miss S. Palfrey (4)	6/2, 9/7
1931	U Mrs D.C. Shepherd-Barron/ Miss P.E. Mudford	Miss D. Metaxa/ Miss J. Sigart (4)	3/6, 6/3, 6/4
1932	Miss D. Metaxa/ Miss J. Sigart (4)	Miss E. Ryan/ Miss H.H. Jacobs (2)	6/4, 6/3
1933	Mrs R. Mathieu/ Miss E. Ryan (1)	U Miss F. James Miss A.M. Yorke	6/2, 9/11, 6/4
1934	Mrs R. Mathieu/ Miss E. Ryan (1)	U Mrs D. Andrus/ Mrs S. Henrotin	6/3, 6/3
1935	Miss F. James/ Miss K.E. Stammers (3)	Mrs R. Mathieu/ Mrs S. Sperling (2)	6/1, 6/4
1936	Miss F. James/ Miss K.E. Stammers (1)	Mrs S.P. Fabyan/ Miss H.H. Jacobs (2)	6/2, 6/1
1937	Mrs R. Mathieu/ Miss A.M. Yorke (2)	U Mrs M.R. King/ Mrs J.B. Pitman	6/3, 6/3
1938	Mrs S.P. Fabyan/ Miss A. Marble (2)	Mrs R. Mathieu/ Miss A.M. Yorke (1)	6/2, 6/3
1939	Mrs S.P. Fabyan/ Miss A. Marble (1)	Miss H.H. Jacobs/ Miss A.M. Yorke (2)	6/1, 6/0
1940–45	No competition		
1946	Miss A.L. Brough/ Miss M.E. Osborne (1)	Miss P.M. Betz/ Miss D.J. Hart (2)	6/3, 2/6, 6/3
1947	Miss D.J. Hart/ Mrs P.C. Todd (2)	Miss A.L. Brough/ Miss M.E. Osborne (1)	3/6, 6/4, 7/5
1948	Miss A.L. Brough/ Mrs W. du Pont (1)	Miss D.J. Hart/ Mrs P.C. Todd (2)	6/3, 3/6, 6/3
1949	Miss A.L. Brough/ Mrs W. du Pont (1)	Miss G. Moran/ Mrs P.C. Todd (2)	8/6, 7/5
1950	Miss A.L. Brough/ Mrs W. du Pont (1)	Miss S.J. Fry/ Miss D.J. Hart (2)	6/4, 5/7, 6/1
1951	Miss S.J. Fry/ Miss D.J. Hart (2)	Miss A.L. Brough/ Mrs W. du Pont (1)	6/3, 13/11
1952	Miss S.J. Fry/ Miss D.J. Hart (1)	Miss A.L. Brough/ Miss M. Connolly (2)	8/6, 6/3
1953	Miss S.J. Fry/ Miss D.J. Hart (1)	Miss M. Connolly/ Miss J. Sampson (2)	6/0, 6/0
1954	Miss A.L. Brough/ Mrs W. du Pont (2)	Miss S.J. Fry/ Miss D.J. Hart (1)	4/6, 9/7, 6/3
1955	Miss A. Mortimer/ Miss J.A. Shilcock (4)	Miss S.J. Bloomer/ Miss P.E. Ward (3)	7/5, 6/1
1956	Miss A. Buxton/ Miss A. Gibson (3)	U Miss F. Muller/ Miss D.G. Seeney	6/1, 8/6
1957	Miss A. Gibson/ Miss D.R. Hard (1)	Mrs K. Hawton/ Mrs T.D. Long (2)	6/1, 6/2
1958	Miss M.E. Bueno/ Miss A. Gibson (1)	U Mrs W. du Pont/ Miss M. Varner	6/3, 7/5
1959	Miss J. Arth/ Miss D.R. Hard (1)	Mrs J.G. Fleitz/ Miss C.C. Truman (3)	2/6, 6/2, 6/3
1960	G Miss M.E. Bueno/ Miss D.R. Hard (1)	Miss S. Reynolds/ Miss R. Schuurman (4)	6/4, 6/0

	Champions	Runners-up	Score
1961	*U* Miss K. Hantze/ Miss B.J. Moffitt (2)	Miss J. Lehane/ Miss M. Smith (3)	6/3, 6/4
1962	Miss B.J. Moffitt/ Mrs J.R. Susman (2)	Mrs L.E.G. Price/ Miss R. Schuurman (4)	5/7, 6/3, 7/5
1963	Miss M.E. Bueno/ Miss D.R. Hard (2)	Miss R.A. Ebbern/ Miss M. Smith (1)	8/6, 9/7
1964	Miss M. Smith/ Miss L.R. Turner (2)	Miss B.J. Moffitt/ Mrs J.R. Susman (2)	7/5, 6/2
1965	Miss M.E. Bueno/ Miss B.J. Moffitt (2)	*U* Miss F. Durr/ Miss J. Lieffrig	6/2, 7/5
1966	Miss M.E. Bueno/ Miss N. Richey (3)	Miss M. Smith/ Miss J.A.M. Tegart (1)	6/3, 4/6, 6/4
1967	Miss R. Casals/ Mrs L.W. King (3)	Miss M.E. Bueno/ Miss N. Richey (1)	9/11, 6/4, 6/2
1968	Miss R. Casals/ Mrs L.W. King (1)	Miss F. Durr/ Mrs P.F. Jones (3)	3/6, 6/4, 7/5
1969	Mrs B.M. Court/ Miss J.A.M. Tegart (1)	*U* Miss P.S.A. Hogan/ Miss M. Michel	9/7, 6/2
1970	Miss R. Casals/ Mrs L.W. King (2)	Miss F. Durr/ Miss S.V. Wade (4)	6/2, 6/3
1971	Miss R. Casals/ Mrs L.W. King (1)	Mrs B.M. Court/ Miss E.F. Goolagong (2)	6/3, 6/2
1972	Mrs L.W. King/ Miss B.F. Stove (1)	Mrs D.E. Dalton/ Miss F. Durr (3)	6/2, 4/6, 6/3
1973	Miss R. Casals/ Mrs L.W. King (1)	Miss F. Durr/ Miss B.F. Stove (3)	6/1, 4/6, 7/5
1974	*U* Miss E.F. Goolagong/ Miss M. Michel	*U* Miss H.F. Gourlay/ Miss K. M. Krantzcke	2/6, 6/4, 6/3
1975	*U* Miss A.K. Kiyomura/ Miss K. Sawamatsu	*U* Miss F. Durr/ Miss B.F. Stove	7/5, 1/6, 7/5
1976	Miss C.M. Evert/ Miss M. Navratilova (2)	Mrs L.W. King/ Miss B.F. Stove (1)	6/1, 3/6, 7/5
1977	*U* Mrs R.L. Cawley/ Miss J.C. Russell	Miss M. Navratilova/ Miss B.F. Stove (1)	6/3, 6/3
1978	Mrs G.E. Reid/ Miss W.M. Turnbull (4)	Miss M. Jausovec/ Miss V. Ruzici (7)	4/6, 9/8, 6/3
1979	†Mrs L.W. King/ Miss M. Navratilova (1)	Miss B.F. Stove/ Miss W.M. Turnbull (2)	5/7, 6/3, 6/2
1980	Miss K. Jordan/ Miss A.E. Smith (4)	Miss R. Casals/ Miss W.M. Turnbull (2)	4/6, 7/5, 6/1

†Twentieth title, the all-time record.

MIXED DOUBLES – FINALS

	Champions	Runners-up	Score
1913	H. Crisp/ Mrs C.O. Tuckey	J.C. Parke/ Mrs D.R. Larcombe	3/6, 5/3 (retd)
1914	J.C. Parke/ Mrs D.R. Larcombe	A.F. Wilding/ Miss M. Broquedis	4/6, 6/4, 6/2
1915–18	No competition		
1919	R. Lycett/ Miss E. Ryan	A.D. Prebble/ Mrs Lambert Chambers	6/0, 6/0
1920	G.L. Patterson/ Miss S. Lenglen	R. Lycett/ Miss E. Ryan	7/5, 6/3
1921	R. Lycett/ Miss E. Ryan	M. Woosnam/ Miss P.L. Howkins	6/3, 6/1
1922	P. O'Hara Wood/ Miss S. Lenglen	R. Lycett/ Miss E. Ryan	6/4, 6/3

	Champions	Runners-up	Score
1923	R. Lycett/ Miss E. Ryan	L.S. Deane/ Mrs D.C. Shepherd-Barron	6/4, 7/5
1924	J.B. Gilbert/ Miss K. McKane	L.A. Godfree/ Mrs D.C. Shepherd-Barron	6/3, 3/6, 6/3
1925	J. Borotra/ Miss S. Lenglen	H.L. de Morpurgo/ Miss E. Ryan	6/3, 6/3
1926	*M* L.A. Godfree/ Mrs L.A. Godfree	H.O. Kinsey/ Miss M.K. Browne	6/3, 6/4
1927	F.T. Hunter/ Miss E. Ryan	L.A. Godfree/ Mrs L.A. Godfree	8/6, 6/0
1928	P.D.B. Spence/ Miss E. Ryan (2)	*U* J.H. Crawford/ Miss D. Akhurst	7/5, 6/4
1929	F.T. Hunter/ Miss H. Wills (2)	*U* I.G. Collins/ Miss J. Fry	6/1, 6/4
1930	J.H. Crawford/ Miss E. Ryan (2)	*U* D. Prenn/ Miss H. Krahwinkel	6/1, 6/3
1931	*U* G.M. Lott/ Mrs L.A. Harper	*U* I.G. Collins/ Miss J.C. Ridley	6/3, 1/6, 6/1
1932	E. Maier/ Miss E. Ryan (4)	H.C. Hopman/ Miss J. Sigart (6)	7/5, 6/2
1933	*U* G. von Cramm/ Miss H. Krahwinkel	N.G. Farquharson/ Miss M. Heeley (4)	7/5, 8/6
1934	*U* R. Miki/ Miss D.E. Round	*U* H.W. Austin/ Mrs D.C. Shepherd-Barron	3/6, 6/4, 6/0
1935	F.J. Perry/ Miss D.E. Round (3)	*U* H.C. Hopman/ Mrs H.C. Hopman	7/5, 4/6, 6/2
1936	F.J. Perry/ Miss D.E. Round (1)	J.D. Budge/ Mrs S.P. Fabyan (2)	7/9, 7/5, 6/4
1937	J.D. Budge/ Miss A. Marble (1)	Y. Petra/ Mrs R. Mathieu (2)	6/4, 6/1
1938	J.D. Budge/ Miss A. Marble (1)	H. Henkel/ Mrs S.P. Fabyan (2)	6/1, 6/4
1939	R.L. Riggs/ Miss A. Marble (2)	*U* F.H.D. Wilde/ Miss N.B. Brown	9/7, 6/1
1940–45	No competition		
1946	T. Brown/ Miss A.L. Brough (3)	G.E. Brown/ Miss D. Bundy (2)	6/4, 6/4
1947	J.E. Bromwich/ Miss A.L. Brough (1)	C.F. Long/ Mrs N.M. Bolton (3)	1/6, 6/4, 6/2
1948	J.E. Bromwich/ Miss A.L. Brough (1)	F.A. Sedgman/ Miss D.J. Hart (4)	6/2, 3/6, 6/3
1949	E.W. Sturgess/ Mrs S.P. Summers (4)	J.E. Bromwich/ Miss A.L. Brough (1)	9/7, 9/11, 7/5
1950	E.W. Sturgess/ Miss A.L. Brough (1)	G.E. Brown/ Mrs P.C. Todd (4)	11/9, 1/6, 6/4
1951	F.A. Sedgman/ Miss D.J. Hart (2)	*U* M.G. Rose/ Mrs N.M. Bolton	7/5, 6/2
1952	F.A. Sedgman/ Miss D.J. Hart (1)	*U* E. Morea/ Mrs T.D. Long	4/6, 6/3, 6/4
1953	E.V. Seixas/ Miss D.J. Hart (1)	E. Morea/ Miss S.J. Fry (4)	9/7, 7/5
1954	E.V. Seixas/ Miss D.J. Hart (1)	K.R. Rosewall/ Mrs W. du Pont (3)	5/7, 6/4, 6/3
1955	E.V. Seixas/ Miss D.J. Hart (1)	E. Morea/ Miss A.L. Brough (2)	8/6, 2/6, 6/3
1956	E.V. Seixas/ Miss S.J. Fry (1)	G. Mulloy/ Miss A. Gibson (3)	2/6, 6/2, 7/5
1957	M.G. Rose/ Miss D.R. Hard (4)	N.A. Fraser/ Miss A. Gibson (2)	6/4, 7/5

	Champions	Runners-up	Score
1958	R.N. Howe/ Miss L. Coghlan (4)	K. Nielsen/ Miss A. Gibson (2)	6/3, 13/11
1959	R.G. Laver/ Miss D.R. Hard (3)	N.A. Fraser/ Miss M.E. Bueno (2)	6/4, 6/3
1960	R.G. Laver/ Miss D.R. Hard (1)	R.N. Howe/ Miss M.E. Bueno (2)	13/11, 3/6, 8/6
1961	F.S. Stolle/ Miss L.R. Turner (1)	R.N. Howe/ Miss E.Buding (4)	11/9, 6/2
1962	N.A. Fraser/ Mrs W. du Pont (3)	UR.D. Ralston/ Miss A.S. Haydon	2/6, 6/3, 13/11
1963	GK.N. Fletcher/ GMiss M. Smith (2)	UR.A.J. Hewitt/ Miss D.R. Hard	11/9, 6/4
1964	F.S. Stolle/ Miss L.R. Turner (2)	K.N. Fletcher/ Miss M. Smith (1)	6/4, 6/4
1965	K.N. Fletcher/ G†Miss M. Smith (2)	UA.D. Roche/ Miss J.A.M. Tegart	12/10, 6/3
1966	K.N. Fletcher/ Miss M. Smith (1)	R.D. Ralston/ Mrs L.W. King (3)	4/6, 6/3, 6/3
1967	GO.K. Davidson/ Mrs L.W. King (1)	K.N. Fletcher/ Miss M.E. Bueno (2)	7/5, 6/2
1968	K.N. Fletcher/ Mrs B.M. Court (4)	UA. Metreveli/ Miss O. Morozova	6/1, 14/12
1969	F.S. Stolle/ Mrs P.F. Jones (4)	A.D. Roche/ Miss J.A.M. Tegart (3)	6/2, 6/3
1970	UI. Nastase/ Miss R. Casals	UA. Metreveli/ Miss O. Morozova	6/3, 4/6, 9/7
1971	O.K. Davidson/ Mrs L.W. King (3)	M.C. Riessen/ Mrs B.M. Court (1)	3/6, 6/2, 15/13
1972	I. Nastase/ Miss R. Casals (2)	K.G. Warwick/ Miss E.F. Goolagong (1)	6/4, 6/4
1973	O.K. Davidson/ Mrs L.W. King (2)	UR. Ramirez/ Miss J.S. Newberry	6/3, 6/2
1974	O.K. Davidson/ Mrs L.W. King (1)	UM.J. Farrell/ Miss L.W. Charles	6/3, 9/7
1975	M.C. Riessen/ Mrs B.M. Court (1)	UA.J. Stone/ Miss B.F. Stove	6/4, 7/5
1976	UA.D. Roche/ Miss F. Durr	UR.L. Stockton/ Miss R. Casals	6/3, 2/6, 7/5
1977	UR.A.J. Hewitt/ Miss G.R. Stevens	F.D. McMillan/ Miss B.F. Stove (1)	3/6, 7/5, 6/4
1978	F.D. McMillan/ Miss B.F. Stove (1)	R.D. Ruffels/ Mrs L.W. King (2)	6/2, 6/2
1979	R.A.J. Hewitt/ Miss G.R. Stevens (2)	F.D. McMillan/ Miss B.F. Stove (1)	7/5, 7/6
1980	B UJ.R. Austin/ Miss T. Austin	M.R. Edmondson/ Miss D.L. Fromholtz (6)	4/6, 7/6, 6/3

†Divided Australian title.

LONGEST SINGLES MATCHES

| 1969 | *Men* | 112 games | R.A. Gonzales bt C. Pasarell 22/24, 1/6, 16/14, 6/3, 11/9 in the first round |
| 1948 | *Women* | 54 games | Miss A. Weiwers bt Mrs O. Anderson 8/10, 14/12, 6/4 in the second round |

LONGEST DOUBLES MATCHES

| 1966 | *Men* | 98 games | N. Pilic/E.L. Scott bt G.C. Richey/T.Ulrich 19/21, 12/10, 6/4, 4/6, 9/7 in the first round |

| 1933 | *Women* | 48 games | Miss P.G. Brazier/Mrs I. Wheatcroft bt Miss M.E. Nonweiler/Miss B. Soames 11/9, 5/7, 9/7 in the first round |
| 1967 | *Mixed* | 56 games | K.N. Fletcher/Miss M.E. Bueno bt A. Metreveli/Miss A. Dmitrieva 6/8, 7/5, 16/14 in the quarter-finals |

LONGEST MATCH SINCE TIE-BREAK INTRODUCED

| 1978 | *Men* | 78 games | J.G. Alexander bt V. Pecci 7/5, 4/6, 9/8, 8/9, 12/10 in the first round |
| 1974 | *Women* | 46 games | Miss C.M. Evert bt Miss L.E. Hunt 8/6, 5/7, 11/9 in the second round (her opening match—she went on to win the title) |

LONGEST SINGLES FINALS

1954	*Men*	58 games	J. Drobny bt K.R. Rosewall 13/11, 4/6, 6/2, 9/7 (2h. 36m.)
1970	*Women*	46 games	Mrs M. Court bt Mrs L.W. King 14/12, 11/9 (2h. 26m.)
1902	*Women*	53 games	Miss M.E. Robb bt Mrs C. Sterry 4/6, 13/11; rain held up play, match replayed next day 7/5, 6/1

LONGEST DOUBLES FINALS

1968	*Men*	70 games	J.D. Newcombe/A.D. Roche bt K.R. Rosewall/F.S. Stolle 3/6, 8/6, 5/7, 14/12, 6/3
1933	*Women*	38 games	Mrs R. Mathieu/Miss E. Ryan bt Miss J. James/Miss A.M. Yorke 6/2, 9/11, 6/4
1967	*Women*	38 games	Miss R. Casals/Mrs L.W. King bt Miss M.E. Bueno/Miss N. Richey 9/11, 6/4, 6/2
1949	*Mixed*	48 games	E.W. Sturgess/Mrs S.P. Summers bt J.E. Bromwich/Miss A.L. Brough 9/7, 9/11, 7/5

LONGEST FINAL SINCE TIE-BREAK INTRODUCED

| 1980 | *Men* | 55 games | B. Borg bt J.P. McEnroe 1/6, 7/5, 6/3, 6/7 (16–18), 8/6 (3h. 54m.) |
| 1978 | *Women* | 30 games | Miss M. Navratilova bt Miss C.M. Evert 2/6, 6/4, 7/5 (1h. 43m.) |

LONGEST SETS

1968	*Men's Doubles*	62 games	A. Olmedo/P. Segura bt G.L. Forbes/A.A. Segal 32/30, 5/7, 6/4, 6/4 in the second round
1962	*Men's Singles*	46 games	N. Pietrangeli bt N. Pilic 24/22, 6/2, 6/4 in the second round
1969	*Men's Singles*	46 games	R.A. Gonzales bt C. Pasarell 22/24, 1/6, 16/14, 6/3, 11/9 in the first round

The longest set in Ladies' Singles is 26 games (in 1948, 1970, 1975); in Ladies Doubles 30 games (1921); in Mixed 30 games (1936, 1967, 1968).

LONGEST SET IN A SINGLES FINAL

1970	*Women*	26 games	Mrs B.M. Court v. Mrs L.W. King
1954	*Men*	24 games	J. Drobny v K.R. Rosewall
1958	*Men*	24 games	A.J. Cooper v. N.A. Fraser

LONGEST TIE-BREAK

| 1973 | *Men* | | B. Borg bt P. Lall 6/3, 6/4, 9/8 (20–18) in the first round (Borg's first match ever on the Centre Court) |

SHORTEST SINGLES FINALS

1881	*Men*	20 games	W. Renshaw bt J.T. Hartley 6/0, 6/0, 6/1 (37 minutes)
1936	*Men*	20 games	F.J. Perry bt G. von Cramm (suffering from a pulled muscle) 6/1, 6/1, 6/0 (40 minutes)
1911	*Women*	12 games	Mrs D. Lambert Chambers by Miss D.P. Boothby 6/0, 6/0 (25 minutes)

SHORTEST DOUBLES FINALS

1910	*Men*	22 games	M.J.G. Ritchie/A.F. Wilding bt H.R. Barrett/A.W. Gore 6/1, 6/1, 6/2
1953	*Women*	12 games	Miss S.J. Fry/Miss D.J. Hart bt Miss M. Connolly/Miss J. Sampson 6/0, 6/0
1919	*Mixed*	12 games	R. Lycett/Miss E. Ryan bt A.D. Prebble/Mrs D. Lambert Chambers 6/0, 6/0

OLDEST LAST-TIME SINGLES WINNERS

Year last won	Men	Exact age in years & days	Year last won	Women	Exact age in years & days
1909	†A.W. Gore	41.182	1908	C. Sterry	37.282
1930	W.T. Tilden	37.145	1900	B. Hillyard	36.242
1914	N.E. Brookes	36.235	1914	†D. Lambert Chambers	35.304
1887	*H.F. Lawford	36.53			
1954	*J. Drobny	32.263	1912	*E.W. Larcombe	33.27
1975	*A. Ashe	31.360	1938	H. Wills Moody	32.269
1880	†J.T. Hartley	31.188	1955	A.L. Brough	32.113
1969	R.G. Laver	30.330	1977	*S.V. Wade	31.356
1946	*Y. Petra	30.119	1975	B.J. King	31.224
			1958	A. Gibson	30.314
			1969	*A. Jones	30.260

In her famous Challenge Round defence against Suzanne Lenglen in 1919, Mrs Lambert Chambers at 8/10, 6/4, 6/5, 40-15 had 2 match-points to become the oldest woman to win the title. She was then 40 years and 304 days old.

* = Only win
† = Played Challenge Round only

OLDEST SINGLES RUNNERS-UP

1912	A.W. Gore	44.188	1920	D. Lambert Chambers	41.302
1974	K.R. Rosewall	39.246	1904	C. Sterry	41.290
			1930	E. Ryan	38.149

OLDEST DOUBLES WINNERS

1957	G. Mulloy (*Men*)	43.226	1934	E. Ryan (*Women*)	42.152
1926	L.A. Godfree (*Mixed*)	41.67	1962	M. du Pont (*Mixed*)	44.124

OLDEST COMPETITORS

1964	J. Borotra (*in Doubles and Mixed*)	65.320	1932	C.O. Tuckey (*in Mixed*)	54.358
1922	A.W. Gore (*in Singles*)	54.177			

YOUNGEST FIRST-TIME SINGLES WINNERS

Year first won	Men	Exact age in years & days	Year first won	Women	Exact age in years & days
1891	W. Baddeley	19.174	1887	L. Dod	15.285
1931	*S.B. Wood	19.243	1952	M. Connolly	17.291
1925	R. Lacoste	20.2	1959	M. Sutton	18.286
1976	B. Borg	20.27	1905	C.M. Evert	19.196
1881	W. Renshaw	20.191	1974	*K. Susman	19.208
1932	*H.E. Vines	20.278	1962	M.E. Bueno	19.266
1939	*R.L. Riggs	21.132	1884	M. Watson	19.284
1956	L.A. Hoad	21.225	1971	E. Goolagong	19.337
1958	*A.J. Cooper	21.291	1919	S. Lenglen	20.42
1974	*J.S. Connors	21.307	1963	M. Smith	20.357
			1978	M. Navratilova	21.260
			1927	H. Wills	21.269

* = Only win

YOUNGEST SINGLES RUNNERS-UP

	Men			Women	
1924	R. Lacoste	19.3	1973	C.M. Evert	18.198
1954	K.R. Rosewall	19.242	1924	H. Wills	18.271

YOUNGEST DOUBLES WINNERS

	Men			Women	
1960	R.D. Ralston (*Men*)	17.341	1961	B.J. Moffitt (*Women*)	17.228
1959	R.G. Laver (*Mixed*)	20.329	1980	T. Austin (*Mixed*)	17.205

YOUNGEST SEEDS

1973	B. Borg (6)	17.19	1980	A. Jaeger (14)	15.18

This was the year ATP withdrew. Borg was again the youngest seed in 1974.

YOUNGEST COMPETITORS

1927	S.B. Wood	15.231	1907	M. Klima	13.?
				W. Klima	14.?
			1977	T. Austin	14.193

HIGHEST NUMBER OF SINGLES TITLES

	Men			Women	
7	W. Renshaw	1881, †1882–6, 1889	8	H. Wills Moody	1927–30, 1932–3, 1935, 1938
5	H.L. Doherty	1902, †1903–6	7	D. Lambert Chambers	1903, †1904, 1906, 1910, †1911, 1913, †1914
5	B. Borg	1976–80	6	B. Hillyard	1886, 1889, 1894, 1897, 1899, †1900
4	R.F. Doherty	1897, †1898–1900	6	S. Lenglen	1919, †1920–1, 1922–3, 1925
4	A.F. Wilding	1910, †1911–13	6	B.J. King	1966–8, 1972–3, 1975
4	R.G. Laver	1961–2, 1968–9	5	L. Dod	1887, †1888, 1891, †1892–3
3	W. Baddeley	1891, †1892, 1895	5	C. Sterry	1895, †1896, 1898, 1901, 1908
3	A.W. Gore	1901, 1908, †1909	4	L. Brough	1948–50, 1955
3	W.T. Tilden	1920, †1921, 1930	3	M. Connolly	1952–4
3	F.J. Perry	1934–6	3	M.E. Bueno	1959–60, 1964
3	J.D. Newcombe	1967, 1970–1	3	M. Court	1963, 1965, 1970

† = Played Challenge Round only

HIGHEST NUMBER OF DOUBLES TITLES

8	H.L. Doherty }	1897, †1898–1901,	12	E. Ryan	1914, 1919, †1920–1, 1922–3, 1925–7, 1930, 1933–4
8	R.F. Doherty }	1903, †1904–5			
7	E. Renshaw }	1880, †1881, 1884,	10	B.J. King	1961–2, 1965, 1967–8, 1970–3, 1979
7	W. Renshaw }	†1885–6, 1888, †1889			
6	J.D. Newcombe	1965–6, 1968–70, 1974			

HIGHEST NUMBER OF MIXED DOUBLES TITLES

4	E.V. Seixas	1953–6	7	E. Ryan	1919, 1921, 1923, 1927–8, 1930, 1932
4	K.N. Fletcher	1963, 1965–6, 1968			
4	O.K. Davidson	1967, 1971, 1973–4	5	M. Court	1963, 1965–6, 1968, 1975

HIGHEST NUMBER OF TITLES

13	H.L. Doherty (5 singles, 8 doubles)	20	B.J. King (6 singles, 10 doubles, 4 mixed)
		19	E. Ryan (12 doubles, 7 mixed)

BEST CAREER RECORDS

Men	Titles Won	Matches Played	Lost	Won	Women	Titles Won	Matches Played	Lost	Won
J. Borotra (1922–64)					B.J. King (1961–80)				
Singles	2	65	10	55		6	99	13	86
Doubles	3	88	31	57		10	82	10	72
Mixed	1	68	28	40		4	63	12	51
	6	221	69	152		20	244	35	209

LOWEST SEED TO WIN SINGLES

1954   J. Drobny (11)   1962   K. Susman (8)

(No unseeded player has ever won a singles title)

NO. I SEEDS IN SINGLES WHO HAVE NEVER WON

1939	H.W. Austin		1959	C.C. Truman
1946	D. Pails		1961	S. Reynolds
1948	F.A. Parker			
1953	K.R. Rosewall			
1973	I. Nastase			

UNSEEDED FINALS

Singles	None	Ladies' Doubles	1974, 1975
Men's Doubles	1960, 1963, 1971, 1975	Mixed Doubles	1931, 1934, 1970, 1976

TWICE OR MORE SINGLES FINALISTS WITHOUT WINNING

F.L. Riseley	1903, 1904, 1906	A.M. Morton	1908, 1909
H. Roper Barrett	1908, 1911	E. Ryan	1921, 1930
H.W. Austin	1932, 1938	L. de Alvarez	1926, 1927, 1928
G. von Cramm	1935, 1936, 1937	H. Krahwinkel	
K. Nielsen	U1953, U1955	Sperling	1931, 1936
K.R. Rosewall	1954, 1956, 1970, 1974	D.R. Hard	1957, 1959
F.S. Stolle	U1963, 1964, 1965		
I. Nastase	1972, 1976		

PLATE EVENT WON BY PAST CHAMPION

1903	A.W. Gore	None
1932	H. Cochet	E. Goolagong won the Plate in 1970 and the Championship in 1971

LONGEST INTERVAL BETWEEN FIRST AND LAST SINGLES TITLE

W.T. Tilden 10 years 1920–30   B. Hillyard 14 years 1886–1900
                                         C. Sterry 13 years 1895–1908
                                         D. Lambert Chambers 11 years 1903–14
                                         H. Wills Moody 11 years 1927–38

LONGEST INTERVAL BETWEEN TWO SINGLES TITLES

W.T. Tilden 9 years 1921–30   E. Goolagong Cawley 9 years 1971–80

(The longest interval of all is in Men's Doubles where A.K. Quist won in 1935 and 1950)

LONGEST INTERVAL BETWEEN FIRST AND LAST APPEARANCE IN A SINGLES FINAL

K.R. Rosewall 20 years 1954–74   C. Sterry 17 years 1895–1912
                                         D.K. Lambert Chambers 17 years 1903–20
                                         H. Wills Moody 14 years 1924–38

SINGLES WINNERS AT FIRST ATTEMPT

1877	S.W. Gore		1884	M. Watson
1878	P.F. Hadow		1887	L. Dod
1879	J.T. Hartley		1905	M.G. Sutton
1919	G.L. Patterson		1919	S. Lenglen
1920	W.T. Tilden		1946	P.M. Betz
1932	H.E. Vines		1952	M. Connolly
1939	H.L. Riggs			
1949	F.R. Schroeder			
1951	R. Savitt			

UNBEATEN IN SINGLES

R.F. Hadow[+]	1878	L. Dod	1887–8, 1891–3
R.L. Riggs	1939	S. Lenglen§	1919–23, 1925
F.R. Schroeder	1949	P. Betz[+]	1946
		M. Connolly	1952–4

[+] = without losing a set   § = she retired in 1924 and 1926

TRIPLE CROWN WINNERS

1937	J.D. Budge	1920	S. Lenglen[+]
1938	J.D. Budge	1922	S. Lenglen[+]
1939	R.L. Riggs	1925	S. Lenglen
1952	F.A. Sedgman	1939	A. Marble
		1948	A.L. Brough
		1950	A.L. Brough
		1951	D.J. Hart
		1967	B.J. King
		1973	B.J. King

In 1901 Mrs A. Sterry won all three titles when Doubles did not rank as Championship events

LONGEST SINGLES SEQUENCE WITHOUT DEFEAT

B. Borg 35	1976–80	Mrs H. Wills Moody 50 1927–38	

(she did not play in 1931, 1934, 1936–7)

LEFT-HANDED SINGLES CHAMPIONS

N.E. Brookes	1907, 1914	Mrs A. Jones	1969
J. Drobny	1954	Miss M. Navratilova	1978, 1979
N.A. Fraser	1960		
R.G. Laver	1961–2, 1968–9		
J.S. Connors	1974		

COMPETED AT MOST CHAMPIONSHIPS

A.W. Gore 35 (excluding 1923)	1888–1927	Mrs D. Lambert Chambers 21 (excluding 1901, 1909, 1912)	1900–27

CHAMPIONSHIPS WON FROM MATCH-POINT DOWN

Year	In the Final unless otherwise noted	No. of match-points
1889	W. Renshaw bt H.S. Barlow in the All-Comers' Final	6
	Mrs G.W. Hillyard bt Miss L. Rice	3
1895	W. Baddeley bt W.V. Eaves	1
1901	A.W. Gore bt G.W. Hillyard in the quarter-finals	1
1908	A.F. Wilding/M.J.G. Ritchie bt A.W. Gore/H. Roper Barrett	1
1919	Miss S. Lenglen bt Mrs D. Lambert Chambers	2
1921	W.T. Tilden bt B.I.C. Norton	2
1926	Miss E. Ryan/Miss M.K. Browne bt Miss S. Lenglen/Miss D. Vlasto in the second round	2
1927	H. Cochet bt J. Borotra	6
	F.T. Hunter/W.T. Tilden bt J. Brugnon/H. Cochet	2
1932	Miss D. Metaxa/Miss J. Sigart bt Miss F. James/Miss M. Heeley in the first round	3
1935	Mrs F.S. Moody bt Miss H.H. Jacobs	1
	J.H. Crawford/A.K. Quist bt W.L. Allison/J. Van Ryn	1
1947	Miss D.J. Hart/Mrs P.C. Todd bt Miss A.L. Brough/Miss M.E. Osborne	3
1948	R. Falkenburg bt J.E. Bromwich	3
1949	F.R. Schroeder bt F.A. Sedgman in the quarter-finals	2
1954	Miss A.L. Brough/Mrs W. du Pont bt Miss S.J. Fry/Miss D.J. Hart	2
1960	N.A. Fraser bt E. Buchholz in the quarter-finals	6
	R.G. Laver/Miss D.R. Hard bt R.N. Howe/Miss M.E. Bueno	3
1976	A.D. Roche/Miss F. Durr bt R.L. Stockton/Miss R. Casals	1

MARRIED NAMES

The following were finalists or are mentioned in the text under both their maiden and married names:

Mrs W.W. Bowrey	=	Miss L.R. Turner
Mrs T.S. Bundy	=	Miss M.G. Sutton
Mrs R. Cawley	=	Miss E. Goolagong
Mrs R.L. Cawley	=	Miss H.F. Gourlay
Mrs D. Lambert Chambers	=	Miss D.K. Douglass
Mrs B.M. Court	=	Miss M. Smith
Mrs D.E. Dalton	=	Miss J.A.M. Tegart
Mrs W. du Pont	=	Miss M.E. Osborne
Mrs M. Fabyan	=	Miss S. Palfrey
Mrs J. Fleitz	=	Miss B. Baker
Mrs A.C. Geen	=	Miss D.P. Boothby
Mrs L.A. Godfree	=	Miss K. McKane
Mrs G.W. Hillyard	=	Miss B. Bingley
Mrs P.F. Jones	=	Miss A.S. Haydon
Mrs L.W. King	=	Miss B.J. Moffitt
Mrs M.R. King	=	Miss P.E. Mudford
Mrs D.R. Larcombe	=	Miss E.W. Thomson
Mrs R.D. Little	=	Miss D.E. Round
Mrs J.R. Lloyd	=	Miss C.M. Evert
Mrs R. Lycett	=	Miss J. Austin
Mrs M. Menzies	=	Miss K.E. Stammers
Mrs L.R.C. Michell	=	Miss P. Saunders
Mrs F.S. Moody	=	Miss H. Wills
Mrs L.E.G. Price	=	Miss S. Reynolds
Mrs G.E. Reid	=	Miss K. Melville
Mrs D.C. Shepherd-Barron	=	Miss D.C. Shepherd
Mrs S. Sperling	=	Miss H. Krahwinkel
Mrs A. Sterry	=	Miss C. Cooper
Mrs J.R. Susman	=	Miss K. Hantze

SINGLES TITLES BY WINNING NATIONS

	Men				Women				
	Pre-1914	1919–39	1946–80	Sub-total	Pre-1914	1919–39	1946–80	Sub-total	Total
GB	32(13)	3(1)		35(14)	29(9)	4(2)	3(3)	36(14)	**71(28)**
USA		9(6)	12(12)	21(18)	2(1)	10(3)	22(10)	34(14)	**55(32)**
A'lia	2(1)	3(2)	14(7)	19(10)			5(2)	5(2)	**24(12)**
NZ	4(1)			4(1)					**4(1)**
France		6(3)	1(1)	7(4)		6(1)		6(1)	**13(5)**
Germany						1(1)		1(1)	**1(1)**
Egypt			1(1)	1(1)					**1(1)**
Brazil							3(1)	3(1)	**3(1)**
Spain			1(1)	1(1)					**1(1)**
Cz'kia			1(1)	1(1)			2(1)	2(1)	**3(2)**
Sweden			5(1)	5(1)					**5(1)**

Figures in brackets show number of champions.

COMPOSITION OF SINGLES DRAWS

	1914		1939		1980	
	Men	Women	Men	Women	Men	Women
Number in Draw	102	51	128	96	128	96
Number of Nations	8	3	24	15	24	10
GB	88	47	56	68	10	10
USA	1	1	6	5	50	51
A'lia	3	0	2	0	19	8
France	2	2	4	4	5	1
Germany	5	1	5	3	0	3
Rest of World	3	0	55	16	44	23

RECORD ATTENDANCES

1932	Over 200,000 for the first time	1979	Record aggregate of 343,091
1956	Over 250,000	1979	Record for one day of 38,291 (first Wednesday)
1967	Over 300,000		

COURT CAPACITY

The Centre Court has 11,739 seats and standing room for about 2750.
No. 1 Court has 5100 seats and standing room for about 1500 (but extra seats are being provided for 1981).
No. 2 Court has 2020 seats and standing room for about 1000.
No. 3 Court has 800 seats.
Nos. 6 and 7 Courts have 250 seats each.
No. 13 Court has a temporary stand for 1450.
No. 14 Court has a temporary stand for 740.
In addition there are some 200 benches around the outside courts, giving a total seating capacity of approximately 23,350.

WEATHER DISRUPTIONS

Play has gone beyond the second Saturday in the following years:
1909   1912   1914   1919   1922 (every day was affected by rain)   1927   1963   1972   1973
In addition 1925 and 1930 were extended to allow competitors to rest following singles finals
Complete days have been rained off in the following years:
1877   1883   1884   1886   1888 (3)   1892   1893   1894   1900   1903   1905   1906   1909 (2)   1914
1952   1954   1963   1969   1972   1973   1978

THE ALL ENGLAND CLUB

Presidents

1907–09	HRH The Prince of Wales
1911	A.W. Gore
1912–14	Lord Desborough
1915–20	H. Wilson Fox
1921–9	H.W.W. Wilberforce
1930–4	HRH Prince George
1935–42	HRH The Duke of Kent
1943–61	HRH The Duchess of Kent
1961–8	HRH Princess Marina, Duchess of Kent
1969–	HRH The Duke of Kent

Secretaries

1868	W.J. Whitmore	
1869	E.B. Michell	
1870	S.H.C. Maddock	
1871–9	J.W. Walsh	Hon
1880–8	J. Marshall	
1888–91	H.W.W. Wilberforce	
1891–8	A.J. Chitty	
1899–1906	A. Palmer	
1907–24	Cdr G.W. Hillyard	
1925–40	Major D.R. Larcombe	
1940–5	Miss N.G. Cleather (Actg)	
1946–63	Lt.-Col. A.D.C. Macaulay, OBE	
1963–79	Major A.D. Mills	
1979–	C.J. Gorringe	

Chairmen

1929–36	Sir Herbert Wilberforce
1937–53	Sir Louis Greig, KBE, CVO, DL
1953–5	A.H. Risely, OBE
1955–9	Dr. J.C. Gregory
1959–74	H.F. David, CBE
1974–	Air Chief Marshal Sir Brian Burnett, GCB, DFC, AFC, RAF (Ret'd)

Referees

1877–85	H. Jones
1886	J. Marshall
1887–9	S.A.E. Hickson
1890–1905	B.C. Evelegh
1906–14	H.S. Scrivener
1919–36	F.R. Burrow
1937–9	H. Price
1946–50	Captain A.K. Trower
1951–62	Col. W.J. Legg, OBE
1963–75	Captain M.B. Gibson
1976–	F.W. Hoyles

Groundsmen

c. 1888–1918	Arthur Coleman
1918–39	Bill Coleman
1939–67	Edwin Fuller
1968–75	Bob Twynam
1976–	Jack Yardley

WIMBLEDON MILESTONES

1868	Club founded as 'The All England Croquet Club' at Worple Road, Wimbledon.	1884	Ladies' Singles and Men's Doubles events introduced into the Championships.
1875	Lawn Tennis first played at the Club	1887	Miss L Dod, aged 15, of Great Britain became the youngest winner of Ladies' Singles.
1877	Spencer W. Gore won the first Lawn Tennis Championship staged.	1888	Overarm service first used by A.T. Myers.

1889   W. Renshaw of Great Britain won the Men's Singles for the seventh time.

1891   W. Baddeley, aged 19, of Great Britain became the youngest winner of the Men's Singles.

1896   Men's Plate event started.

1902   Two matches were required to decide the Ladies' Singles Challenge Round.

1905   Miss M. Sutton of the United States became the first overseas singles champion.

1907   The Prince of Wales (later King George v) visited The Championships and accepted the first Presidency of the Club. N.E. Brookes (later Sir Norman) of Australia became the first overseas winner of the Men's Singles.

1913   Ladies' Doubles and Mixed Doubles added to the programme.

1919   All five titles won by overseas players.

1920   Mlle S. Lenglen of France became first player to win three titles in a year.

1922   Ground moved to present site in Church Road and was opened by King George v. Challenge Rounds abolished.

1924   Simple form of seeding introduced.

1925   Qualifying Competition introduced. Centre Court tickets rationed for the first time.

1926   The Jubilee Championships. All surviving Singles and Men's Doubles Champions attending received commemorative medals from King George v and Queen Mary on the Centre Court.

1927   Full seeding introduced. First radio broadcast. Loudspeaker first attached to umpire's chair.

1929   Miss R. D. Tapscott of South Africa appeared on the Centre Court without stockings.

1931   Men's singles final only final never to take place.

1932   Over 200,000 spectators attended.

1933   Ladies' Plate event started. Two-handed backhand first used by V. McGrath of Australia.

1937   J.D. Budge of the United States became the first man to win three titles in a year. First television transmission.

1938   Mrs F.S. Moody of the United States won the Ladies' Singles for the eighth time.

1946   Y. Petra of France was the last champion to wear long trousers.

1948   Boys and girls junior singles events instituted.

1949   Miss L. Brough of the United States played 117 games on Finals day.

1957   Miss A. Gibson of the United States became first black champion.

1964   Men's Veterans' event started. Finals Days' programme started with a band.

1967   Over 300,000 spectators attended the meeting. The first professional tournament (for eight players) staged a few weeks after The Championships to celebrate the introduction of BBC colour television transmissions. First time reigning singles champion beaten in first round.

1968   The Championships were made open to all players. Prize money given.

1969   R. Gonzales and C. Pasarell of the United States contested record 112-game match.

1971   Tie-break system of scoring introduced at 8/8; changed to 6/6 in 1979.

1973   Nearly 80 members of the Association of Tennis Professionals boycotted the meeting following the suspension of N. Pilic by his Yugoslavian Lawn Tennis Association for failing to play in a Davis Cup tie.

1977   The Centenary Championships. Past Singles champions presented with commemorative medals on the Centre Court by the Duke and Duchess of Kent. Wimbledon Lawn Tennis Museum and Kenneth Ritchie Wimbledon Library opened. No. 1 seeds beaten in all events for the first time. J.P. McEnroe of the United States became the first qualifier (and the youngest man) to reach the semi-finals.

1979   Centre Court roof raised and 1200 seats added. Record crowd of 343,091. Mrs L.W. King of the United States won her 20th title – a record number of titles won at The Championships. First Final (Mixed) to end on a tie-break.

1980   Four new courts on the north side. Magic eye introduced on Centre and No. 1 Courts. B. Borg of Sweden won the Men's Singles for fifth time in a row. Miss A. Jaeger the youngest seed and youngest quarter-finalist. Due to rain play started at noon from the first Thursday. First Singles Final (Ladies) to end on a tie-break. J.P. McEnroe received the first official warning and P. Fleming the first penalty point under the ATP Code of Conduct.

1981   No. 1 Court seating increased.

WHO IS THE GREATEST?

Who has been the greatest player to appear on Wimbledon's Centre Court? A question often asked but impossible to answer with anything near certainty. A man like F.R. Burrow, whose experience spanned fifty of the early years of the Championships, gave only a qualified answer – and that with a humility that he did not always show.

He was a man used to weighing the odds, comparing performances and assessing strengths, yet he was very cautious in coming to his well-reasoned conclusions. They were that, up to 1936, the two greatest players were Laurie Doherty and Tilden and, he felt, had the two met at an equidistant time out of their own peak periods, Doherty would just have won.

Few post-war pundits would agree with Burrow, but how much is that because they never saw Doherty and because the higher tempo and demands of the modern game weigh heavily in the scale of their opinion? In *The Encyclopedia of Tennis* 1974, Allison Danzig, Harry Hopman and Lance Tingay all give Tilden first place, while Laurie Doherty gets one 8th and one 9th in their lists. Tilden himself said Cochet was the best ever.

I am not going to attempt an overall assessment but rather give my impressions of the players I have seen in the last thirty-five years. As a radio commentator on the game, impressions and trying to convey them to the listener are my business – so here goes.

Imagine all the post-war Wimbledon quarter-finalists (110), all at the peak of their prowess. Put them all in a grand draw for the Champion of champions. For a bit of spice add a hot pepper – Gonzales, whose great years were in the pro ranks. Who would dare to do the seeding?

But consider. There is no lack of champion spark or killer instinct or ability in that lot. So what will the winner need? He must survive seven rounds much tougher than any he has played in succession before – and he must have *flair*. Despite Borg's success, there is only one man I would have staked my money on in that situation, Lew Hoad – Hoad, as strong as a tiger and gifted beyond measure. He needed the stimulus of a great occasion to rouse him from the casual attitude his tremendous talents allowed. As his opponent in that Wimbledon Final I would have expected to see – not Laver but Gonzales. What a magnificent match that would have been.

And of the women? My money would be on the girl who was never beaten at Wimbledon – Maureen Connolly. In her three-year reign Little Mo showed over and over again that she had the ability and fighting quality to raise her game whenever needed. In a similar post-war field (92) – with all at their developed best (and she, alas, was cut short by her riding accident) – I think she would have beaten each and every one.

So, very fearfully, I give you my lists – my impressions:

Men: 1. Hoad; 2. Gonzales; 3. Laver; 4. Borg; 5. Kramer; 6. Sedgman; 7. Rosewall; 8. Trabert; 9. Newcombe; 10. McEnroe; 11. Connors; 12. Emerson.

Women: 1. Connolly; 2. King; 3. Betz; 4. Bueno; 5. Brough; 6. Hart; 7. Court; 8. du Pont; 9. Gibson; 10. Evert, Goolagong and Navratilova.

Borg, Connors, McEnroe, Evert, Goolagong and Navratilova cannot yet be properly assessed and all could move in their respective ladders.

The two players who have given me the greatest pleasure to watch were Ken Rosewall and Maria Bueno. Maria at her best was for me the ultimate in tennis perfection.

There's no justice!